Classroom Confidential

Classroom Confidential

THE 12 SECRETS OF GREAT TEACHERS

Laurel Schmidt

Teach with passion.

Laurel Schmidt

HEINEMANN
Portsmouth, NH

Heinemann
361 Hanover Street
Portsmouth, NH 03801–3912
www.heinemann.com

Offices and agents throughout the world

Library of Congress Cataloging-in-Publication Data
Schmidt, Laurel J.
    Classroom confidential : the 12 secrets of great teachers / Laurel Schmidt.
    p. cm.
    Includes bibliographical references.
    ISBN 0-325-00660-1 (alk. paper)
    1. Teaching. 2. Teachers. I. Title

LB1025.3.S38 2004
371.102—dc22   2004010982

Editor: Danny Miller
Production: Vicki Kasabian
Cover design: Night & Day Design
Typesetter: House of Equations, Inc.
Manufacturing: Steve Bernier

Printed in the United States of America on acid-free paper
13 12 11 10   EB   6 7 8

To my greatest teachers,
Robert and Durnford

Contents

Acknowledgments

GOOD BOOKS, LIKE GOOD CAREERS, ARE COLLABORATIVE EFFORTS. THIS IS PARTICULARLY so in the case of *Classroom Confidential*, a book that spans more than thirty years of living and working with children. Since my entry into the teaching profession, I have enjoyed extraordinary friendships with passionate educators, especially Pat Lem, Diana Donan, Susanne Henry, and Peggy Harris. I was fortunate to have two amazing principals to guide my teaching career, Edith Dury and John Shambra. In the course of this project I had the privilege of talking to many great teachers including Barbara Henry, Bill Coate, Rafe Esquith, Anne Brown, Linda Catanzano, Lisa Bartoli, and Ava de la Sota.

I have been supported in all my endeavors, both teaching and writing, by a band of loyal friends—Karen Boiko, Bill Himelright, Paul Heckman, Viki Montera, Christina Cocek, Margaret Maruschak, and Marolyn Freedman. Special thanks to my brilliant editor, Danny Miller—all writers should have a Danny Miller at least once in their lives. And finally to my family—my courageous mother, Dorothy, my beloved father, Robert, my siblings Sheryl, Bob, Richard, and David, my talented children, Thalia and Anthony, and my best friend and coach, my husband, Durnford King.

Introduction

I can't remember a time when I didn't want to be a teacher. It just seemed to be a self-determined fact of my young life. Somehow I understood that teaching involved learning, and learning was what I loved to do, for I was born with an extra gene for curiosity, a gift from my dear father, who was my first and best teacher.

As a teacher, my curiosity manifested itself in a low tolerance for boredom. Every few years I'd cajole my way into a new grade level until finally I'd covered the waterfront from kindergarten through middle school. I loved the chance to tackle a new curriculum, but mostly I just adored kids in any size, shape, or zip code. It didn't take long to discover that my restlessness was incompatible with classroom serenity. As a result, my kids and I became experts at beating the curricular bushes for intriguing projects that occasionally morphed into crusades. We lived and learned contentedly on the barricades, saving murals, defending endangered landmarks, and rewriting the history of our town to include its darker days of racial discrimination.

The most reassuring thing about curiosity-driven teaching was that as my kids grappled with nonstandard topics, their enthusiasm for learning exploded. At times their appetites were so voracious that it took all my energy not to feel like the poster girl for No Teacher Left Behind. Cramming continually to meet the challenge, I was supremely happy.

My greatest fortune was to have a wealth of mentors. Of course, my students were my best and most critical coaches when it came to authentic teaching. And in every school, I discovered a few great teachers who became great friends. In my last years in the classroom I met Dr. Paul Heckman, the quietest revolutionary in education. Actually, it was more like a collision. He pushed me relentlessly to reexamine my fundamental beliefs about teaching, just when I was ready for a good, long rest on my laurels. But I wanted to be a great teacher, so I listened, dismembered my curriculum, and grew.

For twenty-three years I rose each morning and eagerly headed for a classroom. Most nights I fell asleep with a book in my hands, determined to learn more about learning. I was grateful to any author who could zap a few of my weary neurons violently enough to spark an epiphany.

Now I'm returning the favor. I wrote *Classroom Confidential* to help you have a few epiphanies of your own. First, I emptied a quarter century of ideas from my head. Then I went in search of some truly great teachers who could share their excellence with you. You get to meet Ruby Bridges' teacher and a man who cruises graveyards with his kids as an introduction to local history. You even get a recipe for pumpkin bread from the world's best mentor.

Classroom Confidential is your paperback mentor. And although it can never take the place of learning from your students or those intimate conversations with trusted colleagues, it can keep you company late at night and be a silent partner in your quest for greatness. So swing for the fences! Knock yourself out! I swear you'll never regret an ounce of passion or an hour of your life spent on the awesome task of helping children learn. Be a *great* teacher! It's the most amazing gift you can give yourself.

Classroom Confidential

SECRET #1

Great Teachers Are Equal Opportunists

Capitalizing on How Kids Learn

In This Chapter:
- What's the Big Idea About Learning?
- How Kids Are Smart
- Multiple Intelligences Go to School
- Meet Lisa Bartoli
- How Full-Brain Learning Looks
- Thinking with Things—Learning Through Process and Projects
- Equal Opportunity Assessments

In the not-too-distant past, many educators treated curriculum like a zoo for ideas. Students were allowed to view from a distance but never touch, interact, or make their own discoveries. They'd take in the sights, pick up a few souvenirs, and return home, grateful for the familiar comforts of the television, refrigerator, and computer screen.

But that's not learning. It's tourism.

Nonetheless, well-intentioned teachers spent entire summers hunched over books, combing the library shelves, even attending elaborate institutes, in pursuit of the perfect lesson plan. Some of them got really smart in the process. And a few of them got quite excited. On the opening day of school, they were ready to roll. And roll they did, right over any kid who wasn't receptive with a capital R. Or, at the very least, compliant.

Curriculum wasn't about kids. It wasn't even about learning. It was about the presentation of a product. If that sounds like factory talk, you're on the right track. A quick tour of the glossary of twentieth-century education feels more like a visit to an auto assembly plant than a school. Take a look at some of the buzz words that were popularized in the past fifty years to describe the inexplicable, ephemeral act of teaching: *delivery systems, inputs and outputs, units, standardization, targets, structures, outcomes,* and *maintenance.* Instruction became a package exported from its production site—the teacher—to its delivery site—the child.

Let's think a little more about life in a factory. Let's take The Rouge, a massive Ford plant in Detroit. An infant car is propelled along an assembly line. At each stage, tool-wielding workers apply the right parts in the right place in a prescribed amount of time. The tire guys don't talk to the radiator guys, and no one wonders how the car is feeling about the process as it's ferried from one work station to the next. There are periodic checks to be sure that all the cars look exactly the same when they emerge at the other end. Once in a while there's a lemon. Oh, well.

For a long time that's pretty much how it was in education. We would pass kids from grade to grade, attaching prescribed units of instruction in a designated period of time—colonial history, my community, physical science. Teachers talked about "covering" all the material, as if they were in the upholstery business, or "exposing" their kids to concepts. Most teachers just fretted breathlessly about "getting through." All of which required them to speed-teach the last three chapters of their anthology or math book as June approached, so their kids were "exposed" before they moved on. Nonetheless, when the next year's teacher asked, "How do you calculate the perimeter of a square?," knowing full well it had been "covered" the year before, students would adopt the blank stare of a cultist and swear they'd never heard of such a notion.

That's what passed for instruction when we didn't really understand the workings of the brain. Now we do. So if we continue to approach curriculum without thinking about how kids learn, we're essentially spit-shining a Model T.

What's the Big Idea About Learning?

All of this is not to suggest that kids in the past weren't learning. They were learning a hell of a lot. It just wasn't necessarily what the teacher was "delivering." Kids are learning all the time, in prodigious amounts, often with little or no adult assistance. Their brains are learning machines with no off switch.

Great teachers understand this phenomenon and they believe that learning is sacred. Curriculum is not. So when they think about teaching and learning, they start by asking themselves. "Can I create an environment where kids will reveal the ways that they're smart? Can I capture their attention so that we can focus on topics of mutual interest? Can we learn together?" The great ones know that teaching hasn't happened until kids learn.

So how do great teachers create sacred spaces in which all their kids learn? They pay attention. They give kids permission to show their stuff and then they watch. Actually, watch is an understatement. Great teachers are hypervigilant—not a particularly attractive word. It probably conjures up images of a visit from a disapproving mother-in-law or a clock-watching administrator poring over the sign-in sheet like a bank examiner. And a few not-so-great teachers actually use hypervigilance, quite effectively I might say, as an antilearning device—pouncing on kids who are bold enough to experiment with those intriguing science kits *before* getting complete instructions, or surreptitiously peeking at the pictures in chapter 5, when the assignment on the board clearly indicates chapter 4. But great teachers use hypervigilance to discover who their students are and how they learn. They're looking for signs of intelligent life in every child, and they never come up empty-handed.

Signs of Intelligent Life

On my first day of teaching in East Los Angeles, I was staring at thirty-two little faces and they were staring back at me. That was about all we could do at that point, since they were fluent in Spanish and I was not. But I wasn't worried. I'd just transferred from a school that had twenty-four language groups, where I had learned that language was a temporary and very permeable barrier. So I knew what to expect. First we'd talk with pictures and pointing, like tourists asking for directions outside a village train station. Then we'd do single-word exchanges. By the holidays I wouldn't be able to shut them up. That was my goal.

Just one child concerned me. I knew enough Spanish to suspect that Guillermo had a speech impediment, and this was confirmed by the confused looks of his peers whenever he spoke. But he was my student and I needed to understand him. So I watched him like a hawk.

Now it happened that in this same school there was a magnificent principal named John Shambra, who distinguished himself by having a piano in his office. Scarcely a day passed that music didn't drift from his office and into our play yard. One morning I headed for the block cabinet in the corner of the yard, and came upon Guillermo, playing a tune on an invented piano. He had balanced six long blocks on top of a single horizontal plank. When he "played" the six keys, they would teeter back and forth, giving off a musical tone each time they hit the pavement. When he saw my look of surprise, he smiled and said, "Mr. Shambra, Mr. Shambra."

In that instant, I learned a lot about how Guillermo was smart, and if I wanted to know more, all I had to do was put objects in his hands. By the end of the year he'd established a cardboard box restaurant, outfitted with paper plates, pans, and canned food. Swathed in an apron, he'd ask, "What do you want to eat?" and scribble pretend requests on his order pad. He was a real smarty.

Another year, in another town, I was teaching a multiage third, fourth, and fifth grade class. In this class there was a child who almost wasn't there. Everyday he wore a sweatshirt with the hood in the fully upright position, despite the mild weather. Whenever I glanced in his direction he was hunched so far forward that his face hovered just inches from the tabletop. I never heard a word from him. It was like having my own personal monk.

We started the year with a long discussion about art. I hung an empty frame on the wall with the caption, "What is art?" and asked my kids to bring in examples of anything they thought fit the definition. The next morning students arrived with photographs, sculptures, even a three-by-five foot canvas from a mom who was a painter. As we launched into our discussion, I could see my monk shifting in his seat, as if trying to get my attention, but obliquely. So I asked if he'd brought in some art. Without uttering a word, he inched his chair back and stared under his desk. There among the dust bunnies and discarded pencil stubs was an amazing invention. Part Rube Goldberg, part Joseph Cornell, it was a clear plastic liter bottle converted into a fantastic machine, festooned with wires, batteries, flags, and a propeller that actually rotated on demand. I ushered him to the front of the room where he enjoyed, perhaps for the first time in his school career, the unmitigated admiration of his peers. Slowly he described the function of each attachment and its role in a larger system. It was clear to all of us that there was some brand of genius underneath that hood, and it would be an adventure to spend the year with him.

If you take a minute to think, I'm sure you'll discover that you, too, have lots of mental pictures of kids doing curious things. Once you train yourself to recognize these pictures as clues to the way kids are smart, you and your students are on the road to success.

How Kids Are Smart

For the better part of the twentieth century, being smart was measured with a number—your IQ. In IQ land, bigger was definitely better. If you came out of the chute with a hefty three-digit numeral, the world was your oyster, intellectually speaking. On the other hand, if your number hovered around room temperature, you weren't destined for greatness. The dreariest part of the IQ belief system was that IQ was fixed at birth. Intelligence didn't grow. Effort was irrelevant in the silk purse/sow's ear world of intelligence quotients.

IQ was largely determined through math and language tasks that involved high levels of skill with a pencil and paper, so in effect smart meant being good at school stuff. Then along came Howard Gardner, who both expanded our understanding of how the brain works and pushed us to think about how schools could be more brain-friendly. After years of intensive research on the geography and function of the brain, Gardner proposed his theory of multiple intelligences in 1983. At that time, he identified seven distinct intelligences, and has since added two more. These intelligences or ways of knowing include verbal/linguistic, visual/spatial, musical, kinesthetic, logical/mathematical, naturalistic, existential, interpersonal, and intrapersonal intelligence. Simply put, people are word smart, picture smart, music smart, body smart, logic smart, nature smart, life smart, people smart, and self smart.

We all have all of these intelligences, like a mosaic of abilities located in many different parts of our brains. They're interconnected, so we may use two or three to achieve a single task, but they also work independently. Perhaps the best news for teachers and kids is that these intelligences aren't static or determined at birth. Like muscles, they grow throughout your life if they're nurtured, which means that the right environment, kids can get smarter in lots of different ways.

Long before Howard Gardner had shared his theory about how the brain works, many great teachers had intuitively created brain-friendly classrooms by adopting a multiple intelligence approach to learning. Their kids built and drew, danced and debated their way to academic excellence, using the whole brain to get the job done. Let's take a closer look at all the ways your kids are smart.

Word Smart—Verbal/Linguistic Intelligence

Word-smart kids may enjoy an early lead in school, by virtue of their tongues. While other kindergarteners are trying to figure out where their snacks went, verbal kids are complimenting the teacher or camped out in the library corner. In the upper grades, verbal kids jab their hands in the air every time the teacher asks a question. They love to talk and have a lot of ideas at their disposal. Verbal kids are drawn to poetry and finely crafted prose. Many are avid debaters and junior barristers who would spend all day locked in persuasive or even hectoring dialogues designed to change the minds and hearts of their peers or teacher—if you let them. They like jokes, tongue twisters, and any form of humor that relies on manipulating words. A linguistically smart kid might become a novelist, teacher, broadcaster, talk-radio host, advertising writer, tour guide, lawyer, or comedian.

Picture Smart—Visual and Spatial Intelligence

Kids with a high degree of visual and spatial intelligence seem to have eyes on steroids. They notice your new haircut, even if your significant other doesn't. Move your desk a few degrees and they'll give you a full report. They're great mimics. What they do particularly well is think in pictures. Some make exceptional, precocious paintings. Others can solve problems in the physical world, often without lifting a finger. At school, picture-mart kids wow us with their ability to think in three-dimensions and interpret visual images such as globes, charts, and graphs. There's a practical side to this intelligence, too. These kids can fix an ailing machine or assemble a 100-part model without even looking at the directions. If there's something broken in your room, call on your visual kids. When visually smart kids grow up, they might be happy as architects, artists, automobile designers, animators, engineers, landscape gardeners, or skywriters.

Music Smart—Musical Intelligence

Kids who are music smart like sounds the way a gourmand likes food. They recognize tonal patterns, pitch, melody, and rhythms, but they're also sensitive to the emotional or expressive possibilities of sound and music. In class they may be your hummers, tappers, or snappers, so before you "hush" them, try to think of a way to incorporate musical intelligence into your curriculum. Challenge them to substitute the lyrics in a familiar song with information about the Civil War, photosynthesis, or whatever you're studying. There seems to be a strong connection between musical and mathematical intelligence, so if you add music to your curriculum, you may get a bonus during long division season. If you nurture musical intelligence in your students, they may pursue careers as composers, choir directors, music critics, or speech pathologists.

Body Smart—Kinesthetic Intelligence

Kinesthetic intelligence is probably the most underappreciated way to be smart in school. Body-smart kids are movers and touchers. They know the world through their muscles. But many classrooms are brimming with opportunities to sit still and keep your hands to yourself. You see the dilemma. While the rest of us are content to lurch, stagger, and collapse into the nearest chair, kinesthetic kids have a very refined relationship with their bodies. They use their hands to deftly manipulate objects, build models, or learn sign language. Kinesthetic kids might be drawn to careers as choreographers, weavers, athletes, welders, computer repairpersons, or yoga teachers.

Logic Smart—Logical/Mathematical Intelligence

This is the intelligence that people typically associate with "brains." It governs inductive and deductive thinking, numbers, abstract patterns, and the ability to reason. Logic-smart kids relish mental math, estimating, measuring, and calculating. Their brains are never happier than when they're launching an investigation, whether it's how many pellets the hamster can eat in one minute or why an electrical current will run through potatoes but not bananas. They love to construct controlled experiments and are full of questions about natural events. In addition to using numbers for complex mathematical operations, they can also work with abstract concepts to figure out relationships and handle long chains of reasoning. As adults, they might be astronomers, traffic engineers, logicians, forensic scientists, epistemologists, urban planners, or accountants.

Nature Smart—Naturalistic Intelligence

Naturalist intelligence is attuned to the patterns and connections in the elements of nature. Nature-smart kids like to collect, classify, or read about rocks, fossils, butterflies, feathers, and shells. In school, they excel in science, especially biology, astronomy, meteorology, and zoology. They understand the big ideas behind genus and phylum, and they're likely to be the first in your class to launch a campaign to save the whales. They devour books, videos, and outdoor activities that deal with natural phenomena and make the best pet monitors your classroom every had. They might pursue careers as forest rangers, animal behaviorists, veterinarians, environmental activists, or conservationists.

Life Smart—Existential Intelligence

Existential intelligence is the latest region of the brain that Howard Gardner has described. Kids who have existential intelligence are fascinated with questions about life and death. They wonder about where they came from, what comes next, what happens to people when they die. They speculate about ghosts or spirits, and ask questions about what the earth was like a long time ago and if there are people on other planets. Their brains seem to be wired with a spiritual curiosity. These kids may be drawn to philosophy, religion, or writing as adults.

People Smart—Interpersonal Intelligence

Kids who are people smart have strong social skills. They're always noticing, commenting, helping, mediating—sometimes right in the middle of a history lesson. Hence, they tend to be popular with peers but less so with teachers who see them as gadflies or busybodies. Their empathic skills allow them to understand the motives, moods, and intentions of people around them, giving them the fairly unusual capacity to see things from another person's point of view. Interpersonal kids confidently fill leadership roles, like student council positions, where they can use their influence and problem-solving skills to build trust and resolve problems effectively. Kids with this insightful passion might become genealogists, priests, teachers, salespeople, therapists, social workers, mediators, or lobbyists.

Self Smart—Intrapersonal Intelligence

Kids with strong intrapersonal intelligence are particularly sensitive to their own values, purpose, and feelings. This insight makes them independent, confident, focused, and self-disciplined. They can work happily alone or contribute to a group. They may begin keeping diaries when they're very young and do so all their lives. Intrapersonal kids' quiet demeanor may raise concerns until their teachers discover that they're not daydreamers or withdrawn. They enjoy close friendships because they can manage their feelings, moods, and emotional responses with greater skill than many of their peers. Adults often see these kids as "old souls" because they're so aware of their inner feelings, desires, and dreams. Their intrapersonal intelligence might lead them to careers as philosophers, researchers, archivists, theologians, animal behaviorists, or anthropologists.

Multiple Intelligences Go to School

With all these ways of being smart, why do so many kids feel dumb? One big reason is school. School can be a crushing experience for kids who don't have strong linguistic and mathematical intelligence. They may endure years of being mislabeled or simply alienated from learning because the traditional approach to school activities fails to engage the most dynamic areas of their brains.

A prime example of this bias is the way students with visual intelligence are viewed. Parents wince, like they've been handed the consolation prize, if their child's teacher says, "He's very artistic." Yet we know that visual skills can be used to unlock reading, math, or science. Likewise, a child with extraordinary interpersonal intelligence may be criticized for being too social, when she should be encouraged to run for student council. Intrapersonal intelligence is even less appreciated. The quiet child with a rich inner life may win a trip to the school psychologist's office or just get lost in the crowd.

I think kinesthetic intelligence is the most problematic in classrooms where kids are expected to sit still, keep quiet, and perform repetitive mental tasks—in effect, to learn with their brains tied behind their backs. When they don't respond well, the explanation usually involves some deficiency in the child, the parents, or both. You'll hear things like: He's not trying; There's no support at home; She can't focus; Maybe there's a learning disability. But imagine yourself in that environment, six hours a day, five days a week. How well would you perform?

In *Growing Up Inside the Sanctuary of My Imagination* (1994), the award-winning writer and artist Nicholasa Mohr recalls her struggle in school. A bright, creative child, her bilingual outbursts regularly earned her a seat in the corner.

> I would sit on a chair facing the wall, looking for discolorations in the paint, a crack in the plaster, or shadows on the surface. In this way I used my eyes and imagination to adjust these imperfections by making them take on other visual forms. On that wall I remember a variety of scenes, trees and waterfalls, part of a schooner sinking in the sea, and the profile of a horse. I was able to meditate upon these images and sit under the waterfall or walk in the woods. Although I was still embarrassed and angry at the teacher, this game helped ease my punishment. At the same time, I enjoyed sharpening my sense of fantasy.

Meet Lisa Bartoli

The sign on the nondescript portable classroom reads, Room 40. The sign maker should be arrested for felony understatement. If we lived in a world of truth and justice, the plain siding would be emblazoned with three-foot neon letters announcing: Lisa Bartoli's Whole Child Fitness Center. Inside this six-hundred-square-foot prefab box, twenty kids and their teacher pump iron—mentally, socially, and emotionally, often to the strains of disco music or the scrape of homemade tap shoes. This is a no-pain-all-gain third grade community coached by a truly great teacher, Lisa Bartoli.

Lisa is intelligent, articulate, and highly organized. Her smile is as dazzling as her laser-sharp mind. She reads, travels, and works out at her local gym. But primarily she devotes her heart and mind to creating a classroom where children thrive as learners. All of them, without exception. The word *great* springs to mind when you see Lisa, knee-deep in students, though she protests, "I still have a lot to learn." That may be so, but she is clearly a master at creating an environment where every student enjoys what Abraham Maszlow called *peak experiences*—when they feel at their very best. Moments of intense happiness, free from fear, anxiety and inhibition. How does Lisa do it? She has eight rules for nurturing the fortunate students deposited on her doorstep each September.

1. *Every child must be seen.*

Too many kids spend their entire school careers like the invisible man. They're ciphers in a system that only takes note when they're absent—attendance being a budgetary issue. Lisa believes that every day, every child must be enveloped in the teacher's gaze and acknowledged as individuals. So roll call in her class is a joyful time. Instead of a litany of names followed by "here, here, here," Lisa greets her students with "hello" in a variety of languages. On this day, it's Swahili. "Jambo, David," and she looks intently at the child, as if taking stock of a precious commodity. Children arriving late don't receive a glare, or the standard dressing-down about tardiness being the road to perdition. All the students sing out "jambo" and sweep the latecomer into their thrall. From the moment students arrive each morning, they're locked on Lisa's radar, viscerally acknowledged for their personal importance.

2. *Scared kids can't learn.*

Lisa believes that all kids are smart—especially third graders, so she shudders to see the fear that grips her students on their first day of class. Worried faces, "I can't's," even tears stain her early lessons. "I remember as a kid I was almost afraid to breathe in school. That's no way to learn," remembered Lisa. Spurred by that painful memory, she vowed that all the kids in her class would be deep-breathers. "It's my duty to make them feel safe, comfortable, wanted, and secure. It's my job to protect them." Each September she launches a full-scale assault on their insecurities, and inevitably wins them over with a gentleness and grace some are experiencing for the first time in their young lives.

On the first day, she readily shares the fact that she is not a great speller— "never have been, never will be." So, if they see a misspelled word on the board, they can help her correct it. Lisa continually uses the invocation, "Help me out" to encourage thinking or innovation. Eventually, through watching Lisa model trying and learning, even the most timid students become more accepting of themselves, and more willing to tackle new challenges. Lisa comments, "Once they start to shed their fears, then I know I have the beginnings of a lifelong learner."

3. *There are at least eight kinds of smart.*

Lisa lays the foundation for the year with an exploration of multiple intelligences to help her kids identify all the ways that they're smart. The draw pictures, crack codes, do jumping jacks, and analyze poems to test Howard Gardner's theory on themselves. Then they identify their strengths and the areas where they want to get smarter. Armed with this information, students make a personal intelligence rainbow, with their strongest intelligence arching across the top, and all the other skills arranged in descending order. This isn't just a colorful self-esteem booster. They use their rainbows all year long to figure out the best way to attack any learning challenge.

Time for multiplication tables? Musical kids plug in an audiotape of rap songs to have some fun while learning utterly boring math facts. Visual students design books of diagrams to help them see the patterns in the multiplication game. Kinesthetic kids snap their fingers or clap as they recite the patterns. A student with strong interpersonal skills and a flair for acting learns best when she's teaching, so she sets up an impromptu club for mastering those pesky nines.

Ultimately, what Lisa's kids discover is that learning is a process that yields to many strategies. They stop wondering Can I do this?, which only leads to *yes* or *no* and perhaps some performance anxiety or a dead-end. Instead they're trained to be analytic about each task. They now think, What's required and how can I use my intelligences to do this? Then they ask themselves five questions:

1. What are my strengths?
2. Where am I less comfortable?
3. What's my goal?
4. How can I use my strengths to accomplish my goal?
5. Who can help me with the areas where I'm not comfortable?

In the process, Lisa's kids learn that success is just a matter of finding a match between the work at hand and the ways that they're smart.

4. *We all make mistakes.*

Highlighting multiple intelligences is an important strategy, but Lisa knows from personal experience that growth requires risk taking and that inevitably leads to mistakes. Kids can't grow if they're phobic about mistakes. So she re-tools their view of mistakes by bathing them in statements that normalize error: "Is it okay to make a mistake? Yes. Do we all make mistakes? Yes. Hands up if you've ever made a mistake." Hers is the first hand up: "What do we do about mistakes? Practice." This becomes the class mantra, seeping into even the most tentative learners. Lisa told me about a student who would literally have a meltdown if his work wasn't 100 percent accurate. If she pointed to a math mistake, he would push her hand away in angry denial, then surreptitiously erase it when she turned away. After two months with Lisa, he confidently says, "It's okay to make a mistake" and eagerly recalculates.

5. *Warm up your brain.*

Lisa's determination to help all kids succeed means she's the designated hitter in her school when a truly special child needs a regular education setting. She's had some spectacular success with children on the autistic spectrum, thanks to her positive attitude. She's sure "It's just another opportunity to get smarter about how kids learn." In her quest to help all kids succeed, she became fast friends with the occupational therapists who agreed to teach all kids the brain warm-ups designed for kids with sensory-motor issues. Now mornings in Lisa's class typically start with a workout to coordinate the left and right hemispheres of the brain. Here are two simple ones. First, have your kids trace the infinity sign on a piece of paper, in the air, or on the carpet, with the index finger on the left hand, then the right, then put both fingers together as they trace a continuous loopy pattern. Be sure to have them reverse directions to give both sides of the brain a full workout. The second is to get the whole brain in sync. Have your kids sit and touch one elbow to the opposite knee. That may sound easy, but for kid with motor integration issues, crossing the midline of the body is like me trying to catch a fly ball. Forget about it. To help, Lisa puts a green sticker on the left elbow and right knee, a red sticker on the others. Then they literally use the colored dots to guide their muscles to places the brain can't easily go. Eventually the integration of the two hemispheres kicks in.

6. *Community—not competition.*

All of Lisa's kids are bright but some years she has a student who is remarkable even in a room of high achievers. She has one student who does Accelerated Reader at a speed that even has the computer in a panic. He's racked up a phenomenal number of points. In other classrooms, he'd be a pariah. But Lisa's kids are different. They're convinced that they all have strengths, and individual strengths are collective equity. So they proudly acknowledge his achievement by saying, "I know a genius." And when they're in the library, he's busy pulling books off the shelf and saying, "Read this one. It's great." This sense of community permeates the day. Whether they're correcting homework or working through a series of math problems, Lisa stops periodically to check on individual progress and comprehension. At least once a day you'll hear her say, "We're not moving on until everybody gets this. Check to see if your partner needs help."

7. *Each one, teach one.*

On the first day of school, Lisa tells her students that "they are already experts in a lot of things that they do in their lives." She spends a whole lesson helping them identify the strengths that make them perfect teachers for each other. She asks, "Who should we ask if we have a question about baseball? How about math? Do we have anyone who can help if we want to learn to speak Spanish? Who are the artists in here who can give us some ideas about painting?" Eventually every student can say with confidence, "This is what I do well, and I'll teach you." Lisa creates a culture in which every student feels a vested interest in the well-being of their classmates, and knows how to help. Their ethic is to connect and care for one another.

8. *Have fun, for God's sake.*

Just as Lisa believes scared kids can't learn, she's convinced you can increase the learning range of your kids if they're relaxed and happy. "When I was first teaching, I took everything so seriously. I was afraid to let my kids be kids. I thought that if they started laughing or joking, it would get out of control. Now I know it actually helps." Lisa believes that humor is one of the best stress-busters around, so she has a joke board in the room. Kids sign up and when the work gets intense or Lisa sees too many heads propped on desks, she announces, "We need a joke! Who's signed up to tell jokes?" She also keeps a copy of *Kids Are Punny: Jokes Sent by Kids to The Rosie O'Donnell Show* close at hand for laugh breaks. They also dance. "I love disco music, so when the going gets tough, I just pop in a CD and the whole room springs to life." These sixty-second furloughs increase respiration and cardiovascular activity. That also stimulates the brain. And kids who love music and dance are thrilled to find their favorite pastime stuck right in the middle of a long bout of peer editing.

At the end of the day, when the school bell rings, most children fly out of their classrooms like flocks of startled birds. Lisa's kids linger, drift out, then return for a cherished book or one last hug. Who can blame them? Safe in Lisa's fitness center, they consistently experience themselves as valuable people and skillful learners.

Maszlow said that peak-experiences give meaning to life, and make it seem worthwhile by their occasional occurrence. For Lisa Bartoli, teaching is the peak experience. Every day she shepherds her fortunate students through whatever their next challenge might be, and with endless patience coaches them to be curious about the world, to live in a community, and to find their own unique happiness as lifelong learners.

How Full-Brain Learning Looks

Effective classrooms are like gigantic Petri dishes for growing intelligence, and the most critical ingredient is the teacher. Here's what brain-building teachers consistently do to transform their classrooms into think tanks.

- Propose tasks that are both interesting and problematic. The difficulty of the problem is balanced by the level of motivation. This tension generates energy and stimulates creativity.

- Tap into students' innate curiosity about the world and how things work.

- Suggest several different ways that students can approach any task or project, providing varying degrees of depth, novelty, and complexity. Students self-accommodate by choosing tasks that are the most compatible with their intelligences.

- Encourage students to conduct experiments and tackle real-world problems, then talk about what they've learned and what they still wonder.

- Give students the opportunity to develop individual projects tailored to their own interests.

- Press students to test their ideas, draw conclusions, and pool their knowledge in a collaborative environment.

- Model puzzling, struggling, clarifying, challenging, explaining, persevering, and celebrating as characteristic behaviors of thinkers.

- Promote social and communication skills by emphasizing talking together about ideas and sharing responsibilities for group projects.

- Urge students to notice how much they learn when they are not at school.

- Prompt students to constantly assess how various activities help them learn. By evaluating their strategies, students ideally become experts at learning.

Great teachers succeed because they know that kids learn in different ways. Their classrooms cater to the complexity of the mind, the variety of human intelligence, and the infinite potential of youthful brains unleashed. It is not unreasonable then to conclude that the persistent failure of some students is, in reality, the failure of schools to recognize all the ways those kids are smart.

What Doesn't Work

It is disconcerting to realize that some of our hallowed classroom practices actually inhibit the growth of intelligence by discouraging, ignoring, or even punishing kids who don't learn in the usual chalk-and-talk style. Many kids seem to be trapped on a Mobius strip. They can't learn text-based material effectively, so they fall behind. Remediation means they cover the same material in the same way, but s-l-o-w-e-r, or in such a simplified way that it numbs the small part of their brains that still accompanies them to school. If this goes on for years, kids may never break the pattern of being out of step and out of touch, until dropping out seems to be the smartest move they can make.

As brain researchers catalogued the conditions that encourage learning, they also identified the ones that don't. Let's take a look at some of the things in the "Not Effective" column.

- *The brain is highly sensitive to emotions.* Kids don't learn well if they are frightened, bored, resentful, anxious, confused, or depressed. In contrast, the capacity to learn soars when kids feel safe, smart, and appreciated.
- *The brains needs stimulation.* If you insist that kids sit still in a quiet room with little on the visual or verbal menu, their brains will either shut down or invent stimuli that may result in a conversation with the principal.
- *The brain has a voracious appetite for ideas.* Needless repetition and review act like a verbal sedative, whereas meaty questions and fascinating facts deliver a jolt to the brain pan.
- *The brain needs the big picture to make sense of the little details.* Subjects taught in fragments, fact by fact, make it tough for kids to grasp the overarching concepts that run through literature, history, social science, and politics.
- *Each brain processes information at different speeds.* Time limits and emphasis on speed are counterproductive.
- *The brain falters in isolation.* Learning increases when kids get up close and personal with new ideas and opposing opinions.

And while we're on the subject of brain death, let's take an honest look at some of the things we give kids: worksheets, for example. After three or four years of school, kids aren't thinking, Hey, here comes another worksheet. This might be interesting! More likely, they'll recoil, as if you'd offered them a live kidney. Learning ceases when avoidance becomes the goal, but you can lure kids into learning if you make the mind-hand connection.

Thinking with Things—Learning Through Process and Projects

For years education has touted hands-on experiences, but rapid digit motions are not enough. Activity without cognition is just a way to keep kids from smacking each other or engraving their desk with a protractor. Idle hands may be the devil's workshop, but clueless hands aren't much better. Learning happens in the mind, so before you switch on the hands, you must ease the brain into gear and keep it running. The main focus in all hands-on activities should be problem solving, not just moving matter.

When hands-on learning is effective, students develop skills in planning, organizing, analyzing, and decision making. They focus more intently for longer periods of time and continuously assess their own progress. Need some ideas? Here are ten to get you started.

1. *Building*

Very young children instinctively pile blocks up just to see how high they'll go before a spectacular fall. Building still fascinates older kids if they can get their hands on the materials. Before you shrink from this idea as child's play, consider this: Building is a rigorous exercise in managing mass, stress, symmetry, balance, and ever-present gravity. It's physics, engineering, and architecture all rolled into one graceful spire. Here's what's going on inside the cranium when kids build. First, they visualize a whole structure—working from memory or just inventing something that has never been seen. Then they mentally deconstruct it into its component parts, and reconstruct the concrete model, designing or modifying as they go. This is where visual and logical intelligence really come into play. Building lets kids explore form and function, as they construct houses, machines, towers, or vehicles to illustrate concepts from your curriculum. And you don't need proper building materials. Gather up wood scraps, wooden tongue depressors, toothpicks, strawberry baskets, cigar tubes, spools, and that foam packing material that lines appliance boxes. Many pieces have odd-shaped openings that can be notched together or attached with tape, wire, toothpicks or just piled up until they teeter and collapse. Store your building materials in plastic bags or boxes between building sessions.

2. *Patterns*

When kids see a new object or event, their brains immediately ask: Is this like anything I've already seen? They try to fit the new material into a familiar category by noticing similarities or patterns. Pattern spotting is mental shorthand that helps kids analyze, sequence, follow rules, compute, solve problems, see relationships, and reason abstractly. If that sounds like math, you're right. Patterns are the language of math. To explore patterns, you'll need lots of finger food, attractive to the eye and touch. Gather up buttons, marbles, ceramic tile samples, pegs and pegboards, wooden blocks, or tiles, checkers, bottle caps, playing cards, nuts and bolts, spools of thread, toothpicks and pebbles, sample paint chips (free at the paint store), various types of beans. When kids experiment with pattern materials, some start by sorting or categorizing—creating sets. That's the brain showing what it already knows. Then the imagination kicks in and patterns become pictures, abstract designs, rose windows, aerial views of cities, or whole galaxies. You'll be amazed at how long kids, even the older ones, will work at creating beautiful, complex patterns from bits of junk.

3. *Imaginary Play*

In our rush to get kids ready for yet another round of testing, we've nearly snuffed out the spontaneous exercise of the imagination. There's simply no time to waste on fantasy when kids could be huffing and puffing through phonics worksheets or drilling on the times tables. But play, especially imaginary play, is an important component of intellectual and emotional development. It weaves together logic, aesthetics, narrative fiction, autobiography, emotions, and elements of the real world. When kids imagine, they integrate all their intelligences to create a unique story. Louisa May Alcott exercised her growing talent for narrative by putting on original plays in the family barn using dolls and cats for characters. She fed, educated, nursed, and even hung and buried her toys to serve her plots. So gather up a box of props and encourage your kids to go down the rabbit hole to their own invented worlds.

4. *Inventions*

Orville Wright's career as an inventor was off to a brisk start in junior high when he built a printing press with parts scrounged from a junkyard, including an old tombstone, firewood, and the hinged bars from a buggy top. His eye for combining elements of machines helped him make the leap from a bicycle repair shop to trans-Atlantic aviator. Inventors' minds are special in at least four ways. They're fluent, flexible, elaborate, and original. Which means that if you give them a problem, they'll come up with lots of relevant, detailed ideas that would never occur to the rest of us. Inventing builds analytic thinking and helps kids feel self-sufficient, because when faced with a problem, they can invent a solution! To encourage inventing, just make a habit of saying, "I wonder if anyone can think of a better way to. . . ." That's an invitation to invent. Couple that impulse with a box of junk, wires, tape, and almost anything from your building center and you can have an inventors' festival any day of the week.

5. *Junkyard Genius*

You've probably heard that necessity is the mother of invention. Well, junk is the father. So the next time you're about to donate a defunct MixMaster or ancient Hoover to the dumpster, stop! It's easy to turn a broken radio, alarm clock, fan, blow dryer, or scale into a project that could fascinate kids for days and lead to a brilliant career. It did for Richard Feynemann, whose life as a

Nobel physicist began in a childhood of tinkering with junk. He recalled, "As a child I bought radios at rummage sales and I'd try to fix them. Usually they were broken in simple-minded ways—an obvious wire hanging loose, or a coil was partly unwound—so I could get some of them going." It grew into an obsession—"the puzzle drive." Feynemann was bent on understanding the mechanical world by taking it apart. Dismantling is a complex thinking process. While deconstructing, kids observe the relationship of parts to the whole, and closely examine gears, circuits, levers, pistons, springs, and switches. The process begs them to make hunches, test ideas, and try again. It requires eye-hand coordination, patience, memory, and persistence. Expert dismantlers transform and invent new objects, spurred by questions like, "I wonder what would happen if I strapped two batteries to my electric toothbrush?"

6. Collections

Collecting is thinking made visible. It's how kids begin to categorize the world. When they encounter something intriguing, say, the dark boat-shaped seedpod of a Jacaranda tree or a Luna moth, their brains immediately try to fit it into a category of familiar objects. Making that connection expands their definition of the familiar category—it has one more example in it. And the new object gains a context where it belongs. That's how knowledge is constructed. Sometimes collecting looks like random prospecting or prolonged browsing. It's so subtle that you might never guess how fast the wheels are turning inside a kid's head. Here's a partial list of skills that collectors use: close observation, examining, visual discrimination, speculating, memory, making decisions, sorting, categorizing, describing. It's all mental work. Later, collectors will use the same skills to perform science experiments and organize essays.

7. Experiments

Kids love to invent experiments. They start with the question "I wonder what will happen if . . . ," then proceed to fiddle around, observe, and draw conclusions. Experimenting is a hunch made flesh. Logical-mathematical thinkers are particularly fond of experiments because they love to test their ideas and find out what works—that's the heart of the scientific method. Thomas Edison was a perfect example of this. His teachers thought he was too addled to benefit from school, but at the age of nine he invested his entire allowance in chemicals, more than two hundred bottles worth. Explosions stained his bedroom walls and ate holes in the carpet until his mom banished him to the cellar, where he invented, among other things, a potion that he hoped would allow humans to fly.

Having a well-stocked junk center is probably the best way to promote experiments in your classroom. Add some measuring devices, containers, egg timers, stop watches, and string.

Kids who are writers tend to experiment with language, trying out alliteration, exaggeration, humor, and various endings. Artistic students experiment by mixing media, and musical students experiment with sound and instruments, sometimes inventing unique ways to produce a tune.

8. *Show Time*

Words are the standard vehicle for expressing ideas in school. Sadly, in some classes they are the only vehicle. But kids who think in pictures have a head full of knowledge that they would gladly download if someone would just point them in the right direction. As often as possible, encourage your students to empty their heads using visual as well as verbal expression. Let them show what they know by producing their own videotapes, documentaries, slideshows, maps, charts, graphs, illustrations, drawings, sculptures, paintings, or sketchbooks. Visual images can be used to illustrate science findings and important concepts from history. Story maps enliven literature lessons, and sketching is the only way some students can make sense of story problems in math.

9. *Publishing*

Furnishing a permanent publishing center in your room encourages students to think about language arts with their hands. Producing books, newsletters, invitations, announcements, comic books, magazines, websites, even a simple flyer requires skill. Beyond composing the text itself, they make decisions about format, layout, design elements, illustration, color scheme, audience, and distribution. Access to a computer, a desktop publishing program, and a printer can be a serious draw to the reluctant writer and a real boon to the precocious novelist or journalist in your class.

10. *Nature Watch*

By the age of nine, most kids can name twenty-six TV shows, seven fast-food chains, and just two birds. Three if you count pigeons. The city is a tough place to get acquainted with nature, but it's not impossible. Help your kids make the nature connection by learning to look. Go out on a cloudy day and take some time to scan the sky. Ask: What do the clouds look like to you? Look at a tree and ask: What do the branches remind you of? What shapes can you see? Can you make your body look like that tree? Point out that there are patterns on leaves, seashells, spider webs, and butterflies. Look through art books for all the paintings that include nature images. If your kids become bird watchers, crack open a field guide. These books are like avian dictionaries with information about size, colors, habitats, food, migration patterns, and songs. Field guides are plentiful and inexpensive in used bookstores. Prowling through bird books is another way for kids to make practical use of their reading skills. There are also hundreds of organizations dedicated to preserving the natural environment. Some take on huge issues such as global warming or the destruction of the rain forest. Others focus on neighborhood projects. Call your city or town hall or check your local library, community bulletin board, or newspaper for real-life opportunities to learn from nature.

Equal Opportunity Assessments

Here comes the *no-duh* part of this chapter. If you encourage your kids to use brain-compatible methods of learning, you'll feel like an imposter and a traitor if you resort to pencil-and-paper tests when it's time to assess them. Assessment should mirror the learning process. Some people refer to this as different ways of knowing and different ways of showing.

Traditionally, assessment is a way for teachers to find out what kids know, or more accurately, what they remember being told. But effective assessments help kids learn to identify their own strengths, so assessment is a time to celebrate growth and revel in the feeling of being an expert rather than be crushed by "what I got wrong." Authentic assessments reinforce learning styles so students can modify and improve their own learning program.

Great teachers convince their students that assessments answer the question: How am doing now? Not, Who am I? or, How valuable or smart am I? Mistakes are simply the starting point for the next spurt of growth. When students get in the habit of asking themselves, What can I learn from this?, assessment becomes an integral part of the learning process, and students play a major role in judging their own progress.

How Can Assessment Look?

Authentic assessments provide feedback from reality rather than authority. Kids look at their own products rather than simply staring at a B– or C+ on the top of their page and wondering how the heck the teacher came up with that grade. They might think, What's a minus anyway? And how come the kid at the next table got an A when he only wrote two paragraphs? Kids can't really benefit from assessments that seem arbitrary or at the very least inscrutable. It breeds distrust. Another advantage of authentic assessment is that it allows for invention and creative expression in ways that no True/False or essay test can, so your kids can express as much as they know in a variety of ways. Instead of stuffing a disappointing test in the bottom of a backpack, hoping it will remain undiscovered, kids actually retain the knowledge gained from authentic assessments and apply it to real life. Here are some suggestions for different ways of showing.

You can construct authentic assessments using writing by encouraging your students to write a play, poem, short story, novel, storyboards, brochure, diary, and memoirs to convey their understanding of key concepts in your theme. Assessments in the arts may include writing and performing songs, musicals, skits, simulations, drawings, paintings, sketches, murals, books, and picture books. Students can also demonstrate their mastery of curricular concepts by making models, machines, inventions, dioramas, maps, and diagrams.

What's in It for You?

One thing is for sure: Building a classroom environment that's brain-compatible takes a lot more mental investment than cracking open a carton of workbooks and scrawling an assignment on the board. And teaching with things means you're engaged in a perpetual struggle against the inexorable accumulation of junk. *So what's in it for you?*

Smarter kids, for one. Students learn more, and enjoy learning more when they are actively involved in the process, rather than passive listeners. When you concentrate on thinking and understanding, rather than on rote memorization, your kids begin to understand the uses and delights of the mind.

> *I am a teacher at heart, and there are moments in the classroom when I can hardly hold the joy. When my students and I discover uncharted territory to explore, when the pathway out of a thicket opens before us, when our experience is illuminated by the lightning-life of the mind—then teaching is the finest work I know.*
> —Parker Palmer

The process of acquiring and using knowledge becomes more democratic. You're not the only smarty in the group. It's antihierarchical and intoxicating to kids to feel they can be experts, too. They're drunk on learning and you're the designated driver.

By grounding learning in authentic, real-world activities, you stimulate kids to ask questions and apply their natural curiosity to the world. That's a fundamental requirement of citizenship, so you're actually strengthening the society in which you live. The skills your kids learn in a thinking curriculum are portable. Once kids learn how to learn, they can take their confidence and ability anywhere. You equip them for life in the real world, and that's no small contribution.

Here's the biggest advantage to having a brain-compatible classroom, and the thing that sets the truly great teachers apart from the crowd. Instead of impersonating educational TV all day long, you deftly play a dozen roles: mentor, model, provocateur, agonist, and antagonist. Not to mention cheerleader, champion of the underdog, critical friend, and coach. Best of all, you are both teacher *and* learner in the most superlative sense of the words.

Resources

Gardner, Howard. 1983. *Frames of Mind: The Theory of Multiple Intelligences.* New York: Basic Books.

———. 1991. *The Unschooled Mind: How Children Think and How Schools Should Teach.* New York: Basic Books.

———. 1993. *Multiple Intelligences: The Theory in Practice.* New York: Basic Books.

Jensen, Eric. 1998. *Teaching with the Brain in Mind.* Alexandria, VA: Association for Supervision and Curriculum.

Lazear, David. 1991. *Seven Ways of Teaching: The Artistry of Teaching with Multiple Intelligences.* Palatine, IL: IRI Skylight Publishing.

Schmidt, Laurel. 2001. *Seven Times Smarter: 50 Activities, Games, and Projects to Develop the Multiple Intelligences in Your Child.* New York: Three Rivers Press.

Sylwester, Robert. 1995. *A Celebration of Neurons: An Educator's Guide to the Human Brain.* Chicago: Zephyr Press.

SECRET #2

Great Teachers Are Power Brokers

Building a Culture of Eptness

In This Chapter:

+ What's the Big Idea About Eptness?
+ Building a Class Resume
+ Why Great Teachers Insist on a Culture of Eptness
+ Ten Teacher Behaviors That Promote Eptness
+ How Am I Doing? A Self-Assessment
+ Social Safety and Eptness
+ Meet Ava de la Sota
+ Waking Magoun's Brain

Many kids know from the moment they fall in line on the first day of school that they've drawn the short straw in the teacher lottery. By the time they've stowed their backpacks and droned out "with liberty and justice for all," they sense that there will be little of either for the rest of the year. The walls are festooned with charts defining the outer limits of acceptable behavior—every line begins with *Do Not*. The rows of desks look like a precision drill team, there's a vague threat in the dozens of red pencils stockpiled on the teacher's desk, and the homework assignment is already on the board.

It's a crypt with chalkboards.

Savvy students begin to mentally sort through their survival kits. They do a quick survey to see who's smarter and who's not, calculating what it will take to vault over the dead wood and into the Student *du Jour* Club. Kids with a more defiant approach to the world respond to the he-who-must-be-obeyed atmosphere predictably. They pick a rule and break a bit off. Nothing spectacular at first, but definitely a shot over the teacher's bow. Meek students overcompensate with elaborate displays of compliance. A few just want to bite down on a cyanide pellet.

It's culture shock—and they're wondering how they'll make it to June.

Across the hall, another classroom churns with the bustle of reunions and discoveries. A dozen students cluster around their new teacher, examining him from every angle except supine. In return, his gaze is riveted on their faces. Two Kyles—one boy and one girl—explain their predicament, as he begins to match names to faces. No introduction is needed for the third sibling in the same family to grace his roster, or the child who arrived a day earlier "just to check out the room."

On the outskirts of the group is a loner who seems to be gravitationally challenged. While the other students jockey for a place on the rug, he shifts from foot to foot, then executes a modified jumping jack, narrowly missing a classmate's head. Turning abruptly, he motors between two tables, then re-arranges the mouse and keyboard on the teacher's desk, before coming to rest in a tangle of legs. He immediately wins the teacher's attention and—a job. "Would you mind counting all the chairs in here, and then count the kids so we can see if we have enough? Otherwise, we'll have to find some extras. I could really use your help." Suddenly this human whirligig is rooted to the carpet, silent, focused, and counting. He's going through culture shock, too. It's the first time he's felt useful at school since he lost his milk monitor job in kindergarten.

What's the Big Idea About Eptness?

Teachers may not get to set the culture of their school, but they do set the culture of their classrooms. With every word and gesture, from the opening bell of the first day, they define the world inside those four walls. From greetings and furniture arrangement to grades and getting permission to attend to bodily functions, teachers determine "how-we-do-things-in-this-room." They control behaviors, beliefs, conversational style, attitudes, and activities. In short, the culture of the class. Great teachers build a culture of eptness through an unrelenting search for what each student can do and how those abilities contribute to the strength of the group.

Eptness is a combination of capacities and meaningful activity. It resides in potential in all students, but it's unleashed through the deliberate efforts of their teacher.

In a culture of eptness, students:

- Expect to play the roles of learner and teacher.
- Share in making decisions about their learning and learning environment.

- Draw on a wide variety of resources for knowledge.
- See problems as opportunities to feel smart.
- Are willing to struggle to clarify their thinking and speaking.
- Understand the connections between their classroom and the real world.
- Use real-world knowledge and skills in classroom activities and vice versa.
- Feel they are important to the welfare of their classmates and the community.

Gloria Ladson-Billings (1994), author of *Dreamkeepers*, got it right when she observed that good educators possess a "sociopolitical consciousness" that helps students understand that educational achievement isn't just an individual matter. The whole community benefits from an individual's achievement, and an individual's failure to achieve diminishes the life of the community.

The working relationship of teachers and students in a culture of eptness is similar to that of a movie director with the cast and crew. Movie making is not a solo profession. The director relies on actors, writers, cameramen, grips, chefs, and runners—or there's no movie. The final product depends on the abilities of all the players, and their willingness to work together to give their creative best. The director's job is to elicit that, and in the process, shape the whole effort into the creative image she's carrying in her head.

If the director intimidates or denigrates the cast and crew, the process will be an agony. People will rebel, quit, or sabotage, and the project will suffer. If a director sees each person as an essential resource for realizing the vision, then the creative product will be greater than the sum of the parts.

Great teachers understand that kids are the ultimate resource in their classrooms. Whether school budgets are fat or shaved to the bone, every year teachers get an unlimited supply of human potential. That's what they have to work with. So great teachers consistently use strategies that convey their passionate belief that every child is capable of learning, teaching, leading, and becoming an expert. Here's how they get started.

Building a Class Resume

From the minute students arrive at a great teacher's door, they sense that they've entered a new world. The atmosphere is palpably positive and the first order of business is discovering the *can-do* in each kid. An excellent activity that trumpets the eptness agenda is building a class resume. It's a visual inventory of all the things your students can do.

First, explain to your class that the purpose of a resume is to list a person's skills and accomplishments. You may even want to bring in a copy of your own resume to share. Then tell them that since you'll be working together this year, it's going to be important to know all of the things that they know how to do, so they can help each other. Explain that they will need to talk, think, remember, and ask questions in order to write a class resume.

Start by showing your kids some of the skills or abilities that can be part of their resume, using the following list. Ask if they can think of any others and add their suggestions.

- Speak different languages
- Are familiar with or have traveled to other countries
- Know how to: (cook macaroni and cheese, skateboard, feed a baby)
- Know how to draw: (comics, flowers, animals, etc.)
- Play musical instruments
- Sing or whistle
- Have brothers and sisters
- Have grandparents, aunts, and uncles
- Fix things that are broken (repair a bike or computer)
- Can do double jump rope
- Play games/sports
- Know how to use the bus/subway system
- Know how to use tools (list them)
- Operate machines
- Write (genres: poems, short stories, plays, jokes, skits)
- Know how to care for animals or pets (kinds)
- Grow plants, care for a garden
- Run a VCR, boot up the computer
- Have collections of (list them)
- Do tricks, jokes, mime
- Know how to set up a camping tent
- Have a library card
- Can dance
- Know how to play board games (list them)
- Won a contest or prize
- Belong to clubs or organizations
- Other skills

Personalize the list for your students, depending on their ages, experiences, interests, and ethnic and cultural origins. Include lots of real-world skills, not just things we do at school. Make sure there is something for kinesthetic, visual, and interpersonal learners, as well as kids who are strong in language and math. Remember, the categories are prompts to guide your students' curiosity about each other.

Now divide the class into work-size groups. Give them large sheets of paper and marking pens, or any materials that you think are appropriate for this project. Allow plenty of time for them to talk, review the categories, and discover their collective assets. Each group can design its own resume, but if you have younger students you may want to give them a big template that they can fill in. They can use simple sketches along with words to record their information.

The power of the resume activity is that it motivates students to prospect for talents and experiences among their peers to fill up their resume. A group with four bilingual students is suddenly "language rich" in the resume game. So rather than having students view differences as oddities, they are reconditioned to cheer with each revelation.

Another important feature of this activity is that it immediately focuses kids on the class as a community—who we are and what can we do together—rather than an arena in which they compete against each other.

When the groups are finished, display all the resumes and let the students wander around and look over the information. Then take time to discuss what they've learned about each other.

Ask some questions:

- What's the most interesting item on all these resumes?
- What's the biggest surprise?
- What do you see on our resume that you want to learn?
- What do most of us have in common?

Spend some time identifying the "experts" in the class. Who's the linguist? Who's the checkers champion? Who would we talk to if we want to write a musical? This is not to put certain students on a pedestal, but to let the group know to whom they can turn for various types of help. This discussion sends a powerful message: As a group we possess lots of skills that we can use to help each other learn. No one needs to fail in a class with this much talent. We're in this together and so far we're looking pretty spectacular.

Recopy or just cut and paste the group resumes into one big list. Display it prominently and invite students to keep adding to it as they remember more things they can do. And don't forget to list some talents of your own. You're part of the resource pool, too.

Why Great Teachers Insist on a Culture of Eptness

Great teachers are determined to have a rich, intense existence, inside and out of their classrooms. They insist on a culture of eptness because:

- They're success-oriented, and kids are the raw material of their success.
- They enjoy the company of kids, and want to feel like they're allies and companions on an adventure, rather than adversaries in a ten-month tug of war.
- They have a low threshold for boredom. An ept class multiplies the possibilities for expanding the curriculum and investigating new ideas.
- They always have more work than time. Ept students create a support network for each other, expanding the teaching team.
- Great teachers prefer to spend their days with smart, interesting students rather than with dull, predictable ones, so they create the class they want by building a culture of eptness.

Ten Teacher Behaviors That Promote Eptness

If your goal is a culture of eptness, your kids will need to feel smart so that they can achieve at high levels. They need to feel important to the welfare of the class so that they support each other and have the courage to confront socially unacceptable behavior. The trick is to transfer your vision into their heads and hearts. You can't use ventriloquism, hypnotism, sleight of hand, or any other educational jiggery-pokery if you want an authentic classroom. But there are ten techniques that great teachers use to promote a culture of eptness.

1. *Approximations*

No one needs to give teachers pointers on how to observe kids. Teachers are uberwatchers. The problem is that some teachers devote all their ocular energy to watching for transgressions. Not surprisingly, that brand of surveillance just creates problems. First, it gives the teacher a distorted and rather depressing impression of the class. But worse, patrolling for problems highlights undesirable behavior, putting wrongdoers on the marquee, while the other students are left to wonder, But what *does* he want?

Great teachers have mastered the fine art of ignoring bad behavior. They, too, regard their new students with a laserlike gaze. But they're watching for approximations of the behavior they *want*. If a child drops a pencil and another retrieves it, they hear "Thank you for helping, Jeremy." A student says he's not sure of an answer, but he's willing to guess. "I can tell you're really thinking about this. That's great." One student says he lost his lunch box and another pipes up with two suggestions about where it might be. "We're lucky to have someone who can help solve problems." A newcomer notices that there are three kids named Ashley. "Great observation. How do you think we might handle that?" Great teachers literally pounce on these approximations, encouraging effort, thinking, unique ideas, active kindness, and wondering, not just docile behavior. Pretty soon, the behavior multiplies. More comments from the teacher. And so it goes.

When it comes to noticing approximations, we can all take a lesson from new mothers. They're dying to hear their babies say "mama." But do they frown every time they hear a nice bubbly mouthful of syllables that sound vaguely Latvian? No. They just listen all the harder for the first string of "m-m-m-m-m" and then they make a big deal over it. That reinforcement creates pleasure for the child, who then links the accident to pleasure, and does it again and again. Behavior that's not reinforced is abandoned for more show-stopping feats.

It's the same in classrooms. When your kids walk through the door the first day, you'll spot at least a dozen things that bug you. They're noisy. Their social skills are nonexistent. They have a slavering appetite for pencils, but not for writing. Some of them are downright hostile to anything that looks or smells like work.

Don't say a word.

Just remain on high alert for approximations of eptness and trumpet each discovery. Do that consistently, with fierce and relentless enthusiasm, and you'll begin to get the classroom culture that you want.

2. Expectations

Teachers begin to form expectations very early in the year—often on very first day of school. And many of the factors that color their expectations have nothing to do with academic ability. Initial expectations are often based on body type, gender, race, ethnicity, unusual names, attractiveness, home language, and socio-economics. If first impressions are lasting, then some students have a distinct advantage, while others are already on the road to a dismal academic career.

Great teachers don't prejudge kids as more or less able to learn, and then cling religiously to that preconception. They take a democratic rather than Darwinian approach to success in their classes. Darwinians say that it's survival of the fittest, fit being the closest approximation to the teacher's idea of a good student, or perhaps a student who simply resembles the teacher. In democratic classrooms, teachers search for evidence of all students' capacities; kids know that their success is expected and that they will have the opportunity to demonstrate it in many ways.

Studies have shown that a child's at-riskness in school is largely defined by the teacher's attitudes and expectations, not by a child's family, national origin, or pigment. An ethnographic study (Rist 1975) of a kindergarten class in an inner-city school showed that within eight days the teacher had already grouped the children—not by academic assessments, but according to skin color, behavior, clothing, hygiene, and previous experience with siblings. When the teacher got around to using academic assessments, the outcome was consistent with the teacher's early hunches, and by the end of first grade the teacher's initial expectations were virtually set in stone.

This idea is sometimes referred to as the *self-fulfilling prophecy* or SFP. The term was first coined by sociologist Robert K. Merton in 1957. As part of his explanation of the SFP, Merton embraced the assertion that, "If men define situations as real, they are real in their consequences." Here's how SFP works in a classroom:

1. The teacher forms expectations about each student.
2. The teacher tailors the treatment of each student, based on those expectations.
3. The teacher's treatment tells each student what behavior and achievement the teacher expects.
4. If this treatment is consistent, it will tend to shape the student's behavior and achievement.
5. With time, the student's behavior and achievement will conform more and more closely to what the teacher expects of him or her.

This theory has been tested repeatedly in a broad range of educational settings. And the outcome is always the same. What teachers expect of students has more effect on what they achieve than any other factor—no matter what teaching method is being used. A stunning example of this was documented in *Pygmalion in the Classroom* (Rosenthal 1968). In this study, inner-city elementary school teachers were told that certain students in their classes were likely to blossom academically in the coming year. In truth, the students' names had been randomly selected from the class roster. Sure enough, in a year's time the identified students had shown marked gains—children who were Latino and African American even more than those who were white or of Asian descent. Expect kids to be smart and they perform.

3. Encouragement

Encouragement is the most potent tool you have for creating a culture of eptness. The word alone tells it all. While praise is clearly a commodity bestowed upon, encouragement means to call forth the courage within. It's not judgment. It's activation. High-quality encouragement sends a message of confidence along with some compass skills. The immediate effect is that kids know what to do, and how to do it. The long-range effects of encouragement are greater confidence and independence.

The opportunities for encouraging are boundless in any classroom if you simply tune in. Kids deserve encouragement when they:

- Recognize a problem and speculate about how to investigate it.
- Try various solutions until one works.
- Approach situations with an attitude that's analytic rather than judgmental.
- Volunteer to help peers solve problems.
- Enlist the help of peers to solve problems.
- Seek out several sources of information when investigating a topic.
- Cross-check information.
- Share skills and knowledge effectively, so that peers learn from them.
- Admit when they're stuck or puzzled. (That's an essential step in learning.)
- Ask questions that probe the thinking of their peers.
- Refer to knowledge from outside experiences during classroom activities.
- Apply real-world skills to classroom tasks.
- Acknowledge feelings and needs of peers.
- Acknowledge accomplishments of peers.
- Identify topics they wonder about for personal investigation.

When encouraging students, convey your delight in whole sentences, not just smiles and nods. And be explicit. Tell them precisely what they did that was notable. "That was very clever the way you used those crayons to outline the floor plan of a Mayan temple, and then took Hector on a tour. I think that really helped him picture how Mayan architecture worked." Kids get smarter when you describe what they did and explain why it's important.

It's hard to overestimate the power of encouragement, especially in the early stages of building a classroom culture. In the first weeks of school, this tumult of encouragement will create curiosity among many of your students, if only of the what's-she-raving-about-now variety. But that's a start. They make a mental note of what you're drooling over, and sooner or later, they'll try it, too, because when it comes to encouragement, kids are hungrier than a group of teachers at a faculty meeting. The harder you look, the more capacities you'll find. If you make your students' eptness the centerpiece of every classroom conversation, it will proliferate. It's simply a matter of time and persistence.

I have deliberately avoided the word *praise* because it conjures up lackluster utterances doled out to the deserving and the not-so, with almost no effect. Useless, even harmful praise takes a number of forms:

• *Praise as Verbal Sedative.* These comments are so bland and nonspecific that they put the learning part of the brain to sleep and keep it there. Words like *nice, good, fine, okay* are the equivalent of a pat on the head. A mechanical smile and eyes that look through rather than at a child complete the tranquilizing effect.

• *Pavlovian Praise.* In this case the teacher is one who's become conditioned. She doles out empty phrases in response to routine performances, as if to let students know she's still on the job. "Good job" is about as threadbare as a phrase can be, and kids can see right through it.

• *Praise as Chew Bone.* The class is starting to get out of hand. They're frisky. Bored. Eyeing the furniture with destruction in mind. The teacher quickly picks out one of the nonparticipants in the premelee activities, loudly praises that child, then begins a litany of, "I like the way . . ." remarks designed to rein in the rest of the group. This isn't recognition. It's crowd control and everyone knows it.

• *Skinnerian Snacks.* Periodically the teacher throws out a scrap of praise to promote and reinforce conditioned behavior. This comes with a host of visual aides—gold stars, stickers, happy faces, checkmarks, marbles in jars— all of which have the effect of reducing teaching and learning to a rather labor-intensive exercise in accounting.

The problem with all of these techniques is their inherent emphasis on judgment—what the teacher thinks is good, what the teacher likes, what the teacher wants. Comments like "I'm so proud of you" and "I like the way you're sitting" promote compliance, not capacity. They focus kids on pleasing the teacher as the primary activity when they should be devoting all their energy to discover how to get both hands on the steering wheel of their brain and then driving like crazy.

4. Feedback

When you give feedback, you encourage students by providing both affective and cognitive information about the work they've produced. Effective feedback is positive and includes details that help students appreciate the effectiveness or accuracy of their efforts. When you're giving feedback to students, try whenever possible to quote their own words back to them to make your point. For example:

> "I noticed you used the word *theory* when you were talking about life on Jupiter, and that was very smart because we can't know for sure right now. We just have our theories."

> "You said your character was having trouble deciding whether to leave home or stay and support her family, and that's what makes a good story—conflict."

> "You mentioned that it took you five books and two Internet sites to find that information about Magellan's death. You're really becoming an expert in doing historical research."

Here's a very simple example of feedback in action. Students spend hours learning to print or hand write the letters of the alphabet. And unfortunately for them, there are many ways for a letter to be wrong: too fat, too loopy, not touching the line. Scanning a student's work and saying a letter is "not great" or "try this again" leaves a wealth of questions on exactly what's wrong, and no good model for how to do it right.

On the other hand, you can identify their best efforts and say, "Now that's a perfectly beautiful capital *M*. And there's another one." Point to or touch the examples of what you are looking for. Then the student immediately has a model for how to succeed again. And *again* is the key word. They don't have to wonder *if* they can do it because they have the evidence right before their eyes. They're confident and motivated to do it again. Particularly in tasks such as handwriting, this avoids the prospect of students spending five minutes writing and fifteen erasing, until their papers look bullet-ridden.

During creative writing sessions I used to wander around the classroom and mumble *wow, whoa, fabulous,* as I pointed to a word or line. If we were focused on adjectives or opening lines, I'd simply say, "You got it—that's great!" If my students were doing a series of math problems, I'd walk around with a yellow highlighter and put a dot on several problems that were correct, saying, "That's right, and so is that."

Using unusual words to encourage students gets their attention, too, because it feels like your remarks are tailored to their efforts. Use words like: *unique, interesting, curious, brilliant, impressive, clever, insightful, picturesque, vivid, sharp, amazing, inspiring, unexpected, surprising, novel, creative, inventive, fresh.* Students may pause to think about why that word applies to their work, and that moment of reflection improves their understanding of the ways that they're smart.

5. *Input*

Input goes beyond feedback to teach the next level of skills, or push students to think in more refined ways. It combines observations with guiding questions. The goal is to help students evaluate their own efforts by asking themselves better questions. Input must be tailored to the work at hand, and consider the student's existing skills. The following are examples of comments that provide input.

- It seems like adding dialogue really helped us understand your character's problem. Is that what you were trying to do?
- What part of this graph seems to really work for you? Why?
- What other sources might you use to learn about Atlanta during the Civil War?
- Maybe you could look at some more local maps to decide what kind of legend you want to draw.
- This area of your design looks less detailed than the rest. What do you think?
- Tell me more about . . .
- Have you thought about looking at Custer's diary to get ideas for quotes you might use in your short story?
- Your portrait reminds me of a Picasso. Are you familiar with his Blue Period? You might find the similarities interesting.
- I heard you mention that the weight of your materials was the reason why you won the model boat contest. That's a good hypothesis. How could you test it?

6. *Model Being a Learner*

Kids sometimes have the mistaken impression that teachers have all the answers. They surmise that school would be a lot easier if they knew those answers, too. So school becomes a fact-grab. Some kids take a Roman approach—shove the information in, regurgitate for the test, start all over. That's not learning.

Kids need to know that learning is what the brain does, naturally, continually, involuntarily. Lungs breathe. Stomachs digest. Brains learn. Teachers' brains, too. So take every opportunity you can to reveal yourself as a learner. Bring in the books you're reading. Remark out loud when you make a discovery. Wonder aloud. Pose your own questions at the beginning of a lesson and ask your students to be on the lookout for information that might help you answer them. Your students should hear you say with delight, "I never knew that!"

7. *Model Risk Taking*

Learning in public is risky business. Ask any closet tap dancer. It's one thing to hoof and flail in front of a bedroom mirror, quite another to pull on tap shoes and give it a whirl in a room full of strangers. Paralysis is often the result. And yet, that's what we ask kids to do every day—grapple with challenging tasks in front of their peers. So we need to give them a safety net by modeling how adults handle uncertainty and failure.

As often as possible, try new things in class. Let your kids know if you're taking them on a maiden voyage in mathematics, and you're not sure where it will all end. If the activity is a flop say so, and immediately go into learning mode. "Now what went wrong there? How could we do that differently? Can someone figure out why this didn't work? Did we learn anything from that?" And don't forget, "Help me think this through."

Here are some other phrases that your kids should hear.

- I'm not sure if this will work. I've never done it before.
- We may be wrong, but let's try it anyway.
- Here's my hypothesis. What do you think?
- We may have to start all over.
- There's something wrong with our approach, but I'm not sure what. Let's try a couple of different methods.

8. *Challenge Old Habits*

Schools are like ritual factories. There's an abundance of robotic behavior and no one seems to know where it came from. For example, there's that weird sing-songy way that kids say, "Gooood moooorr—ning, Mrs. Mergatroid," as if they're trying out for the Eddie Haskell choir. And as teachers, we also do some things that our own teachers did decades ago, without asking if there's a better way, or if they need to be done at all. The biggest question we should be asking about any unconscious, unchallenged ritual is, Does this promote eptness and authentic learning?

Here's a perfect example. One day, while giving a spelling test, I realized I'd wandered into the land that time forgot. I was a dead-ringer for my fourth grade teacher, on autopilot, pacing slowly around the room, clutching the spelling list to my chest. Why? She probably did it to prevent cheating, but my kids weren't into cheating. And that stupid, say-the-word, say-it-in-a-sentence, say-the-word-again format was a complete waste of time. Most of my kids knew the words by Tuesday. Here it was Friday and I sounded like an audiotape for a beginner's course from Berlitz. What the heck was I doing?

So I told my kids we were going to try something new: a mental spelling test. They would number their paper, as usual. Then I'd say "Go" and they'd write all the spelling words they could remember from our list. In effect, they gave themselves the test from memory. After five or ten minutes, I'd read the list of spelling words out loud and they could write down any words they'd left out. So there was absolutely no downside to the game.

The upside was that this simple twist on a tired, old procedure stretched their memory skills, and most of all, made them feel smart. They could feel their brain working and it felt good. And here was a real bonus: They got so good at it, they didn't want to stop. Since all of our spelling words were taken from our humanities studies, there were dozens more words that we'd been using all week in discussions, journals, and essays. So when they finished the official spelling list, they could keep on writing any other relevant words, as many as they wanted. A stupid, lumbering twenty-word test turned into a silent, exciting memory tournament with some students writing fifty to sixty words. I never droned a spelling list again.

9. *Never Too Late*

Teachers that emphasize eptness have a deeply held belief that it's never too late. Never too late to learn. Never too late to save a friendship. Never too late to have a better idea. Never too late to revise your work. They have created a culture that celebrates breakthroughs. As long as your heart's pumping, there's still time to improve.

You see this never-too-late ethic at work throughout the day. For example, in many classrooms, the first order of the day is correcting and turning in home-work. Not a great way to start the day for some kids, but it can be a positive experience if everyone is operating under the never-too-late policy. Then correcting homework becomes a time for editing, reworking, recalculating, and having those small epiphanies that make students jump up and cheer "yes!" The marked-up paper you get when it's finally turned in documents growth, not failure.

You simply have to keep your eye on the prize. Do you want kids to learn to self-correct, complete more work, and feel smart, or rack up a bunch of errors, and feel anxious and humiliated? It's your call, and it's an easy one. It's never too late to create opportunities for kids to succeed.

10. *Do Nothing for Students That They Can Do for Themselves*

Great teachers frequently look like employment counselors because they're constantly putting their kids to work. Their students refine classroom systems, do routine maintenance and bookkeeping, organize projects, and solve their own problems. Great teachers refuse to do anything for students that they can do for themselves. The do-nothing rule is a basic principle in working with any group where independence is the goal.

One morning I saw two first graders solemnly walking down the main hall, their tiny hands cradling a ball of fluff. When I inquired, they informed me that they were on their way to the assistant principal's office. He'd made an announcement that morning on the PA system and they disagreed with his idea. In their class, when students disagreed, they talked it out while holding the "warm fuzzy." It was the most natural thing in the world for them to make this journey to negotiate with a six-foot-four-inch administrator. To his credit, he met them on their level and the problem was solved. The only thing their teacher did was sign their hall pass.

If you want kids to discover their own capacities, they have to explore the gap between what they're currently doing and what they can accomplish with persistence, research, collaboration, invention, creativity, and thinking. The only way they do that is if you hold back and let them stare into the gap. Don't finish their sentences, solve their engineering problems, or tell them how their poems should end. Leave it up to them, even if you have to sit on your hands and bite your tongue. It takes longer to do nothing, but the result is a room full of resourceful thinkers.

How Am I Doing? A Self-Assessment

It's nearly impossible to overstate the importance of monitoring yourself if you are trying to build a culture of eptness. You need to consciously assess your expectations, utterances, and activities to see how they're helping your students develop the skills, interpersonal behaviors, attitudes, and habits of mind that characterize a community of confident learners.

Observe yourself. Pay attention to what you do and say. Then ask yourself some good questions:

- Do I plan with all students in mind or just the high achievers?
- What do I model?
- What do I reinforce through recognition and celebration?
- Do I value effort, thinking, and persistence, or only the finished product?
- What do I encourage—ingenuity, great questions, empathy, courage, curiosity?
- What do I assess?
- How do my assessments incorporate a variety of learning styles?
- Do students share in the power and responsibilities of our class?

An honest response to these questions will give you a sketch of how you're doing at building a culture of eptness.

Social Safety and Eptness

No matter how earnestly you promote a culture of eptness, your message will fall on deaf ears if your students don't feel safe in the classroom. I don't mean that they're worried about terrorists or wondering when the next earthquake will send the furniture dancing across the floor. Those concerns certainly do plague students from time to time and interfere with learning, but research tells us that the most persistent safety concerns for students are emotional mistreatment and social cruelty.

Typically, students are mistreated by other students because they're part of a disfavored class: unattractive, poor, physically disabled, homeless, meek, clumsy, learning disabled, foreign-born, or possibly homosexual. Students who are routinely mistreated spend their days in a defensive crouch, focused on survival skills, and even the potential for mistreatment or bullying can render a child unavailable for learning.

Bullying is a tragic reality in American education. Yet many teachers, particularly in elementary school, think that their classroom has been spared of this scourge. In reality, 7 to 12 percent of all students report that they've been the target of significant bullying. So if you have thirty students in your class, three or four of them may be suffering at the hands of their peers.

Parents often wonder why teachers don't prevent the social maltreatment going on right under their noses. One reason is that much of it is invisible—a mocking gesture or simply being treated like a piece of furniture. And many instances of mistreatment are dismissed as *kidding*. We hear kids say after a nasty remark—"Just kidding"—in an offhanded way that bears no resemblance to an apology. In fact, it rehumiliates the victim by suggesting that he can't tell a joke from an insult. The root word *kid* makes it sound benign, even developmentally appropriate, as if it was a rite of passage.

Despite its prevalence, social maltreatment is not a rite of passage, nor is it constructive. Bullying and social cruelty do not build resiliency. Instead, they increase vulnerability. Students who have been victimized repeatedly are strip-mined of all self-esteem. They suffer from loneliness, increased anxiety, self-blame, and social withdrawal. They cannot contribute to their classroom community for fear of being ridiculed. Nor can they learn from their peers when all their efforts are devoted to avoiding contact. While other students are building eptness, these kids are working on their armor, which is why it's critical to eradicate social maltreatment in your classroom. Most teachers make a real effort to do this, but are frustrated by the fact that it usually happens when their backs are turned. Here's a teacher who found a way to help her students feel safe.

Meet Ava de la Sota

Ava de la Sota is a beating-heart liberator. Loves kids. Can't stand to see them suffer. "Gratuitous cruelty drives me crazy," she says. So she set out to invent a program that would free kids from social and emotional mistreatment. Because she spends her days in an elementary school, where taunts and put-downs are more common than skinned knees and peanut butter sandwiches, she knew she was fighting an uphill battle. Some colleagues said it was a losing proposition. Others suggested that she give up and find a hobby.

But to Ava, this crusade against cruelty seemed like a good use of her time—"better than pulling tearful kids out of the bathroom every afternoon, and doing first aid on shattered friendships when I should have been teaching writing." Some of her brightest students spent their days dodging insults and humiliations that gradually had a crippling effect. "Too many students were struggling, and didn't have Clue One about strategies that would help them cope with stress in their social interactions," she lamented. But Ava knew that advocating harsher punitive measures wouldn't create the haven her students needed. "It's not enough to say we need more rules or tougher standards. We need to take time to listen to students and to use these incidents as opportunities for education."

So like any great problem solver, she devoted her brainpower to analyzing the social problems kids face, and then she created a set of tools to match those problems. But what do you put in a tool kit for the tiny but powerful cold shoulder of a kindergartener who says to a newcomer, "You can't play with us"? What could address eye-rolling, conspiratorial whispers, pointing, and giggling? Or the more aggressive offenses: name-calling, threats, racist remarks, and perhaps one of the most insidious forms of bullying—rumors? Silently mouthing the word *gay* when a student stands up to read in class or flinches at a fly ball?

Many adults who live in a world of road rage and industrial-strength indifference, where self-absorption and getting ahead seem like virtues, doubt whether children can give up their taunts and learn to manage conflict humanely.

Not Ava. "Children live in the world we create around them. If they're taught that kindness is the code, they learn to be kind. If they experience the balm of concern and apologies, they learn compassion." The responsibility is clearly on adults, particularly those working with young students, to build, teach, and model a humane universe. Adopting the motto, "It's not cool to be cruel," Ava called her invention *Cool Tools*.

She started with a single ground rule—*no put-downs.* Any word or gesture intended to hurt was unacceptable. That included practical jokes played at one child's expense as well as physically excluding a kid from a game and the whole range of mocking gestures that ridicule without a word being said. In their place, Ava promoted *put-ups.* Compliments, nods, inclusive body language, and smiling. She even gave her students a 5:1 formula. It takes five *put-ups* to heal one *put-down.*

Early in the school year, Ava shares *Leo the Late Bloomer* by Robert Kraus (1971) or *Odd Velvet* by Mary Whitcomb (1998). As she reads, she asks students to signal silently when they hear a put-down by turning their thumbs down. They signal with thumbs-up when they hear a put-up. Then she brings out a life-size butcher paper silhouette of a child and reads the story again. But this time, when students hear a put-down, she has a volunteer come up and tear a bit off the body. When they hear a put-up, volunteers try to repair the torn person, using band-aids, tape, glue or heart stickers. In the class discussion that follows, students acknowledge that despite their best efforts, the tears don't disappear. Put-downs leave scars that can be easily reinjured by another put-down.

Recognizing the power of concrete objects to help kids learn and retain abstract ideas, Ava created an actual toolbox of visual props that represent the social skills kids need to successfully manage interpersonal conflict—communication, compromise, tone of voice, coping, compassion, and the all-important closed-door exit. Each object is a cognitive cue to prompt appropriate behavior. The toolkit contains:

• *Nice Dice.* Kids use colorful foam dice to practice giving compliments. Roll a 2, then give two put-ups. This activity reinforces the ability to prevent conflict through positive communication.

• *Inflatable Microphone.* Kids practice changing their tone of voice while talking into the microphone to drive home the message that their tone of voice can calm or inflame situations. In fact, 90 percent of any message is delivered through volume, tone, and body language. A snippy "Thanks a lot" is not a thank-you at all. Students practice a single phrase such as "Let me see it," using different intonations until everyone is willing to own their tone. When teachers overhear kids talking in a provocative tone they cue their students by saying: "microphone voice."

• *Kaleidoscope.* This tool represents a concept that's tough for many adults—multiple points of view. Kids peek through the kaleidoscope and make drawings of what they see. Inevitably, all the drawings are different, demonstrating that in human interactions there is rarely a single point of view. Ava coaches, "We all see situations differently. The only way to solve the problem is to compromise. What can we agree on?"

• *Inflatable Foot.* This prop teaches kids to recognize when it's time to get out of a situation. If a conflict heats up and the chance of compromise goes down, exit skills are in order. Researchers believe that many students, particularly adolescents, are injured or killed simply because they lack exit skills. They stay too long in dangerous situations because they don't want to lose face. In some cases they lose their lives. Ava teaches one-liners to get kids out the door and close it behind them, while maintaining their self-respect.

• *Ice Cube Tray.* Using the tray as a cue, kids develop a repertoire of "chill skills." They brainstorm ways to calm themselves down and cope with their feelings after exiting a conflict, so they don't hold on to the pain or surrender to the temptation to reengage their adversaries.

• *Toothpaste.* Students squeeze toothpaste out and then try to put it back in the tube to grasp the idea that once harmful words are spoken, it's impossible to take them back and it may take a lot of work to clean up the hurt feelings.

• *Big Eraser.* A hefty three-by-five-inch eraser helps students focus on the difficult task of forgiving mistakes that other people make and forgiving themselves. Erasing represents compassion and lets them move on.

So how does this work? Ava is only one person among hundreds of kids. She can't be everywhere, wielding her eraser or microphone like a big stick to keep order. But she doesn't need to. *Cool Tools* is a safe school system—every child learns the tools, and in a very short time they internalize the concepts. Of course, remembering to use them takes practice, but all the adults have been trained to cue kids using shorthand—a child using a harsh voice simply hears "microphone voice." Children caught in the classic tug of war over a toy, arguing about who had it first, hear "kaleidoscope" to nudge them toward the appropriate solution. In time, the tools become a self-managing system that provides kids with proactive, prosocial behaviors, face-saving one-liners, and even lifesaving strategies.

With *Cool Tools* under their belts, Ava's students learn to think constructively and strategically about challenging social situations. With practice, they can extract themselves from aversive encounters and then ask: "How can I keep this from happening again?" The ultimate goal of *Cool Tools* is to give kids an explicit understanding of self-reliance, kindness, integrity, empathy, fairness, self-respect, patience, responsibility, forgiveness, and perseverance.

But does it work? Schools that use *Cool Tools* experience a dramatic drop in playground disputes. Teachers report that the program doesn't take time, it makes time. Once their kids know the tools, behavior management is reduced to a trickle of single key words, leaving lots of time to praise kids for managing conflicts successfully. How deeply do these *Cool Tools* influence a young child's worldview? When war was declared on Iraq, a puzzled second grader asked his teacher, "Doesn't the President know about *Cool Tools*?"

Waking Magoun's Brain

I once read about a brain researcher named Magoun who identified a part of the brain that only responds to novelty. Its job is to announce to all the neurons and synapses, "Hey, here's something we've never seen before! What do you make of this?"

Great teachers are constantly waking Magoun's brain. They avoid empty routines, like roll call when all the seats in the room are clearly full. Instead they start the day with discussions, quotes or headlines, a strange word or juicy question, even a glimpse at a curious object. The goal is to jump-start the brain and get students thinking, "I wonder what else we're going to learn today?"

> We were lucky to grow up in an environment where there was always much encouragement to children to pursue intellectual interests, to investigate whatever aroused curiosity. In a different kind of environment, our curiosity might have been nipped long before it could have borne fruit.
>
> —Orville Wright

Now I know that some educators are big believers in structure for kids. But isn't it enough that students come to the same twenty-by-thirty-foot room, 180 days a year, sit in the same seat, have snack, lunch, and recess at the same time, are surrounded by the same twenty to thirty faces, with the same books, paper, homework, and bus ride? Enough! Magoun's brain wants to commit suicide.

Try to invent each day. The first minutes of the day should not be predictable in content, but they should be predictably interesting. Program your students to have a sharp, positive association when they walk through the door of your class. They see you and they're conditioned to feel smart, optimistic, and curious. Their first thought is—Something interesting is going to happen, and it will happen to me.

Resources

Kraus, Robert. 1971. *Leo the Late Bloomer.* New York: Windmill Books.

Kozol, Jonathan. 1991. *Savage Inequalities: Children in America's Schools.* New York: Crown.

Ladson-Billings, Gloria. 1994. *Dreamkeepers: Successful Teachers of African American Children.* San Francisco: Jossey-Bass.

Palmer, Parker. 1998. *The Courage to Teach: Exploring the Inner Landscape of a Teacher's Life.* San Francisco: Jossey-Bass.

Whitcomb, Mary. 1998. *Odd Velvet.* San Francisco: Chronicle Books.

SECRET #3

Great Teachers Are Ringmasters

Nurturing Free-Range Students in a High-Stakes World

In This Chapter:

- ♦ What's the Big Idea About Behavior?
- ♦ Understanding Self-Accommodaters
- ♦ Understanding Camouflagers
- ♦ Meet Linda Catanzano
- ♦ Eight Strategies for Ringmasters
- ♦ The Roots of Free-Range Behavior
- ♦ The Law, Special Education, and 504s
- ♦ Hope for Free-Rangers in a High-Stakes World

If you're determined to be a teacher, I heartily suggest that you start with a full-frontal embrace of the Boy Scout motto—*Be prepared.* Manning a classroom in the twenty-first century can feel suspiciously like presiding over a banana republic—with revolution brewing right below the surface. In any room, on any day, students demonstrate a dazzling array of free-range behavior the minute the teacher goes for the chalk. First, a human cannonball flies across the room. Alert peers dive for cover, but a slow-moving tyke is bowled over by his missilelike progress toward the pencil sharpener. Several dozen noisy rotations produce a lead point sharp enough to etch diamonds. Now maybe he can think about working. Another student does a passable imitation of someone in an electric chair. There's a sprinkling of the perpetually confused and velocity-challenged, working earnestly, but at a glacial pace, with little to show for their efforts. Finally, there are the students who spend most of their day staring at the ceiling, as if they were in a planetarium.

You don't need to travel to observe this natural phenomenon. Just cast an appreciative eye around your own classroom.

You announce it's math time, and immediately an unfocused buzz of energy runs through the group. One student lunges for his backpack, as if he's suddenly remembered an important appointment—elsewhere. But no. Like many kids, he enjoys nothing so much as a good long hunt for his favorite pencil, without which he cannot attempt the simplest calculations. A proudly defiant math-phobe noisily scrambles to locate her book, which is a major undertaking since her desk is the Bermuda Triangle of the classroom. Anthologies, manipulatives, and especially homework assignments disappear without a trace, despite daily searches that require more time and industry than she ever devotes to your lessons.

Another desk is strewn with clutter, its occupant intent on creating a galaxy of entertainments, principally involving tissues, a juice box, and three paper clips. He's far too busy to notice something as subtle as you, teaching. Even on your best day, you're just elevator music.

In a far corner, a student—gender undecipherable—is draw-stringed into a hooded sweatshirt and hunched over a book, oblivious to anything in the room. Nearby, the bookworm's polar opposite observes every detail of human and mechanical activity—the fan is a source of complete fascination, and every passing hall monitor draws her gaze.

Just when you think you've captured the group's fragile attention, a limp and slumping scholar sits bolt-upright and grips the sides of his chair. He presses until both arms are stiff and his body hangs suspended above the seat, rocking slowing to and fro. Then with a single deft movement he pulls his feet up, and settles lightly on his sneakers. Seconds later his head swivels, exorcist-style, scanning his neighbor's desk for amusements. If he was in a car instead of a classroom, this child would be screeching, "Are we there yet? How much longer? I think I'm getting sick."

It's free-range behavior served up by a gaggle of out-of-their seat, out-of-turn, charmingly funny, or downright difficult outlyers who can drive a teacher out of her mind. How's a person supposed to teach with all that going on?

Teachers cope with free-range behavior in different ways. Some view these students as the only downside of an otherwise perfect job, so they reduce student-teacher contact to a trickle of widely spaced monosyllables. They fill the day with assignments as crowd control, then pore over their grade books—looking more like accountants than teachers. Time creaks along.

Then there are the no-controllers, whose behavior management techniques would be a hit under the big top, but utterly fail to capture youthful attention. Lights flash on and off, like cheap special effects. The plaintive warning, "I'm waiting . . ." only encourages misbehavers to take their time reforming.

Some teachers don't manage behavior at all. Impervious to everything, including an impromptu boxing match in the library corner, they're busy surfing the Internet for home mortgage rates.

In some classrooms, free-range behavior is an equal opportunity event. Kids yell at the teacher and the teacher yells back. On tough days, the hostilities escalate to include an impressive repertoire of bad manners—slamming doors and slamming books, exchanging dirty looks, exchanging everything but gunfire.

In other "good" rooms, students are subjected to purgatories of worksheets, punctuated with hollow praise. Stars next to their names and smiling faces on their papers let them how they're doing, as if they're unable to sense their own accomplishment, even if it's the same accomplishment every day. These students have been reduced to a docile herd, wending their way slowly through a joyless, lingering event that passes for an education.

But in great rooms, teachers deftly micromanage classroom behavior to highlight the best in every child. They appear to control the classroom by sleight of hand, transforming a potentially unruly troupe into a brigade of youthful scholars or in the best of all worlds, students with a lifelong appetite for history, poetry, and learning in all its wondrous forms.

What's the Big Idea About Behavior?

There are lots of reasons why kids adopt free-range antics in the classroom. New explanations are being invented every day, as scientists and psychologists explore the connections between the brain and behavior. There are too many theories to capture in a single book, let alone a single chapter. But there is one big idea that will help you look at your kids' behavior in a more analytic and productive way. Here it is.

All behavior is motivated by one of two basic instincts:

1. To seek pleasure.
2. To avoid pain.

That's it. Everything else is elaboration.

So when you see a student veer alarmingly out of control, or invent routines that would be breathtaking even on the late-night comedy channel, you need to forego the usual questions: What the hell is wrong with that kid? Why didn't anybody warn me? And of course, Exactly how early is early retirement? Instead, train yourself to ask: Is this child seeking pleasure or avoiding pain?

The drive for pleasure may not be apparent at first glance, since most classrooms are stark affairs with very few amenities. To most observers, pleasure doesn't live here. But the pleasure that free-range kids are seeking comes from being able to fit in by doing what the teacher expects—what other kids seem to do with ease. They employ odd, even annoying behaviors, in the hope that they, too, can experience satisfaction, recognition, and maybe even garner a little praise. They're making self-accommodations to gain their share of school's simple pleasures.

As for avoiding pain, that can be subtle, too, since we no longer administer attitude adjustments via canes or paddles. Nonetheless, many schools utterly fail to qualify as pain-free zones, as some children routinely experience exclusion, humiliation, disappointment, self-loathing, and even despair because they cannot "do" school. To protect themselves, they employ a variety of tactics to hide their inabilities from the teacher. They use camouflage to avoid the pain of school failure.

So when kids are acting out in your classroom, apparently oblivious to your game plan, it's likely that they're either *self-accommodating* to perform the tasks you want, or *camouflaging* the fact that they can't.

Unfortunately, their motives often get lost in translation, and we simply see a troublemaker or a kid who won't try. Sometimes we even take it personally, as if the child is out to get us. That's not the message behind free-range behavior, but it takes a patient and analytic mind to plow through the smoke screen kids generate to discover what they're trying to accomplish. In addition, it takes superhuman self-control to view classroom disruptions as opportunities to become a better teacher, or even a great one. But it can be done.

Great teachers understand that free-range students want to learn as much or more than their well-adjusted peers. Indeed, they may be trying twice as hard as the scholarship boy who gets straight As without breaking a sweat. They long to enjoy, at least occasionally, the sense that they are good and valued members of the classroom community. Your role as a teacher is to empower free-range kids to accomplish their learning goals by:

1. Creating an environment in which they can learn using appropriate accommodations.

2. Helping them develop the courage and confidence they need to give up their camouflage and tackle the real job of learning.

Let's take this piece-by-piece.

Understanding Self-Accommodaters

I live in Los Angeles where traffic is plentiful and as an added bonus, unpredictable. A twenty-minute drive can take upwards of ninety minutes, if I time it just right. Now, I love driving, but I detest crawling across the city at ten miles per hour as an involuntary member of a commuter drill team.

So I have a PhD in alternate routes. If the freeway is at a standstill, I escape onto a parallel highway. If that's choked, I head for the hills, dart through several sleepy neighborhoods and arrive at my destination sooner, less frustrated, and justly proud of my navigational ingenuity. But if my husband were in the car, he'd fix me with a quizzical expression each time I wandered farther from the direct route.

For many kids, school is one long traffic jam, particularly if they have physical, emotional, or learning challenges. Forward progress is hard won. While their peers zoom through assignments, they creep toward an ever-receding horizon. Some take left turns when almost everyone else heads right, ending up in limbo or trouble. Not surprisingly, many such students are labeled as difficult, slow, or unreceptive to classroom instruction.

Great teachers truly believe that all kids want to learn, and they can be astonishingly productive if they're encouraged to invent alternate strategies that help them accomplish classroom goals. Smart but challenged students have devised hundreds of ways to help themselves get the through school, like drumming a pattern on the tabletop to remember their multiplication facts, humming a jingle to remember history dates, or standing hunched over their table and gnawing on a plastic straw to maintain focus during a spelling test. Great teachers recognize these curious behaviors are actually self-accommodations that reveal strengths that can be used to leverage learning in other areas of your curriculum. I had a student who began every writing assignment by doodling in the margins of his paper. Or at least that's what I thought he was doing until I asked. He was actually making tiny sketches of his ideas as a way to brainstorm and remember what he wanted to say. Since he was a visual learner, sketching was his language of choice. Once I caught on, we found ways for him to use sketching as a thinking and planning tool across the curriculum. He made storyboards to show a sequence of historical events, and comic strips or story maps for literature.

The trick with self-accommodations is that adults have to pay attention and figure out the purpose behind this unschoolish behavior. Unfortunately, rather than congratulating kids for persisting in their attempts to learn, we're frequently irritated by their originality and imagination. How many times have you seen a proud, young mathematician rebuffed by the curt dismissal "you have to show your work" with the clear implication that there may be some cheating afoot?

Great teachers openly acknowledge that there are many ways to learn. Instead of stigmatizing children for failing to respond to traditional methods, at the average speed, while sitting like the star pupils in a Prussian posture academy, they look to their students as the experts on what works. Instead of just guessing how to tailor the curriculum, or providing the same generic accommodations for all students—do every other math problem on the page—great teachers become experts at spotting and implementing accommodations tailored to each student's strengths and needs.

What Do Self-Accommodations Look Like?

If you think kids are the only self-accommodaters, just take a look around at your next faculty meeting. These gatherings typically feature overcrowding, uncomfortable chairs, dead air, and agendas that range from annoying to verbal sedation. If you scan the crowd, you'll see a sprinkling of catatonics, seditionists, and of course, the designated whiner. But mostly you will see industrious captives arriving with bulging Land's End tote bags, intent on plowing through their appointed tasks. It looks like a study hall for teachers, with a pesky administrator trying to attract their attention.

The goal for most teachers is to stay awake, stay under the radar, and get home as soon as possible without aggravating their principal, so they make dozens of self-accommodations to cope with the relatively simple task of sitting through a meeting. Some teachers take the busy-hands-are-happy-hands approach. They scrawl smiling faces on hundreds of papers, correct tests, and record grades. Birthday cards circulate and checkbooks are balanced. Manic knitters labor over baby sweaters. Others just kill time by fidgeting in socially acceptable ways. They swig on water bottles or gnaw a hangnail. Some jiggle one foot, rock back in their chairs, twist their hair, or readjust their glasses. Occasionally, there's a discreet nap. No one would call this fun, but all survive and swear that they heard and understood every announcement. Now, if the principal asked them to "sit up straight and tall" with their hands folded on a naked table for ninety minutes, she'd be lucky to escape with her life.

Many kids find the classroom more challenging than a faculty meeting by a factor of about ten, so they spend their days devising accommodations that will allow them to execute the seemingly endless parade of tasks required to progress from kindergarten through high school. You need to be familiar with this intriguing repertoire of physical, social, and cognitive accommodations so that you will stop scolding kids for doing the very things that help them cope with your expectations. Here's a beginning list.

Physical Accommodations

Students may:

- Drag a finger under the text as they read, trying to compensate for poor tracking skills, which result in skipped words, phrases, or lines or completely losing their place on the page.

- Tear bits of paper and roll them into neat ball or grind erasers on the table top as a way to focus.
- Turn sideways when asked to write so that their papers rest at the side of the body, not in front of the torso. These students may have a brain/motor difficulty that prevents their hands from crossing over the midline of the body. Their hands only work in their respective hemispheres—right on the right side of the body, left on left.
- Chew on their clothing while working, putting pressure on the muscles and joints in their face and jaw to help them concentrate.
- Hum, whistle, tap, fidget, lean their chair back on two legs, rock back and forth, drum with fingers or a pencil on the table top to keep the brain awake and stimulated.
- Arrange all their materials in a precise order before starting work to organize their minds.
- Put their heads down on the desk while working.

Social Accommodations

Students may:

- Look at what other people are doing before they start work.
- Talk over the directions with a partner.
- Ask for help from the teacher before even starting.
- Ask to work with another student.
- Pass notes.
- Offer to give assistance to another child.

Cognitive Accommodations

Students may:

- Flip through books and look at pictures.
- Make lists.
- Doodle and draw pictures.
- Talk out loud about what they need or plan to do.
- Talk while they work.
- Read aloud.
- Mark up the text with highlights and notes.
- Reread portions of the text or assignment repeatedly.
- Scribble notes on scraps of paper.

Getting Smarter About Accommodations

Left to their own devices, students invent a fair number of accommodations, but they may be so distracting or inefficient that they only complicate their problems, leading to more frustration and less success. So part of your job is to devise effective ways to adapt the work in your room so that all kids can succeed.

Making accommodations requires task analysis. You look at the assignment in question and break it down into its component parts—including the invisible steps where students are just thinking. Ask yourself what needs to be done first, next, and next. Then ask if there are other ways your kids can master this material—reading an alternative text or looking at photographs to gather historical information; building a model or drawing a map to demonstrate concepts; listening to story tapes or watching a video. At first, it takes time and patience to come up with effective accommodations. But happily, there are many resources, and with a little research you can incorporate them into your best practices and help all your kids exchange free-range behavior for achievement.

For example, many bright students have sensory-motor issues that make handwriting a torture. They write slowly, so slowly, all the while strangling their pencils in a death grip. Despite their best efforts, their work is almost illegible—as if written with the left foot. Your first move should be to investigate the program, *Handwriting Without Tears* developed by Jan Olsen and then think about using any of the following accommodations. Give your students big foam pencil grips, tape their paper onto the desk to prevent it from moving, replace standard worksheets with wide-lined paper, and use a three-ring binder as an elevated slant board on which they can write with greater ease. It also helps to seat the slower writers together, so they don't get so frustrated observing peers writing at lightning speed. Remember, this is a physiological problem that responds very well to accommodations and encouragement, and not at all to admonishments and criticism.

There are hundreds of accommodations that teachers can make to help students succeed. Here are a few of the most commonsense ones:

- Break directions into discrete steps, then give them verbally and in writing, highlighting critical words with yellow.
- Allow for additional time to finish schoolwork or take tests.
- Use audio textbooks (available through Recordings for Blind) if students have difficulty reading.
- Provide students with auditory difficulties with copies of notes from a classmate or let them use a tape recorder during lessons.
- Provide graph paper for math calculations to help students place numbers in the correct columns.

- Color-code each column in a multiplication problem to help students align numerals.
- Have students highlight information with a yellow highlighter as they read. If possible, photocopy pertinent chapters from textbooks so the material is consumable.
- Let students with writing difficulties use a computer with spell checks or grammar checks whenever possible.
- Teach key words or phrases in written directions then highlight with a color.
- Provide models to help students with multistep tasks. Post the models and refer to them often.
- Teach through multisensory modes, giving information in visual, auditory, and kinesthetic formats.
- Use buff-colored paper rather than white to reduce glare.
- Teach students to use an egg timer, hourglass, or other visual cues to stay on task.
- Ignore inappropriate behaviors that are not drastically outside classroom limits and reinforce appropriate behavior relentlessly.

The Internet is an amazing source for accommodations. Just type in a specific disability, such as ADD, and the word *accommodations*, and you'll get dozens of citations explaining how to make schoolwork more accessible to students with that disability. For example, the Sevier County Schools has a tremendous website with ideas for accommodating students with learning disabilities. Just go to www.slc.sevier.org/ldaccom.htm for hundreds of specific ideas. Or visit the *What You Need to Know About* website on special education http://specialed.about.com/cs/teacherstrategies. This website has links to at least twelve other sites where you can find accommodations for every area of the curriculum. With just a few clicks of the mouse, you're on your way to being an accommodations expert.

Maybe cyberlearning doesn't work for you. If you do better with face-to-face mentoring, look up some of the experts right on your campus or in your district. If you're a regular education teacher, seek out a colleague in special education and make a date for coffee. Special education teachers have advanced knowledge about different ways of knowing and they can suggest dozens of effective strategies without batting an eye.

Another way to get smarter about accommodations is to track down a school psychologist. You'll probably find them behind closed doors, since they spend lots of time doing student assessments, but it's well worth the effort to make an appointment. I can almost guarantee that you'll get a warm reception once you announce that you're not there to refer another kid for testing, but to learn about instructional strategies to enhance learning for all kids! You may be able to negotiate a consultation, where you brief the psychologist about several kids, then he or she comes to your room to observe and make suggestions for accommodations. A simple visit like this can mean major breakthroughs in teaching a broad range of kids.

If you can find an occupational therapist (OT), you're really in for a treat. Occupational therapists have dozens of simple techniques that help kids who are struggling with attention, focus, and writing. Here's a quick trick I learned from a great OT. If your students' handwriting resembles chicken scratches because their grip is all wrong, pull out the tissue box. Crumple up a tissue, put it in on their palm, and ask them to hold on to it by folding down three fingers—middle, ring, and pinky. Now they grab their pencil with their two free fingers and they have a perfect grip. Try it!

Parents can also be a great source of ideas for helping you understand how their kids learn best, since they've been dealing with these challenges for years. Ask, "What have you found that works?" and "How can we work together?" Some parents will be so grateful to have a teacher who understands and cares that they will go to great lengths to help with homework, test preparation, and behavior contracts. Having parents as allies is a lot more fun than making phone calls to report bad behavior or discuss failing grades.

Understanding Camouflagers

Many kids are unable to perform the work you propose, even with self-accommodations, so they camouflage their disability to avoid looking like failures. They've invented a dozen ways to duck scholastic tasks, including outright defiance, because attempting and failing is more painful that any discipline you can mete out.

Not surprisingly, camouflage is often confused with character. A kid feigns disinterest at math time because he knows he doesn't understand fractions. He lolls on his desktop, as if someone spiked his juicebox. The verdict: "He's smart but lazy. He simply doesn't try." A student with ADHD struggles from one incomplete task to another, with occasional junkets to seek eraser guidance from a peer or make impromptu inspections of the hamster cage and fish tank. When the teacher finally declares it's choice time, he makes a dive for the Legos and builds quietly, intently, for twenty-five minutes. Rather than remarking on the complexity of his construction, or the ingenuity of his heli-car design, frustrated teachers are likely to declare, "You see? He can concentrate when he wants to!" Disability is reduced to an act of will.

Rather than resorting to judgments, concerned adults should be looking for more reasonable explanations. After all, what kid really prefers to be the outcast over belonging to the group? It's more useful to simply ask: What's he hiding?

What Does Camouflage Look Like?

Many of your students with achievement challenges camouflage their disabilities to avoid embarrassment and rejection. For them, going to school is less an education than a vanishing act. They're wary, on guard, and worried most of the time. That's not an emotional state that's conducive to learning or even appropriate social development. So your goal is to find the real child underneath the camouflage. To do that, you need to sharpen your ability to spot the ploys kids use to hide their inability to meet your expectations. Here are six of the most common ones you'll encounter.

Class Clown

When there's an accident at the circus, if an entertainer tumbles from the tightrope or a lion turns on his trainer, the manager sends in the clowns to distract people and restore the good mood. That's exactly what's going on in your classroom if you have a camouflager who's acting like a clown. Clowns broadcast nonstop comedy routines to divert attention from what they can't do. But since their humor is often based on extremely perceptive observations, quick thinking, or plays on words, they may look smart and seem connected to the life of the class, if not the exact topic you're discussing. Somehow their outbursts count as participation, so they manage to hide the fact that they don't really understand what's going on.

Truly savvy clowns set up a playful power struggle with their teachers to avoid exposure. After a few side-splitting performances, their teachers treat them as fissionable material. They stop calling on them during most academic lessons, for fear that their raucous comments will disrupt the entire class. So this clown doesn't have to worry about being called on to execute a math problem on the board or explain how the House differs from the Senate. If they're flamboyantly funny, clowns may earn resentment as a rival to the teacher and be labeled as a behavior problem. But in their minds, that's better than being seen as dumb.

Frequent Flyer

Frequent flyers are students who accumulate dozens of miles each day, circling your room or darting back and forth from their desks to the tissue box, trash basket, or water fountain to evade assignments that may reveal their incompetence. I totally identify with this behavior because it's exactly what I do when I'm about to start writing a new chapter. I sit down at my computer, intent on writing, and immediately notice the dust on my bookshelves. Then I think about doing a load of laundry, or remember that the newspapers and bottles need to be loaded into the car for recycling. All of this is just to postpone the agony of tackling that huge, amorphous jumble of ideas and beating them word-by-word into a coherent statement. It's fear and loathing time, and I'm on the move.

You have kids like me in your room. Every time you propose a task that's difficult for them, like doing long division or grammar, they pop up as if their chairs are spring-loaded, just to avoid the frustration or embarrassment of tangling with an assignment that's sure to defeat them. Instead, they fill the time allotted for work making pilgrimages from one peripheral, perhaps helpful activity to another. When time is up and their work is unfinished, they simply claim that they ran out of time, which is a whole lot better than admitting that they still don't get division, no matter how many times you explain it.

Teflon Tyke

Teflon students are convinced that they can't perform like their peers and their defeatism is like a painful religion. Typically, they've spent years trying, failing, being scolded and repentant, then failing again. To avoid more pain, they've developed a Teflon exterior. Your words slide right off. It looks like they don't care. It may even look like contempt. No matter what you do—plead, beg, cajole, or threaten—there's no apparent response. The only person likely to be moved by all this railing is you. You get frustrated, short-tempered, maybe even a little careless with your language, so beware. You don't want to sacrifice your effectiveness with the rest of your students or even scare them by snarling in frustration at a student who isn't doing anything—just sitting like a stone—and waiting for you to give up and go away.

Charmer

There is a handful of less-than-stellar students who live by their wits, and their wits tell them that what the world needs now is love, sweet love. They make their way in school by being complimentary, attentive, helpful, seductive, unusually kind, or self-sacrificing. It's hard to see past this charming exterior to the struggling student underneath. It's another false-face, but such a sweet one, that these students often slip by, getting mediocre grades in academics and high, high marks in effort and citizenship, rarely having to reveal their difficulties.

Bad Boys and Victims

This is an intriguing combination because their camouflaging techniques are so overt and high-profile, that it's as if they're hiding out in the open. Bad boys and victims have a symbiotic relationship that gives both of them an out when it's time to do schoolwork. The bad boy or girl looks around for someone to annoy. The victim is feeling frustrated or daunted by the task at hand, and looking for someone to blame, or simply waiting for an affront that is sure to come. The bad boy is happy to oblige. The chemistry is perfect. The first time you sense a problem is usually when a howl goes up from the victim—"He took my pencil, he hit me, he's staring at me." Then the bad boy takes up the refrain—"I didn't do anything." Once you jump in the middle, you're in their arena and they'll keep you there as long as possible, or until it's recess time. Even if you give both of them a tongue-lashing, or time-out, they'd quietly agree that it's better than pawing through a book they can't read for answers they can't write.

These aren't all the tricks in the book, but you get the idea. When you see bad behavior, train yourself to immediately ask, "What are they hiding?"

Getting Smarter About Piercing Camouflage

The only thing that will break through your students' camouflage is to discover what they're good at, and have them do it. You must be willful and persistent in exposing their competence, even discovering their expertise. Each time you construct activities that allow them to succeed, the camouflage recedes. Eventually, it's unnecessary.

Great teachers use humor to relax and disarm camouflagers who come to class slouching under the weight of their defensive armor. Years of feeling like they screwed up in school have taught them to get the jump on the situation. If they think the teacher doesn't know they have a disability and they're intent on masking their misfortune, they may act out preemptively to keep the teacher at bay and in the dark for as long as possible.

If they've been considered a discipline problem in the past, perhaps because of impulsivity, they're ready to be scolded before it ever occurs to you that something's amiss. You may just look in their direction and they bristle—"What? What did I do? Jeez." Don't withdraw. Lean in. Smile. Make a positive comment or kid them. They'll go into a mild form of shock and start reevaluating the situation—maybe you aren't the same brand of enemy as the teacher last year. That's the first chink in their defensive armor. It will take repeated positive exchanges and no yelling to get them to trust you, but it will happen.

In the process of being disarmed with gentleness and humor, students begin to feel safe. Then you can talk about what's going on underneath their camouflage. Many times kids are so grateful to be understood that their motivation and mood improve dramatically, and the problems diminish.

Sometimes kids have a reputation to uphold. They've played the subversive, queen bee, or the smart mouth for years. Then you come along and fail to take their disruptive or dysfunctional persona seriously. You're unphased by the less than attractive parts of them, and drill right into their good and useful core. If you stick to your guns, they'll change. In fact, it's fascinating to watch kids do a double take or look over their shoulders to see who you're talking to when you accept their offhand remarks as valuable—"Now that's very interesting. Tell me more about that." Within seconds they find themselves at the center of an academic conversation, perhaps for the first time in years. They're momentarily stunned by your perceptiveness, then surprised at how good it feels to be on the winning side of a conversation. Pour on the encouragement. Don't let them out of your sight. The comfort that comes from being validated outweighs the discomfort of trying, and eventually they can turn in their camouflage for membership in your class.

Meet Linda Catanzano

Every time I watch Linda Catanzano at work, I get flashbacks of high school. She is young, but that's not the association. It's about the cheerleaders. The way they were always bursting with energy. The constant flow of motivational phrases meant to galvanize a group of lumbering football players into goal-driven, point-gaining action. Clearly, those girls had a powerful belief in their unique blend of invocation and kinesis, and many times, miraculously, it worked.

In a similar fashion, Linda trains her extraordinary teaching prowess on struggling learners and they respond like linebackers in the thrall of a pert pom-pom girl. They listen. They're motivated. And they get moving—toward academic success. Linda's secret lies in a three-part formula—order, challenge, and support.

Her classroom is a marvel of organization. Every desk sports an array of colored folders, one for each subject. Most students are guided through their daily schedule by a small printout with times, topics, and places to be. A few have laminated strips stuck to a Velcro frame, which indicate tasks to be accomplished. Students remove, count, and reorder the strips as they meet their goals. One child checks his schedule, pulls a hat down to his eyebrows, and stuffs a hank of sweatshirt in his mouth, preparing to leave for math in his mainstream classroom. "Is your desk neat?" Linda inquires and he wordlessly executes a quick inspection before departing.

Life in this classroom community is regulated by a set of simple rules that the kids have devised with Linda: Help each other. Be a good listener. Golden rule. Mind your own business. Each child's signature is scrawled across the bottom, rather like the signers of the Declaration of Independence. But an orderly room can be a mind-morgue if compliance is valued over the unique learning needs of each student. Linda has a deep respect for the minds and feelings of her students. She respects even their instincts of rebelliousness and subtly trains them to think about their problems. Her constant mantra is: "What is our question? What should we ask to solve this problem? How could you figure this out? How could you help yourself solve this?"

And there's plenty of thinking to go around in Linda's class, as students move through the day from one rigorous task to the next. Linda never apologizes for the difficulty of the work. She simply offers industrial-strength support. "You can do this. You've been having a great day." As a student struggles to get the hang of long division, pausing at the "goes-into" step, she gently coaches the others, "Give him a second to think. He needs a little wait time. So do you sometimes." She sits head-to-head with a child who has chosen a library book that is just slightly beyond his skill level. After he stumbles on several words in a row, Linda reframes the difficulty, "You're almost there. You're so close. You're catching up really fast." The hesitant steps her kids take can be thrilling and heartbreaking at the same time. But she is a one-person booster club and the results are frequently life-changing.

Linda teaches with an unusual focus from the minute her kids hit the door until they head for their bus at the end of the day. But she approaches reading with an intensity that is nothing short of messianic zeal. She's convinced down to the soles of her running shoes that all kids can crack the code and she will not sit still until the job is done. Her well-deserved reputation among her colleagues is that she "could teach a stone to read"—including words like *igneous* or *metamorphic*. With only months separating some of her students from middle school, she will not rest until she helps them achieve an irrevocable membership in the world of the literate. Reluctant readers become bibliophiles and timid learners gain confidence because Linda believes there are no learning disabilities, only learning challenges, and she never met a challenge she didn't like.

Eight Strategies for Ringmasters

Some days even great teachers feel like they flunked Crowd Control 101. It's just human nature. But you can reduce the incidence of free-range behavior and increase the number of days when you say, "God, I'm lucky" by using techniques that help your students' gain pleasure by succeeding in school. Here are eight strategies that can help your free-range students get into the honor society.

1. *Provide Choices*

Choice is a powerful factor in getting frightened or reluctant kids unstuck. Instead of staring at you like a deer in the headlights, they can weigh their strengths and choose the option that seems most doable. For example, you can ask them to write a story problem, draw a picture or make a diagram that illustrates how multiplication works. Students do more real thinking while evaluating their choices than they would just obediently performing a task. Sometimes students counter with additional ideas—"Can I do a comic strip or invent a multiplication board game?" More cerebral activity is going on. And wasn't that your goal?

2. Change Formats

Great teachers realize that doing half of a really hard task is still really hard. Writing three sentences can be a full-body workout for a kid with ADHD, while his peers can knock out three paragraphs with glee. So less is not always the answer. Instead, consider giving work in different formats. The surprise of a new approach catches kids off guard. They're thinking, "I haven't resisted this before, nor failed at it." That's your window of opportunity. For example, while some students write a paragraph about the setting of a story, other students produce annotated maps, drawing the settings and adding key words for detail and clarity. Both tasks address the topic and reveal what students understand about setting, but one relies on verbal skills while the other capitalizes on visual and spatial intelligence.

3. Defer to the Experts

Great teachers are the first to admit that they don't know everything, so they call on the experts—their students—whenever they can. Most elementary classrooms, even kindergartens, sport at least one *computer-savant*, so let her be in charge of booting up your computer and restocking the printer each day. Let the *materials organizer* run the art cabinet and check your paper supply. Find the kid who needs to run errands and dub him the *communications specialist*. Moving and cleaning furniture is a perfect task for kids with attention issues because putting pressure on muscles, joints, and sinews by lifting, pushing, or scrubbing focuses the mind for academic tasks. Moving sets of books is another task that dramatically calms fidgety kids. Some teachers keep a stack by the door, and have a colleague who graciously takes delivery of the books any time of day, knowing it's helping your *distribution manager* regain control.

4. Teach Self-Encouragement

Great teachers know that the most powerful affirmation comes from within. You can heap praise on kids until they are buried up to their clavicles, but if they believe they're defective or stupid or worthless, your words will fall on them like acid rain. But if you can get your kids to recognize the ways that they're smart, and have them verbalize their observations, then they're on their way to mental health for life. Psychologists call it *cognitive restructuring*, but I prefer the term *positive self-talk*. Coach your kids to say out loud what they're doing well. At first you may prime the pump by saying, "You wrote 153 words in your journal on the computer today. Twice as much as yesterday. How do you feel about that?" Encourage them to do silent cheers—raising their fists in the air and whooping soundlessly—every time they feel good about their work. Explicit mental health techniques reduce the need for camouflage.

5. *Use Body Language*

Some quantum physicists believe that they can change the behavior of a neutrino simply by observing it. Great teachers would probably endorse that notion, since they can modify even the most outrageous student behavior with a glance or simply by clearing their throats. Proximity is the most basic move that great teachers use to encourage, comfort, and redirect students. Getting closer or just moving energetically around the room shedding positive comments along the way is a powerful way to help all your kids feel noticed, connected, and energized. Touching the edge of students' desks can have an immediate impact on their behavior without murmuring a single, corrective syllable. They may not know if you are sending a message or just resting, but it's safe to say, they'll be intently focused on their work as long as you're in the neighborhood.

Eye contact is another stealth item in a teacher's toolkit. Without a word, teachers can encourage or redirect students from clear across the room. Children respond best when eye contact is direct, sincere, and encouraging, but it is also true that a steady inquisitive glance can help kids rethink their behavioral plans. Sign language also works to redirect students toward more productive behavior. Pointing at your watch reminds kids who need to refocus. Raising an index finger to the eyes can cue a child who's working on making eye contact in a social skills group to keep it up. Sometimes you can work out a private sign with a student, which increases their awareness because they own the plan.

6. *Provide Supportive Redirection*

Knowing that disruptive or counterproductive behavior is often the result of fear, insecurity, or embarrassment about academic incompetence, it's critical that you help kids change their behavior without sacrificing their sense of self. That doesn't mean that you overlook inappropriate behavior, but you will gain more if you address it constructively.

• Comment directly on the specific behavior that needs to change, rather than making global statements about deportment. Saying, "Please don't kick your neighbor's chair" is more instructive and less critical than "Why do you keep disturbing everyone?"

• Talk about behavior privately or at a very low volume. Broadcasting a child's misdeeds causes humiliation and resentment. Other kids in your class may identify with the misbehaver and feel conflicted or scared, so you unintentionally damage your relationship with a number of students, while doing little to improve the behavior of the free-ranger.

• Your comments should reflect concern for the child. "I know you love to talk to your friends, but I want you to be able to finish your beautiful painting today, so I'm moving you because I think you'll be able to focus better at this table." The child hears that a change in behavior has the potential to benefit him.

• Compliments and constructive redirection are most effective if they're made at the moment when the behavior occurs, because the actions and words get linked in a child's brain. If you wait too long to address behavior, you may get a genuinely puzzled child demanding to know, "What did I do?" Delayed feedback has little ability to change or reinforce behavior.

• If you have to speak to a student fairly often, check privately to be sure she understands your comments and the reasons behind them. Ask if there's a signal you could use to remind her about her behavior, or words that would be easier for her to hear. Students are more likely to respond if they help create the interventions.

7. Devise Alternative Assessments

Occasionally, you will hear someone say that accommodations on assessments aren't fair. Some ask, Why should a kid get extra time to complete tests, or have fewer items, or have a reader or scribe? The answer is that these accommodations are necessary for the teacher to learn what the student knows. They don't provide an unfair advantage, any more than audiotaped textbooks give blind students an edge over their sighted peers. Here is a sampling of alternative assessment strategies you can use to accommodate students:

• Reduce that amount of work needed to demonstrate mastery.

• Give oral tests in which the teacher or another adult reads the test questions and listens to or writes the student's answers.

• Allow open book tests for students with memory deficits so they can use notes, books, maps, and pictures to formulate a response.

- Tape tests and let the student listen to the test questions and record his answers on tape.
- Give many short quizzes instead of cumulative tests for students with memory and attention deficits.
- Suggest demonstrations, building models, or other projects to let students show mastery three-dimensionally.
- Have students present their research findings in an oral presentation rather than in writing.
- Encourage group efforts rather than individual presentations to allow division of labor that highlights the talents of all students.
- Evaluate through daily participation in class.
- Teach test-taking skills explicitly and use practice exams to refine those skills
- Provide computers, calculators, and other appropriate tools whenever possible.

8. Reenergize Students

One of the biggest challenges free-range students face is completing tasks—even the ones that they like to do because it's difficult to get their minds and bodies synchronized for work. Focusing is one hurdle; energy is the other. Their energy may drop so low that you find them sprawled on their desktop, blowing eraser crumbs from side to side. Or they're so wired that they create their own climate—a human tornado. Either way, productivity ceases. Great teachers have a huge menu of activities that they use like snacks throughout the day to help their kids tune their energy to the right level so they can focus and produce. These activities may look like recreation, but they are actually brain-friendly strategies that:

- Relieve stress before it erupts.
- Create balance between right and left brain.
- Release energizing hormones and endorphins.
- Open blocked thinking.
- Present alternative challenges and the satisfaction of solving them.
- Create new links between ideas.

Musical Energizers. Performing brief musical activities calms and energizes kids by increasing the flow of blood to new areas of the brain through deep, forceful breathing. Even listening to a single track of a favorite CD can do the trick. In a matter of two or three minutes, you can have all your kids pumped up and back on track. Once kids learn to use music to reenergize, individuals can step outside with an instrument or pop on the earphones, then get back to work without a lot of downtime or negative consequences. Teach your students to improvise with any of the following instruments:

- Harmonicas
- Kazoos
- Plastic ukelele
- Silent drum—wooden mixing spoons on a mousepad
- Rainstick

Kinesthetic Energizers.   Movement of any kind, even jiggling a foot, activates the sensory-motor system, bringing stimulation to the brain through the muscles, joints, and sinews. Kinesthetic activities are particularly effective for helping overactive students slow down, reorganize their energy, and focus. Some require a bit of space, but others are so soundless and subtle that students can do them at their desks whenever they need a boost. They could:

- Jump rope.
- Juggle scarves.
- Chew on a plastic straw.
- Play paddleball (ping pong paddle with ball attached by elastic cord).
- Touch, sort, and arrange buttons into designs.
- Play pick-up sticks.
- Knead a squeezy ball or Hacky Sack.
- Play a round of hop scotch on the carpet.
- Lift small, soft dumbbells.

Mental Energizers.   You can reenergize a brain that's stuck by giving it a new problem to solve. When kids experience frustration with one type of work, switch briefly to a completely unrelated task. They often experience a break-through with their original problem during a time-out. Envourage them to switch gears and try out:

- Board games such as checkers, chess, or Chinese checkers
- Crossword puzzles
- Comic books
- A box full of maps for browsing and fantasy traveling
- Internet research
- Magnetic poetry kit

Visual Diversions. These activities shift the brain away from the language centers to the areas that are expert in noticing the nuances of shapes, lines, and colors. The activities combine relaxation, stimulation, and focus. Suggest:

- Puzzles
- Catalogues and magazines
- Collections of interesting objects to manipulate and organize
- Models to assemble
- Photo album of class activities and events to look at, arrange pictures, or write captions
- Kaleidoscopes
- Travel slides with an individual viewer
- Building cubes or colored tiles.

The Roots of Free-Range Behavior

What's the explanation behind the struggle of free-range students? For a start, I think it's helpful to rule out ignorance, orneriness, or lack of character. I simply don't know any kid who comes to school with the determined thought, "I want to screw up and fail today." But clearly free-rangers have a tough time managing "school stuff." Many of these kids are intelligent but struggle to decipher simple words, or make their tongue pronounce *th*, while being watched by a concerned teacher and an audience of puzzled peers. Their responses to the constant challenges of school are often avoidance, wandering, noisy diversions, confusion followed by frustrated outbursts, even embarrassment that turns to hostility or tears.

You may have eliminated many of these behaviors with a fine-tuned program of accommodations, but still find that some of your free-rangers are not making satisfactory progress on their learning goals. You're trying hard. They're trying hard. But something more is needed. This may be the time for you to do some research on the seven major hurdles to learning that result in free-range behavior. They are sensory-motor integration issues, learning disabilities, ADD/ADHD, autistic spectrum disorder, trauma, emotional disturbance, and conduct disorder. You can get smarter about any of these causes during a quick search on the Internet. Start at ERIC and work your way out to the articles and websites that are most useful for understanding your kids.

The Law, Special Education, and 504s

Can you remember a time when IDEA meant something brilliant you had while shaving or taking a shower? Well, think again. IDEA—Individuals with

Disabilities Education Act—is a complex set of federal regulations that provide protection for the disabled in school settings—generally called special education. Ensuring the rights of students in special education is a huge responsibility. Providing appropriate services is a matter of law, so you can't afford to be casual about this topic because what you don't know about special education law can disadvantage students, impede learning, enrage parents, and even result in personal lawsuits against you. My advice? Embrace IDEA and recognize its potential as a powerful tool for helping your students.

There are lots of ways to get smarter about special education. As with so many other topics, I learned on the job. Some, IEP meetings at my school looked like senate subcommittee hearings, with as many as twelve experts, advocates, specialists, service providers, and school staff huddled in a stuffy room, discussing goals and services. Some meetings were wildly successful—truly a team effort. Others were agony, and months or even years later, we'd have a grim reunion at a due process hearing. If you're starting from scratch, read the parent rights booklet that must be offered at every IEP meeting. Check websites, go to conferences, and keep asking questions. Then train yourself to think like a diagnostician and document like a lawyer.

There are thousands of websites, public and private, government and advocate, devoted to special education issues and laws. Sites sponsored by parent organizations are excellent sources for learning about cutting-edge interventions and what's-in-the-pipeline research. Here's a sampling.

Office of Civil Rights, www.ed.gov/offices/OCR

Office of Special Education, www.ed.gov/offices/OSERS/OSEP

IDEA Practices U. S. Department of Education, www.ideapractices.org

National Council on Disabilities, www.ncd.gov

Center for Law and Education, www.cleweb.org

Center for Special Education Advocacy, www.cseadvocacy.com

Education Law Center, www.elc-pa.org

If you do nothing else at the beginning of each school year, insist on having a copy of the most current IEP for each of your students with special needs. If it's more than one year old, it's out of compliance. Insist that the team schedule an IEP meeting as soon as possible. Know your students' goals and analyze how they intersect with your classroom curriculum. Talk to your kids privately about their specific challenges and how you intend to help them achieve their goals. And remember that you are a critical member of the IEP team. If your kids aren't making progress despite your best efforts, you can ask for an IEP team meeting to set new goals, increase services, or plan for assessments that can give you the information you need to crack the code with each child.

Hope for Free-Rangers in a High-Stakes World

Most kids want to do well in school. It's the big event of their day, five days a week, just like your job is for you. From the time they're five or six years old, school is also a major contributor to their identity. So persistent struggles and failure in school can take a tremendous toll on kids that may last well into their adult years with significant psychological, emotional, and social effects.

Without treatment, accommodations, or support, students with learning and behavior challenges are vulnerable on many fronts. The obvious concern is school failure. They simply won't have the academic skills or motivation needed to plow through twelve grades and on to higher education. This can cause bright kids to feel isolated or give up and join the permanent underachievers group. Elementary students may become dropouts with training wheels, taking less and less interest in school because school doesn't seem to be interested in them. Progressive problems with disabilities or emotional disturbance can lead to poor social adjustment, deep and abiding unhappiness, early exits from school, delinquency, and other self-destructive behaviors.

It is a tragic but consistent comment on the vulnerability of these students that the majority of incarcerated youth suffer from disabling conditions. But it is also true that some of the most productive minds and creative people in this country are learning or emotionally disabled. They've mastered the fine art of making accommodations to meet their special challenges and excel in screenwriting, filmmaking, computer programming, and yes, teaching.

I think kids know the ways that they're smart and they struggle to give us clues, seeking our validation and guidance. The challenge for all educators is to find ways to adjust our perspective because in the majority of cases the problem isn't so much in the learner as the learning.

Nothing Succeeds Like Excess

Great teachers also know that these unique students need more of everything—more praise, more nudging, more opportunities to invent, and more structures that let them feel safe. They thrive on a high-calorie diet of intellectual stimulation, clear expectations with appropriate support, and jubilant celebrations. And what do you get in return? Some of the most satisfying teaching you will ever do, and the devotion of some very special kids.

> *Nine-tenths of education is encouragement.*
> —Anatole France

Resources

Books

Ayres, A. J. 1979. *Sensory Integration and the Child.* Los Angeles: Western Psychological Services.

Greenspan, S. I. 1995. *The Challenging Child.* New York: Addison-Wesley.

Levine, Mel. 1992. *All Kinds of Minds: A Young Student's Book About Learning Abilities and Disabilities.* New York: Educator's Publishing Service.

———. 2002. *A Mind at a Time.* New York: Simon and Schuster.

Other Resource

Teacher Expectations and Student Achievement (TESA) is a research-based program that focuses on behavioral change and encourages teachers to interact equitably with all students. The premise is that through questioning, feedback, and affection, teachers can transmit to students the feeling that they can succeed.

SECRET #4

Great Teachers Are Curiosity Seekers

Fostering Success in Multicultural Classrooms

In This Chapter:

- What's the Big Idea About Culture in the Classroom?
- Meet Rafe Esquith
- Culture-Blind or Just Confused?
- Seeing Your Class Through Culture-Colored Glasses
- Navigating in Multicultural Settings
- Culturally Responsive Teaching Strategies
- Cultural Awareness and Your Curriculum
- Culturally Inappropriate Materials

I was born under a lucky star, and my good fortune was firmly in place the day I accepted my first teaching assignment. Fresh out of college, I got a call from Edith Dury, an amazing principal and mentor. I still remember my interview, which was remarkable for how uninterviewish it was. There were no canned questions about pedagogy. I wasn't required to discuss phonics, the current crop of textbooks, or how I would handle an unruly parent. Instead, Edith and I huddled in her office for over an hour, talking passionately about student-centered learning. I eagerly scribbled diagrams of learning centers on scraps of paper. She shared her vision of the school she was trying to build. Then she clinched the deal with the promise of a "teaching adventure." So I cheerfully signed on the dotted line, accepting a first grade assignment and a sixty-minute commute—longer if it rained—for the pure joy of teaching with Edith in Tinsel

Town. That's right. On a clear day you could see the Hollywood sign. Never a movie star.

I quickly discovered that the surrounding neighborhood was *Diversity* personified. My kids covered the socioeconomic waterfront, from a diplomat's offspring reverently delivered each morning by her gloved chauffeur, to students crowded into one-bedroom apartments with ten members of their extended family. There were refugees and social climbers and one brilliant, boisterous student who proudly announced the first day, "I'm an Okie from Oklahoma!" The halls of the prewar building echoed with voices chattering in twenty-four languages. It was a cultural smorgasbord, and I feasted from one end to the other for fifteen years.

Now you might think it would be daunting for a novice teacher to tackle the three Rs with thirty-two first graders from fifteen cultures. But I couldn't wait. In fact, this was exactly what I'd been longing for since my sophomore year in college, when a rather unremarkable professor recommended that I read *Teacher* by Sylvia Ashton-Warner (1963). Eager to do well in her class, I headed for the library and snatched the book off the Reserved shelf, with nothing more than brownie points in mind. Within minutes I'd fallen over the edge of my world, and landed in a sunny New Zealand schoolroom full of Maori children and their brilliant teacher, Sylvia. I sat riveted for hours, and emerged from the library with one thought in mind. I want to teach Maoris—or the closest equivalent in Los Angeles!

Instead, I got a class that would have made the UN swell with pride— Korean, Cantonese, Japanese, Armenian, German, Mexican, Hungarian, Croatian, Persian, and Soviet Unionists—it wasn't called Russia in those days. But it seemed to me that the ideas I found so appealing in *Teacher* still applied— exponentially.

In essence, Ashton-Warner believed that it was her role to build a bridge between the culture of her students and the European school system through which they would travel—if they managed to stay in school. The bridge was made of words. By prospecting deep inside her students for their thoughts, and capturing them in words, she used their cultural experiences as the foundation material for learning in her classroom. She recognized, well before others, the importance of building on the language and knowledge that her students already possessed. Her recipe for success was simple: See your students as capable learners, tap into their world, then link school learning to who they are and what they know. Guided by her approach, I fell in love with my kids, and they fell in love with learning.

That first experience in my classroom at the crossroads of the world made an indelible mark on me. It drummed into my young head notions about the politics of poverty, race, and privilege. It enriched me as a person by radically altering the way I saw and still see the world. But most of all, it instilled a deep and abiding curiosity about the many cultures that embroider life on this planet.

To this day I keep a copy of *Teacher* by my bedside. In the years since, many more books—and people—have added to my understanding of kids and cultures. There's *Dreamkeepers: Successful Teachers of African American Children* by Gloria Ladson-Billings (1997), *Other People's Children* by Lisa Delpit (1995), and the many writings of James Banks. *Hunger of Memory* by Richard Rodriguez is a fascinating evocation of his childhood in two worlds, his Spanish-speaking home and the world of an Anglo school.

All of these writers reinforced that early epiphany I had in the shadow of the Hollywood sign. There isn't just one world out there. There is the world as each of us sees it, and that vision is shaped from birth by our own culture. It's the way we were raised *to be and to see.*

What's the Big Idea About Culture in the Classroom?

One of the great tensions in the conversation about teaching children from diverse cultural backgrounds has been the tug of war between highlighting their cultures as an important part of the curriculum, and insisting on a rigorous academic program that would allow children to succeed in a kindergarten-through-college system that staunchly reflects the values of the dominant culture. Some educators refer to this as the struggle between self-esteem and skills. Great teachers contend that one is useless without the other, so they don't choose. They tackle both.

Every morning your students arrive at school through a visceral corridor of their culture, surrounded by sights, smells, sounds, words, and gestures of their family, extended family, and neighbors. If you have multiple cultures in your class, students are taking distinctly different routes to your room. Having arrived, two things can happen.

1. You can view their cultures and practices as assets.
2. You can view some students as burdened with deficits—not proficient in English, underschooled, poor—and by extension, burdens to you, their teacher.

Great teachers reject the deficit model and recognize that all kids have personal strengths that spring directly from their families and the culture in which they were raised. It's the teacher's job to prospect for those cultural strengths, and construct an environment in which they are not viewed as oddities or points of interest, like a theme park of the underprivileged, but counted as assets that are critical to the success of the entire class.

Great teachers realize that all the kids in their class started as infants—totally helpless and dependent. Within a few short years they can walk talk, feed, and dress themselves. They ride bikes, figure out how to con sweets from grandma, and learn which big kid to copy if they want to get really good at soccer. In short, they learn how this human being game works. And they learn all of that in the context of their own families and cultures. When they arrive at school, they're learners. For great teachers, there is never a question about this—their kids are already proficient learners.

Then the question is: How did they learn all those things, and how can that knowledge be used to drive learning here in school? Teachers launch an investigation to discover who their students are, what they know, and how they learn so that they can use their students' diverse learning skills to tackle new material and help them succeed in the majority culture.

Great teachers know that in order for low-income students and students of color to capitalize on their education, they have to master a dual curriculum. First there's the standard academic content—reading, writing, math, and so on. The second is a stealth curriculum, equally necessary for school success. It consists of expectations about conduct—language, gestures, taboo words, dress, and manners—that are dictated by the white majority culture. They are deeply ingrained in the culture of schools and in the teaching staff, 90 percent of whom are white.

Lisa Delpit (1995), an award-winning teacher and researcher, examined the phenomenon of the stealth curriculum in her book, *Other People's Children*. She looked at the culture of power and the rules people must follow if they want to get their share. Those rules are created and maintained by the people in power, including the rules about the way we "do" school. She asserts that schools are fundamentally unequal because minority children don't have access to the rules about power, unless their teachers or other caring adults explicitly supply that information. Great teachers help their students crack the code and master the knowledge they need to succeed in school and gain access to the systems that lead to economic success in society.

Meet Rafe Esquith

It's early on a cold-for-L.A. morning. The streets are still pedestrian-safe, and the latte stand is waiting for the first wave of mocha-seekers. But as the clock clicks over to 7 AM, thirty-some students begin piling into a fifth-grade classroom and cluster in small groups at tables or perch on stools and bookcases. It's a Thursday during Christmas vacation, but in Room 56, school is in session.

Room 56 is a typical public school classroom, battered and unlovely. Paint is chipped. The doormat curls dangerously to catch a passing toe. Tennis balls muffle the scrape of metal chairs on standard institutional linoleum—beige with a vomit motif. Each closet is secured with a hank of heavy-duty chain and a jumbo lock. The closest thing to an amenity is a mini-refrigerator, stocked with water and Diet Coke.

But once you pass over the threshold, it seems like you've wandered into a cross between a music studio and a college souvenir outlet. In the northeast corner is the gleaming chrome expanse of a professional drum set. The opposite corner is gridlocked with two keyboards, a quartet of microphones, two electric guitars, a sound-mixing panel, a CD player, and a dozen CDs. Cords crawl everywhere. But it's the walls that announce you're not in Kansas anymore. They're festooned with college pennants from places most of the students in this neighborhood will never see. Yale, Penn, Columbia, Harvard, and the list goes on. It could be a half-hearted college awareness strategy or a visual nod to the district's drive for high expectations, but each pennant trails a string of small white plaques—dozens and dozens—bearing the names of every Room 56 alum who's been accepted to that institution. A sprinkling of green plaques herald the degree holders, including one from Yale Law School.

The names on the wall, the Monday through Friday fifth graders, and the dozens of graduates who still call Room 56 home, are all part of an extended community created and carefully tended by Rafe Esquith, teaching savant.

Rafe is an impressive, impeccably dressed six-footer. He walks with a gait that you couldn't accurately call a lumber because it has too much velocity—the heels of his shoes rarely touch the floor. Perhaps it's the urgency of his task that animates him. After all, he's living on the frontier of middle school, hypercognizant that he has just one short school year in which to reach his students and begin their transformation. That would explain the fact that he arrives at school by 6 AM each morning and prepares for the day with the meticulous concentration and dedication that suggests an artist at work.

But what explains the arrival of his students shortly thereafter? Two full hours before other students are robotically saluting the flag, Rafe's kids file into their classroom, orderly, eager, and prepared for the wonder. And he never disappoints. The first order of business this day is christening the new Ovation guitar. A student so small she could pass for a third grader perches on the edge of a table and plays "Paranoid Android" from Radio Heads. Rafe is visibly impressed, since he taught her that tune just the day before. "How long did you practice last night?" She quietly volunteers, "Two hours." "But you missed all that television, and you know those people on TV really care about you." The class dissolves into laugher and their day is underway. It will be crammed with a full academic agenda—literature, writing, history, geography, math, acting, keyboarding and guitar, singing, sign language, and sports. "That way there's something for every child. They get to do something they love at least one part of each day—and so do I," Rafe explains.

Watching Rafe Esquith at work, the image of a wizard comes to mind. He's larger-than-life, noisy, and powerful. His kids are clearly mesmerized. But there's more than wizardry here. Rafe is a life force who possesses and is possessed by the most refined instincts of a teacher. Every interaction, from the mundane task of passing out bottled water to parsing Renaissance poetry, is imbued with high expectations, a love of learning, and unwavering confidence in his kids.

Rafe has succeeded in creating an expanded universe inside this urban classroom that is as unique and unexpected in this part of L.A. as the Emerald City would be. His students are Korean or Hispanic, all second-language learners, most from low-income households headed by a single parent. The neighborhood is diversely nonwhite, and has its share of crime after dark. Yet his kids' test scores consistently exceed the ninetieth percentile in a school where 45 percent would be cause for celebration.

So what brand of magic is this wizard using? Like the head honcho of Oz, Rafe is convinced that his students can do it all, and well, because the ability is already inside them, just as the Scarecrow was smart and the Lion possessed courage long before they ever won an audience with the great Oz. Rafe tells his kids over and over, from day one, that they have everything they need to achieve their goals, and Doubting Thomases have only to look at the names on the walls to know that it can be done. Then he tells them that they're going to do lots of hard things, just like all the Room 56 kids before them, but they're not to worry. It's his job to teach them, and teach he will. With this two-pronged strategy he convinces them that they're safe, and urges them to take chances. Otherwise, they can't make the big leaps that he knows are possible. His goal is to help all of his kids develop into confident, capable people who can hold their own in middle school, private school, and on the campus of any university they choose—if they're willing to be as devoted to their own success as he is. "I tell them that I will open lots of doors for them, but they have to walk through." This collaboration is the central feature of Rafe's classroom. There's the demanding, inspiring, revelatory enterprise of teaching, along with the equally demanding, inspiring, and revelatory work being done by his kids: learning and growing up.

Codes of Power

But for my money, the most dazzling thing about Rafe Esquith is his transparency. It's like his kids spend the year with a really smart person whose brain is on speakerphone. He doesn't just teach. He externalizes his thinking all day long. Through a constant narrative he explains: the politics of education, handling conflicts, evaluating ethical dilemmas, the tricks of the academic trade, how their class work relates to the world at large, and the obstacles they'll face as they move on.

When I asked one student what's so special about Rafe, she whispered conspiratorially, "He teaches us things we're not supposed to know—like equations." She has no idea how right she is! Rafe is willfully and persistently teaching his kids the stuff they would be unlikely to learn in any school, anywhere, and it's not about equations! What are they learning?

- The how and why of reading, practicing on works by Mark Twain, Tolkien, and Malcolm X.
- How standardized tests are constructed and how to take them successfully.
- How to make a mistake and take responsibility.
- How to decide if a movie is good or just mediocre.
- How smart people organize their time.
- The importance of music in an educated person's life.
- Table manners and how to order from a menu.
- Rules of hospitality and telephone etiquette.
- How to check out of a hotel and wait in an airline lobby.
- How effort relates to accomplishment.
- How to support each other.
- And his favorite question, which he attributes to his wife Barbara: What will you do when things in life go wrong?

He's the instruction manual to life that few minority students ever receive, and without it they are forever at a disadvantage. Through narratives, conversations, jokes, and direct instruction, he gives them access to the unstated rules and intricacies of the dominant culture and explicitly tells them how they can make it work for them. This information, the "things we're not supposed to know," is what Lisa Delpit calls the "codes of power." The game plan is simple: Prepare kids to succeed in school, jobs, and life.

Here's a single example of code sharing from the dozens strategically inserted throughout the day. Rafe writes a math problem on the board—subtracting fractions—and tells his kids that they can do it horizontally or vertically, but in middle school the teacher might not accept horizontal. He begins, "Suppose the teacher says, 'That's not acceptable. You have to show your work.' What should you say? I'll give you three answers. A. Okay, I'll do that. B. But I have the right answer, or C. Get out of my face." There's a quiet chorus in the room—"A." "That's right—A." He elaborates—"even if your math teacher is substandard or can't find his way around a calculator, arguing with him is a battle you can't win, and it will only get you in trouble, no matter how good you are at fractions."

There's also a continuous theme about moral development woven throughout the daily dialogue. Like all great teachers, Rafe shapes character through hundreds of iterations of his simple classroom ethic: Be nice, work hard. In fact, the overarching message is about being a good person. He says, "I can get high test scores, but what does it mean if my kids aren't good people?" His students can recite like a mantra Kohlberg's Six Levels of Moral Development—in shorthand. They call it the six reasons we do things: to avoid trouble, for the reward, for someone else, it's the rule, I don't want to hurt someone else, it's my code. And they're encouraged on a daily basis to make the long stretch toward Level Six—it's my code.

On this day they're preparing to serve lunch to five hundred homeless people on Christmas Eve and serenade them with the fifty holiday tunes they've been practicing for months. Rafe reviews Level Six behavior: "Are we expecting them to say thank you? That's not why we're doing this. Feeding the homeless is your code. You don't get a thank you. You don't call the newspaper." Then he goes a step beyond to prepare them emotionally for the event, previewing the situation with a direct question: "What will it be like in a room full of homeless people who may have some serious mental problems?" In a brief discussion he gives them clues for making sense of the behavior so they'll feel safe. Finally, he ends with a remark that is as compassionate as it is matter-of-fact: "They're people. They're our species, so let's take care of them."

Essential Esquith

Periodically, spontaneously, Rafe launches into soliloquies that blend history, strategies, and the explicit recognition of his students' potential. Here's a perfect example. His kids were FOILing with polynomials—an acronym that guides them through a complex mathematical process. As students caught on and announced their breakthroughs, Rafe stoked their growing enthusiasm. "Algebra is the glue the holds all math together—and it's fun! It's a wonderful subject, but they just teach it badly." With a note of wonder he continues, "Algebra. It's how we got to the moon. It's how we cure cancer. It's amazing, and it's just problem-solving." After a pause. "We're coming up on a very important date in American history. December 17, when two men from Dayton, Ohio, walked out on the sands of Kittyhawk, North Carolina, and took off into the sky. And they did it with algebra. I look at your faces and I wonder what you'll discover. Shakespeare was a kid once. Steinbeck was a kid." Gesturing at one student, "Maybe someday you'll write the book that everybody will want to read."

Granted, Rafe is a math enthusiast. He devours equations like a hungry man scans a fast food menu. But the same litany is repeated over and over throughout the day—every new task gets a corresponding injection of focus and energy. As his students prepare to attack a long section of Henry VI, he confides, "Shakespeare is a terrible read. Not meant to be read. Nobody read it when Shakespeare was alive." He rattles off a brief history of Shakespeare in America, citing performances in the pre-Revolutionary colonies and amateur productions in Gold Rush bars. "Shakespeare was always mass entertainment. If he were alive today, he'd be writing for television." Then in a lightning segue to the text, "Why is Richard so ticked off?" The lesson consists of listening to an excellent CD recording of *Henry*, punctuated by Rafe interjecting questions ("What's his argument?"), making connections ("Check your chart of the Houses of York and Windsor"), and stabbing at the buttons on the CD player.

He applies the same voracity to baseball—his love. Many schools send their students to baseball games—usually as a reward—where they spend most of their time cruising the bleachers for social experiences or forfeiting scandalous sums of money for Dodger Dogs. Then they leave after the fifth inning. Rafe's students make a study of baseball. They play it with him in physical education, ardently follow their favorite teams in the newspaper, and unfailingly master the math of it. When he finally takes them to a flesh-and-blood game, their eyes are riveted on the action and they're keeping score—all the way to the bottom of the ninth.

The Saturday Academy

Most of Rafe's graduates don't actually leave after fifth grade. They simply exchange daily attendance for a spot in their old classroom on Saturday. By eight o'clock each Saturday morning, at least sixty teenagers return to Rafe's room, ready to work. What catapults these kids out of bed on a weekend morn? Pretty much the same things that motivate other Americans to *carpe diem*—calculus, intellectual companionship, and a line-by-line examination of a four-hundred-year-old text. All before noon.

"This is my favorite day of the week," notes Rafe, as he bounds between adjacent rooms, checking on sixth graders' reading comprehension, then tossing calculators to high school students as they tackle equations so clogged with letters that I'm tempted to volunteer "sound it out" when Rafe asks if anyone has a strategy for solving the first problem. "These are the true believers," he tells me. Some of these students have spent every Saturday for the past four years pursuing goals that will require as many years to accomplish as they've already lived, and thousands of hours of work. The banner at the front of the class says it all—*There are no shortcuts.*

This is where the Esquith saga shifts from *Oz* to *Field of Dreams*. Rafe realized years ago that a single year with him would not get his kids to the finish line. They needed continuous support for years to make it through the ivy-covered gates of America's best colleges and universities. So he offered a tutorial program on Saturday mornings. Through his passion, persistence, and the alchemy that often emerges in the struggle between willpower and adversity, his Saturday program has grown to include annual college tours back East; a trip each summer to the Shakespeare Festival in Ashland, Oregon; and intensive coaching on how to apply for private schools, qualify for scholarships, and master the SAT. But there's more. These students are offered investiture in an extraordinary community that spans fifteen years of Room 56 graduates, toiling toward their dreams. Inspired by the nameplates on the walls, these Saturday scholars experience increasing levels of responsibility, opportunity, and mutual support. They benefit from and contribute to this amazing enterprise that is now orchestrated by the foundation Rafe established, The Hobart Shakespeareans. After years of working four jobs to fund the quality of education he felt his kids deserved, he now has a following of well-deserved supporters who champion his cause.

P. S. They Do Shakespeare

The day-to-day reality of what Rafe Esquith does with his kids is truly of epic proportions. The volume and variety of work, the early morning intensity that hasn't waned through the afternoon and on to dinnertime, the fierce dedication to high standards that local bureaucrats largely ignore, as if befuddled by the evidence of what a single, determined, autonomous teacher can do. Every kid dreams of having a teacher like Rafe; most teachers long to be like him. But there's a final dazzling piece. Room 56 is an Elizabethan Enclave. Every child speaks Shakespeare fluently. It's the second language of the classroom.

Each year Rafe and his kids select one of the bard's plays—it's *Hamlet* this year. Then they slowly and methodically devour the text, debating the characters' moral choices, examining the politics at play, piercing the peculiar vocabulary to unearth what it all means, examining every metaphor and symbol. Eventually they audition for parts and then crawl inside their characters for the rest of the year. In the spring they give fifteen performances right in their classroom. They dress down—T-shirts are the only costumes, but they augment the bard's plays with a soundtrack of a dozen or more contemporary songs, some in sign language. It's a standing-room-only event every night attended by luminaries from Hollywood and the theatre world.

It's clear that Rafe Esquith is concerned with no ordinary form of education. With every breath, he broadcasts his undying affection for his work and the children he shepherds tenderly and tenaciously toward adulthood. His life is a testament to education as a form of calling and a demonstration of the painstaking process of imparting knowledge. Though he talks openly of the loneliness of his job, it is abundantly clear that he would be content to be among children until he breathes his last. He recently published *There Are No Short-cuts* (Pantheon, 2003), a candid account of his irreverent assault on the institution of education. You won't be able to put it down.

Culture-Blind or Just Confused?

Teachers who haven't come to grips with the challenge of cultural diversity in their schools are inclined to take one of two approaches toward their non-majority students. They are either culture-blind or confused. If you approach your students in either of these ways, you may unwittingly interfere with the very work you're trying to do because cultural blindness and confusion reduce the chances of school success for minority students and by extension their opportunities to have a useful and satisfying life.

That may sound overly dramatic, but I offer a single glaring statistic to consider in this regard. An African American boy who was born in California in 1988 is three times as likely to be murdered than to be admitted to the University of California. The persistent failure of our schools to provide minority students with a quality education that respects their cultures *and* teaches them the codes of power deprives them of tangible routes to social and economic success.

The Perils of Being Culture-Blind

Being culture-blind is not a virtue, although it is frequently used to suggest that a person is immune to bias, as in "I treat all kids the same, no matter what their culture, and I don't see color." It's an ostrich approach to diversity that refuses to consider that culture shapes children, as people and learners, and it shapes your reaction to them, whether you realize it or not.

One result of a culture-blind approach to education is the exclusive use of a majority-centered curriculum—particularly literature, history, social science, and art presented from the point of view of white people of European origin. This monolithic approach can alienate students of color by sending the message that when important events were happening—discoveries, inventions, creations, elections, and victories—people of their culture weren't in the starring role or pulling the levers of power. They're on the outside looking in with not an entrance in sight.

Faced with cultural blindness at school, many smart students simply withdraw. They think, "You're not interested in me. I'm not interested in you."

Unfortunately, some teachers read students' withdrawal as laziness, indifference, or a room-temperature IQ, so they lower their expectations. Instead of stimulating students with challenging dialogues and meaty problems, the work slows down and is watered down. There's even less to attract and keep students' attention, resulting in lower achievement, which reinforces the teacher's original incorrect assumption that the lights are on but nobody's home. It's a vicious circle.

Students of color who feel alienated from school may retreat into the protection of their culture by embracing or even exaggerating differences between themselves and the majority culture. Through clothing, music, language, and attitudes, they protect themselves from feeling like failures. If you ask, they'll say they didn't fail, but that they just weren't trying because they have no interest in that brand of success. School failure becomes a kind of cultural solidarity. The dropout rate among minority students is high—11 percent for African Americans, 24 percent among Native American students, and 27 percent for Hispanics by a recent government survey. Even if minority students do remain in school, their education may have no meaningful connection to their real life—it's just a place to hang from eight to three.

The Perils of Being Confused

Some teachers notice that there are significant cultural differences at play in their classrooms, but they lack the information to transform their awareness into effective practices. The result of their confusion can be mistakes or missed opportunities.

One mistake that springs from cultural confusion is that we may misidentify cultural learning styles as learning difficulties. For example, you may listen to children who come from a culture that favors storytelling as a mode of communication. Directness and economy of speech are less important than characters and dialogue. Certain phrases may even be repeated for emphasis. You may observe this cultural difference but conclude that the explanation lies in weak communication or critical thinking skills.

Cultural confusion is a likely suspect in the overidentification of minority children in special education programs. For example, in 1992, African American students accounted for 16 percent of the total U.S. student population, but represented 32 percent of students in programs for mild mental retardation (MMR), 29 percent in programs for moderate mental retardation, and 24 percent in programs for serious emotional disturbance. African American children were almost three times more likely to be labeled "mentally retarded" than their white counterparts.

Cultural confusion can also cause teachers to misinterpret interpersonal responses. For example, teachers often insist on industrial strength eye contact from students, particularly if they're explaining an idea or admonishing them. But in some cultures, it's a sign of great disrespect for children to meet your gaze directly, especially if you're busy delivering a vigorous scold. This is such an ingrained practice, that even if you stoop to their eye level, they will not be able to comply. Not knowing that this is a cultural taboo, you may get emphatic but still fail to win even a furtive glance. So you conclude that this child is op-positional or simply doesn't get it. The last thing to enter your mind is that he's being respectful, *and* showing strength of character by sticking to the rules of his family and culture, despite your insistence.

Missed Opportunities

Most teacher preparation programs do a good job of exposing the perils of an exclusively Anglocentric experience for minority children—always seeing them-selves on the margins of the curriculum, as occasional contributors to white society. But basing your curriculum and teaching practices on the majority culture also has serious disadvantages for students from the *majority* culture. If we create classrooms that overwhelmingly reflect the majority culture, we unwittingly send a message that this is the superior culture. By extension, that makes many majority students feel superior, reinforcing implicit attitudes of racism that most teachers so earnestly try to eradicate. Having a majority-heavy curriculum denies students the chance to study other cultures, and view their own culture as one among many. Only through a broad-based look at many cultures can students be analytic about their own cultures, appreciating their unique aspects and the features that they share with other cultures.

Seeing Your Class Through Culture-Colored Glasses

No one can make you culturally aware and responsive. That's a gift that only you can bestow on your kids and yourself. To achieve that, you will need to teach yourself to see anything that's different as potentially interesting or instructive to you as a teacher. You'll need to devote specific, conscious energy to expand-ing your cultural awareness—and awareness begins at home. Start by asking:

- *Who am I?* What is the effect of my culture on the way I view this thing called teaching?
- *Who are my students?* What is the effect of culture on the way they approach learning?
- *Who are we together?* What advantages can all my students gain by learning about and in the manner of different cultures?

The teaching profession in the United States is predominantly white, which means among other things, that most teachers can walk into a faculty meeting and expect to see a lot of people who look like them. If they tell people that they work at a school, people won't automatically assume that they're a gardener, custodian, or clerk. They open textbooks and see people of their race widely represented in positions of importance. And most likely, they give little thought to any of this because in the United States, being white is "normal." This notion of white as the norm is brilliantly explored in an article by Peggy McIntosh (1988) titled, "White Privilege: Unpacking the Invisible Knapsack." The entire text of McIntosh's article is just a google away on the Internet and well worth your time. It will definitely change your day and could change your life.

In the article, McIntosh illustrates the many aspects of daily life that people in the majority culture get to take for granted. They can shop without being followed, and rent or purchase housing in any area that they can afford, and go to a music store or a grocery store and find the products that fit with their cultural traditions. A major conclusion in McIntosh's work is that if you're white, it's nearly impossible to step outside the majority culture and feel the challenge of being a minority. But you must do this if you are going to be the conduit through which your students learn the codes of power.

What's My Culture?

In order to know what your kids are up against, you need to inventory the elements of culture that you bring to your classroom. So let's start at the very beginning. Who are you and what aspects of your culture shape you as a teacher? I know that culture is woven into every aspect of your life, from grocery shopping to the kind of music you play and how loud you play it, but I want you to focus on the ways that your culture shapes you as a teacher. Consider each cultural element in the following list. Ask yourself the questions and make notes. Try to be specific in your responses. If you feel a twinge of hesitation or discomfort, note that, too.

- *Belief systems.* What's right and wrong in a classroom?
- *Biases.* What's important to learn to do in a classroom?
- *Communication patterns.* How should students speak and write at school?
- *Customs and rituals.* What's polite, respectful, or rude?
- *Expectations.* How should students and parents respond and participate at school?
- *Gender roles.* What can or can't students and parents do because of gender?

- *Language.* What languages do I feel comfortable speaking or hearing in my classroom?
- *Learning styles.* What do I think is the most effective way to learn?
- *Nonverbal communication.* What gestures and looks are acceptable or offensive in my classroom?
- *Religion.* What's the effect of my religion or my students' religious on the way I interact with them?
- *Values.* What's nonnegotiable? Who and what are most important in my classroom?
- *Family history.* What did my family do or say that influenced my success as a student?
- *Family structure.* What family structure do I think is best to support students as learners?

Review all your notes, then ask yourself: If my students and their parents were doing this exercise, how might their notes differ from mine? The next question is the truly important one: What is the effect of those differences on students in your classroom? For a start, consider the following.

If you were raised in a culture that values punctuality, and a student comes from a culture where "on-time" means give-or-take fifteen minutes, do you see that family as not caring about education, and label the child as disruptive because she arrives late?

If your culture values an independent approach to learning and enjoys learning for learning's sake, and your students' culture emphasizes group learning related to real-life experiences, using dialogue and hands-on process, do you see these kids as less able academically and unlikely to complete high school?

If you were raised to obey authorities such as teachers, and your students come from a culture that values logical argumentation, do you see them as disrespectful when they launch a debate with you over a low grade or an incorrect answer?

If listeners in your culture signal their attention by making eye contact, and your students come from a culture where listeners are expected to avert their gaze to indicate respect and attention, do you see those kids as daydreamers, easily distractible, or disinterested?

You see the dilemma. Kids may be judged and labeled as a certain type of not-so-good student, simply because they fail to leave their cultural practices at the door and adopt yours, when they may not even know what yours are. So if you want to succeed as their teacher, you need to know as much as possible about the cultures of your students and be explicit with them about the culture of school. Then they and you can make informed choices that lead to success.

Navigating in Multicultural Settings

Everyday you have an opportunity to get smarter about cultures from your students and their families. You can learn more in one afternoon with parents who are eager to share than from an entire week in a graduate class on culturally relevant pedagogy—because you're talking to the experts. So you have two choices. Glide across the campus, waving and smiling as if you're in a Popemobile, or dig in and get an authentic education. You can't get this kind of smart through osmosis. You have to pay attention. So round up some parents and declare yourself a student of their culture. Here are six skills that will help you in the process.

1. *Develop your tolerance for ambiguity.*

First encounters with new cultures leave most smart people with a head full of questions. Why is she looking down? Why do I feel invisible? Why is he shouting? Why doesn't that mom ever talk to her baby? Why doesn't that one ever stop? And your brain obediently sets about looking for answers, even if it has to make them up from fragments of unreliable information animated by a huge speculative leap. Train yourself to stop looking for answers and simply *look*. Instead of focusing on how puzzling things appear, replace that thought with ". . . this is very interesting" "I wonder what this is about?" "I wonder what I can figure out by watching?"

2. *Quell the urge to judge.*

Most classrooms have parties at the holidays. The simpler versions feature cookies and punch—all the way up to enough take-out pizza and chips to feed the whole neighborhood. A colleague related a story about watching her Hispanic students gather handfuls of holiday cookies into napkins to take with them. *Greedy* was the first word that came into her mind. In fact, it was the opposite phenomenon. These children were thinking about how they could share this party with their families. It's simple to see the lesson here. You're always wearing those culture-colored glasses, and they affect how you see your kids. The feeling that your way is right must yield to a more tentative approach if you are going to learn about and appreciate other cultures. If you notice something that makes you feel uncomfortable, train yourself to ask: "Could this be a cultural practice?" Simply inserting that question into your inner monologue will reduce the inclination to jump to conclusions.

3. *Discover ways to communicate respect.*

It's tough to learn about other people's culture if they think that you're dissing them. You can find yourself on the receiving end of a truckload of attitude in no time if parents or students feel you don't respect them. Or you'll just get a blank stare or nervous laughter, without knowing why. Communicating respect is complicated. One size doesn't fit all. Speaking directly to the mother of a student at a parent conference may seem respectful, but could make her very uncomfortable if she feels you should be addressing her husband. What about eye contact? Locking gazes can be confrontational. Looking away a sign of disinterest. This is very subtle stuff and you need to talk to experts in the cultures you're studying to learn trust-building strategies.

4. Practice changing places.

I have a magnificent colleague, Sylvia Rousseau, who is a superintendent, holds a PhD, is a community leader, a minister's wife, and a mother. Sylvia makes me want to be a better person, and that effect is pretty universal. But if she went shopping in white neighborhoods, she and her children were routinely tailed through department stores as potential shoplifters. Here's an exercise that can help you develop cultural awareness and empathy. Choose an ethnic or cultural group other than your own and imagine for a week that you're a member of that group. Which group would you choose and why? What is one value from that group that attracts you? Is there anything about being in that group that concerns you? Each day try to think of at least one concrete way that your life would be different if you were a member of that group. This would be a great time to review Peggy McIntosh's article.

5. Keep your eyes on the prize.

If a student says to you, "Can I aks you something?" your answer should be an enthusiastic "Sure." If you stop at that moment to deliver a pronunciation lesson—"You mean *ask*. Can you say ask?"—it's doubtful you'll ever hear that question or any others. When working in a multicultural setting, you need to have a dual focus. It's critical that you authentically acknowledge what your students are thinking, attempting, and creating. When they talk to you, notice how much of the message is getting through and the tone of their communication. Appreciate that their willingness to try something new or difficult reflects their growing trust in you. Then tackle the codes of power. Teach students what else they need to know to communicate successfully, and be sure to help them understand the potential benefit to them of adopting different standards of language or behavior depending on the situation.

6. Keep trying.

Learning about other cultures is tricky. So much is invisible and unconscious. Sometimes you're afraid to inquire because your questions cross the line into issues of race, a difficult topic for many people. Teaching students about the codes of power requires utter clarity, so they don't get a message about cultural inferiority. It's very tough work and you have to be fully conscious all the time. You will make some mistakes. They will, too. Don't give up. When students feel that you care about them and want them to get an excellent education, their trust and efforts grow.

Culturally Responsive Teaching Strategies

The way that you organize learning in your classroom can have a profound effect on whether your kids will listen to you, talk to you, and ultimately learn. Cultural awareness can be the key to your success. Unfortunately, most classrooms in the United States are still a two-sided affair. Kids on one side, teacher on the other. The teacher gets the whole group in his sights, then lectures, leads, or demonstrates something from the curriculum. What follows is some flavor of student response. Kids individually replicate what the teacher has done, often to the tenth power. After sufficient practice, there's an assessment, judgment is rendered, shame descends on those who don't measure up, and the whole thing starts over again.

This is a familiar system that rarely inspires academic zeal in any student. But it is particularly ineffective with children from nonmajority cultures. In response, many simply treat the teacher and the lesson as so much wallpaper, and prospect for other diversions among their friends. The possibilities are dazzling. Unfortunately, from the teacher's side of the room, this looks like an unmotivated or unskilled student. The blame rarely falls where it belongs—on the complete inability of some lessons to grab kids by their brain stem and make something happen.

So whether you're planning lessons, units, excursions, or even the simplest writing assignment, stop and think. Then try to incorporate some of these strategies to support the vigorous learning of all your students, and particularly those from different cultures.

- Teach abstract concepts by linking them to familiar, culturally meaningful contexts.
- Explain how the curricular content is related to students' everyday experiences.
- Encourage flexible grouping that allows students to closely observe and work with students from different cultures to increase achievement and awareness of diversity. Students learn that "how we do things" in other cultures may be unique and very effective.
- Use cooperative groupings to support students from cultural backgrounds that value community over individuality.

- Organize curriculum around big ideas or themes so that students whose cultures approach thinking holistically can grasp the overall concept and then address the component parts.

- Invent activities that incorporate motion and emotion.

- Arrange your room so that lower-achieving students are close to you, and use the proximity to encourage and support their efforts, not to surveil and criticize them.

- Be extremely vigilant about including all students in your discussion, not just the talkative, eager, or ambitious ones.

- Encourage students to express their opinions and cultural points of view.

- Provide various forms of reinforcement—smiles, explicit phrases, nodding, and appreciation.

- Pay individual attention to your students. Greet each one personally as they arrive. Whenever possible, hand papers, books, and learning materials to each individual rather than passing them down the row. Imagine spending a whole day without ever hearing your name, as if you were invisible.

- Use open-ended questions to increase quantity and quality of participation in discussions.

- Be conscious of wait time during discussions because in some cultures there is a distinct pause between questions and answers. Silence is evidence of thinking.

- Encourage peer tutoring so students can share culturally diverse strategies for learning and all students can be seen as learners and teachers.

Cultural Awareness and Your Curriculum

My esteemed colleague Peggy Harris, who has been my mentor about culture in the classroom, often refers to the Three Fs approach to multicultural education—*food, fiestas,* and *famous people.* Great teachers eschew this limited approach and use cultures as an overarching theme in their classrooms. Their goal is not to specifically "teach" the cultures, as if preparing for a citizenship test, but to expand students' awareness of multiple cultures as a given in our history and in contemporary life.

But there are some very real barriers to this approach that even great teachers must overcome. Teachers often report that they simply don't know enough to make timely and relevant connections between various cultures and their curriculum. This leads to a feeling of insecurity about where and how to integrate cultural references. If you factor in too few materials, little planning time, and no room in an overcrowded curriculum, culturally inclusive teaching can seem like a real challenge. And it is. But the benefits to you and your kids can be immense, so the trick is to stop thinking of ways to add culture on, and start thinking of ways to use culture to teach all the things on your current agenda—literacy, critical thinking, writing, history, and the arts. The following are ten starter activities that blend culture and learning.

1. *Read Aloud*

All good teachers read aloud because they know that it is the single greatest predictor that kids will become readers. Great teachers use their read-aloud time to teach about cultures using literature, poetry, biography, and autobiography. A good children's librarian can help you locate the folktales and myths from various cultures that all tell the same story or have the same motif. Reading a wide range of multicultural literature helps students see social and historic issues from multiple perspectives and develop empathy for the struggles of various cultural groups.

2. *Family Interviews*

This activity builds thinking and language skills while your students dive into the particular culture of their families. Talk about the elements of culture and help your kids develop a list of questions that would uncover data about cultural practices in their homes. Then let them conduct family interviews with parents, grandparents, aunts, uncles, and family friends. They can record the data with pictures, sketches, lists, or complete narratives. When they come back to school, have them share in pairs, and then with the larger group.

3. *You, Too? Graphing Cultural Overlapping*

To process all the data from family interviews and let your kids begin to look at cultures analytically, set up an activity where they chart what they have discovered. For example, you can make a chart with lines, columns, or categories for different aspects of culture. Then give your kids a stack of adhesive tags on which they write their names. As you point to a category, for example, "Grandparents Live with Us"—they come up and put the paper with their name in the column to indicate that their family shares that trait. The final product is a chart that shows the ways that families in your room are similar.

4. *Venn Diagrams*

Once you identify all the cultures in your class, make a Venn diagram with one circle for each group, and have all the circles overlap in the center. Students can use words or pictures to display the data gathered in family interviews. Students will soon discover that while each culture has some unique elements, many practices overlap with other cultures. The center represents what all cultures have in common—who we are together.

5. *Home-Grown Literacy Materials*

Some teachers of younger students have found a way to include more culturally relevant reading material in their curriculum by transcribing stories told by their students from different cultures and using them as reading material. For example, you may ask students from different cultures to describe how they celebrate birthdays.

6. *Holistic Reading Versus Comprehension Checks*

In our zeal for comprehension checks, we often interrupt stories, poems, even read-aloud activities to ask questions and elaborate. But many children have better comprehension when they are allowed to read or hear the whole story, uninterrupted, before focusing on details and concepts. So try various approaches with your students, and observe their responses.

7. *News From*

Many teachers include current events in their curriculum to boost geographic, political, and environmental awareness, and with the Internet as your newsstand, you can literally log on to hometown newspapers from all over the world. Articles about ancient ruins near Mexico City, hurricanes in Puerto Rico, as well as pictures of local holidays and festivals from far away can increase your students' global and cultural awareness.

8. *Roots*

You can create a highly integrated cross-curricular project simply by encouraging students to investigate their cultural roots. This is not an investigation of their specific families, but a broader look at the ethnic or cultural groups from which they are descended. As they investigate, students will learn about the location, geography, and climate of their ancestral homeland. They will need to study maps, look at reference books, videos, and the Internet. They can concentrate on the art, music, and drama, or investigate people who made significant contributions to their culture. They can present their findings with murals, dramatic performances, cooking demonstrations, scrapbooks, and oral presentations. Family members may join in the culminations.

9. *Rewriting History*

As your students become attuned to the notion of the dominant culture, guide them to examine their history textbooks to see how many points of view are consistently presented. Whose view is most favorably represented? What groups are generally excluded? Then challenge your students to take a piece of writing that reflects the majority point of view and rewrite it from other points of view.

10. *Cultural Awareness Through Music*

Music is a universal language and a powerful type of intelligence. It is one of the easiest ways to introduce cultures into your classroom because there's no language barrier—kids just need ears to get it. So ask parents to lend you recordings of music that they play in their family. Your kids will begin to appreciate that all cultures create music but every group has its own special ways of doing it. Talk with the children about how different music sounds: loud, soft, fast, or slow. Listen for the different instruments. Ask your music teacher or parents if they have any instruments that your kids could use for impromptu performances. The Internet is a great place to sample music from many cultures. Start with "Ethnomusicology as Advocacy" (http://otto.cmr.fsu.edu/~cma/Advocacy/music_cultural_survival_index.htm), a group that teaches the Internet public about the music, dance, and other creative arts of many cultures.

Culturally Inappropriate Materials

Despite decades of multicultural emphasis in our schools, you may still be the proud owner of a closet full of textbooks and curriculum resources designed for consumption by students in the majority culture. Minorities may be included in anecdotes, sidebars, or illustrations, but the text is overwhelmingly seen from the majority perspective. You can sharpen your ability to spot bias in classroom materials by asking yourself questions like:

- Whose voice, experience, or perspective is represented in these materials?
- Does the curriculum represent the contributions of all people, including women and people of color?
- Are there accurate historical accounts of shameful periods of U.S. history, including slavery, the destruction of Native American cultures, the internment of Japanese Americans?
- Whose voices are missing?
- What voice or perspective do I need to add?
- How can I locate materials that represent other voices and perspectives?

What if you come up with a pile of culturally lopsided books? You don't have to host a book burning. If fact, biased materials can be very powerful learning materials if you put them to work for you. Issue a challenge to your kids: Does anyone see any problems in this statement or illustration? Let your kids gnaw on the problem for a while. Think of this exercise as a chewbone to strengthen their social justice muscles. Once your kids tune in to the language of exclusion and bias, they'll ferret out examples that even got past you. That's authentic critical thinking that will eventually make your kids better consumers, media observers, and voters.

Even officially adopted textbooks have their low points, so review your reading materials, texts, and tests carefully to identify culturally biased materials and take action. Have your kids write to the school board, administrators in charge of instruction, and the publishers. This is a great way to motivate kids to sharpen persuasive writing skills. But don't stop there. Have your kids rewrite a section of the offensive material to demonstrate their demands. Spend time with your colleagues discussing the problem of bias in learning resources, policies, or procedures that inadvertently penalize certain races, cultures, sexes, or disabilities. Bring them to the attention of school officials and work with them to make changes.

The Culture of Inclusion

What's the point of all this cultural awareness? Does it mean that you have to become a cultural chameleon, changing your expectations and responses from moment to moment in order to accommodate the many cultures of your students? Should you adopt, adapt, and accept anything that your kids shoot your way in the name of cultural sensitivity or tolerance? Absolutely not. But great teachers firmly believe that children from other cultures are advantaged in many ways—unless schools insist on making their nonmajority status a cause for concern in and of itself. And to ensure that all students succeed, great teachers make explicit for their kids the parts of school that are firmly cemented in the majority culture, so that they can learn how to use the codes of power to realize their potential

> *Social equality cannot be attained merely with material resources. Those who have knowledge and education must be ready and willing to share it with those who lack them, for inequality in money and property is not always the most tragic. There is an even more crying inequality—between those who know and those who do not know.*
>
> —Golda Meir

in the world. If we do any less, we end up creating a culture of exclusion, forcing children to undergo rituals of failure, until they simply give up on school.

Resources

Ashton-Warner, Sylvia. 1963. *Teacher*. New York: Simon and Schuster.

Banks, James, ed. 2001. *Multicultural Education: Issues and Perspectives*, 4th ed. New York: John Wiley & Sons.

Delpit, Lisa. 1995. *Other People's Children: Cultural Conflict in the Classroom*. New York: New Press.

———. 2003. *The Skin That We Speak: Thoughts on Language and Culture in the Classroom*. New York: New Press.

Howard, Gary. 1999. *We Can't Teach What We Don't Know: White Teachers, Multiracial Schools*. New York: Teachers College Press.

Jacobson, Tamar. 2003. *Confronting Our Discomfort: Clearing the Way for Anti-Bias in Early Childhood*. Portsmouth, NH: Heinemann.

Ladson-Billings, Gloria. 2001. *Crossing Over to Canaan: The Journey of New Teachers in Diverse Classrooms*. San Francisco: Jossey-Bass.

Paley, Vivian. 2000. *White Teacher*. Cambridge, MA: Harvard University Press.

Rochman, Hazel. 1993. *Against Borders*. Chicago: ALA Books. A survey of children's books with multicultural themes.

Great Teachers Don't Take No (or Yes) for an Answer

Teaching by Asking Instead of Telling

In This Chapter:

Kids don't have to be in the gifted club or even wide awake to answer most of the questions their teachers pose. In fact, the level of dialogue in some classrooms is so rudimentary that many bright kids have completely abandoned the notion of school as a cerebral experience. That's why in many classrooms you encounter the phenomenon of the DA—the Designated Answerer. Designated Answerers have a single purpose in school—to answer any question the teacher asks. They spend most of the day with their arms in an aerial position, waiting expectantly, cooperatively, even slavishly, to field the next volley.

What's the capital of Iowa?

Des Moines!

What is the major export of Alaska?

Oil!

What do pandas eat?

Bamboo!

How many toes on your left foot?

Uh, five? (Seems like a trick question.)

Some classrooms have just one DA, tirelessly playing verbal ping-pong with the teacher from early morning through the closing bell. Other rooms are DA-rich. Three or even four contenders semaphore vigorously to catch the teacher's eye, or gasp as if being garroted to catch her ear. All for the honor of delivering the "right" answer, so the game can move on to the next round.

And where are the rest of the students? AWOL. Having a rich fantasy life. Working on a series of Baroque doodles, or drafting the great American novel, one clandestine note at a time. They're bored. Indifferent. Ripe for rebellion. Can you blame them? The teacher has made it clear that their presence is only required so that the body count matches the attendance sheet. Participation is strictly optional—maybe even unwelcome from students with inquisitive minds or an argumentative streak. And that's fine with them. School is simply a rehearsal for retirement, without the cane or walker.

The only thing that disturbs the metabolism of most students is when the Designated Answerer is absent or unexpectedly transfers to another school. Who's going to keep the teacher busy all day? The teacher may get a little nervous, too. Who *is* going to answer her questions? What will happen when she asks where Kenya is located, and no one volunteers "right on the equator" or leaps up and gestures toward the middle of the map? Luckily, teachers have a robust repertoire of emergency moves for situations just like this. Faced with stony silence, they repeat the question, "Who can find Kenya?" but louder, as if they've suddenly been transferred into a class for the hearing-impaired. If the silence persists, they're likely to bear down upon a hapless student and demand, "Adrianne, find Kenya!" or simply stab at the map with a yardstick, sputtering, "Right there! We talked about this last week."

Not a pretty picture. But it's pretty accurate. Too many schools and instructional programs that tout critical thinking seem to be fundamentally critical *of* thinking as a basic classroom activity. It takes a long time. It's messy. The outcomes are uncertain. And how do you assess something that has no right answer? The instructional day is so crowded with "experts," from textbooks and videos, to prescribed, scripted, time-driven curriculum that there's simply no place for students or teachers to say, "Wait a minute, I don't think I agree. Let's take a closer look at that."

What if teachers do want to dig in and try some rigorous thinking? Really probe kids to find out what they're wondering besides "Is it lunchtime yet?" They're not likely to get many takers. Any kid who's old enough to tie his shoes without assistance is too savvy to play that game because from the first day of kindergarten, we teach kids how to *do* school. The teacher asks a question. It has one answer. He already has that answer, but he wants to hear it from a kid. In return for the right answer, the respondent will get a smile or a saccharine "that's right" and the class will get another question to answer. That's how you do school, and woe unto the student who breaks the rules, gives the wrong answer, or worse, asks a question back! Questions posed by students frequently earn the curt reply, "We're not talking about that now."

This is a graveyard for thinkers.

So kids protect themselves by not volunteering unless they're certain of the answer. If you decide to change the rules by asking open-ended questions that seem more like an invitation to ruminate than simply recite, kids think it's a trick. Their response? Industrial-strength silence.

Here's the saddest part. That silence in your room is an echo of the silence in their heads. Their brains are gridlocked—intrigued by the notion of a question that really could have some interesting possibilities, and paralyzed by the skepticism that there's just one right answer after all, and they don't have it.

Enter Socrates.

What's the Big Idea About Inquiry Teaching?

Socrates was one of the first educators to conclude that learning cannot be delivered. Like most great teachers, he believed that people learn best when they're involved, and the way Socrates got them involved was to ask a great question. He spent his life asking and asking, annoying almost everyone in town, until finally they quenched his thirst for knowledge with a cup of hemlock. Happily, teachers who use Socrates as a model rarely share his fate.

The way that Socrates taught is called the Socratic or inquiry method. The word *inquiry* tells it all. It's about motion—probing, eliciting, pressing for, searching, seeking, scrutinizing. Inquiry is an interactive, give-and-take-ish way to pursue learning with your students. It's the opposite of those monologues called the didactic approach, where the teacher delivers large shipments of information to students who are apparently "learning." In reality, many students simply gaze in the approximate direction of the speaker and silently refuse delivery. Occasionally the teacher breaks the monotony by firing a low-level question over their heads—Who was the first president of the United States? How many inches in a yard? Which is bigger, a molecule or an atom? Who fought in the War of 1812?—more as a check for consciousness than comprehension.

The inquiry method uses questions, too, but they're open-ended. That means there's no one right answer, since the purpose is to elicit students' thoughts, and then help them examine their thinking. The answers to inquiry questions are knowable to anyone within earshot, if the question is well-crafted and the students work at it by thinking.

Let's look at some didactic questions translated into the inquiry mode.

Didactic Questions	Open-Ended Inquiry Questions
What shape is this leaf?	What do you notice about this leaf?
How was this tool used?	How might this tool have been used? By whom?
What color is this?	How would you describe this color?
What is bark?	Why do you think trees have bark?
What animals migrate?	Why do you think creatures and people migrate?
Who invented the first writing system?	Why do you think people invented writing?

Words like *think, would, could,* or *might* embedded in a question indicate inquiry in progress. They signal that there are many ways to answer the question, and typically the answers themselves stimulate more questions. So instead of the tidy game of ping-pong that occurs with didactic teaching, inquiry stimulates talking, puzzling, risking, and debating. Students feel confused, frustrated, tense, puzzled, affronted, shocked, determined, and sometimes triumphantly surprised at their own cognitive accomplishments.

Inquiry demands effort. Teachers have to work hard devising great questions, but the good news is that kids have to work harder because inquiry forces them to root around in their heads and come up with details, examples, evidence, ideas, theories, and speculations. In an era when sound bites have replaced communication and thought, this is revolutionary. The teacher listens, thinks, and asks another question and perhaps another to push students' thinking. The result is that kids get smarter through their own efforts. They construct meaning by interacting with others, rather than waiting in a persistent vegetative state for another delivery of information.

Where does inquiry fit in your teaching day? Great teachers are perpetually in inquiry mode. They use inquiry in the moment, to respond to students' remarks. For example, if a student complains, "I don't get why we have to study history, anyway. All these people are dead, so what's the difference?" An inquiry-type response would be, "That's an interesting question. Why might it be useful for us to learn about things that happened in the past?" If you train yourself to consistently respond to questions and remarks with probing questions, students learn to think first, or pose better questions geared toward finding an answer, not just registering a complaint.

Many teachers use inquiry to introduce a specific topic in a content area, such as understanding winter migration routes, examining the cause of low voter turnout, or analyzing strategies to combat discrimination. Great teachers take inquiry much farther, using a set of inquiry questions as the engine to drive an entire unit of study, such as the rise of civilization, the Civil War, or adaptation in animals and plants, which may last all year. Inquiry, done well, stimulates full-throttle cognition. There are few things a teacher can do that are more exciting or exhausting. Inquiry teaching truly is a contact sport.

The Three Basic Moves

There are three basic moves in an inquiry approach to teaching. Master these and you're on your way to creating a gymnasium for youthful minds.

1. Ask initiating questions.
2. Ask questions to respond and follow-up.
3. Insert information at key points.

Move Number 1: Ask Initiating Questions

Teachers who use the inquiry method launch their lessons with an open-ended question that identifies the topic and jump-starts the discussion. For example, if you were starting an inquiry lesson on the history of your community, you might say: "Our town was founded in 1793, just over two hundred years ago. Why do you think people came to live here?" Given time and encouragement, students will comment on the location, resources, weather, climate, geography, proximity to other places, exile, adventure, vacation, health, opportunity, accident, or luck. They may go for fifteen minutes, rummaging for reasons. How do you get this much discussion out of kids who are used to relaxing in the shadow of the Designated Answerer? Each time students volunteer an answer, you acknowledge their interesting contribution and then say, "What else? What's another reason people would come here?"

What else? is one of the most powerful questions you have to galvanize all of your students, not just the smarties. *What else?* trains your kids to treat the obvious, superficial answers as warm-up for thinking rigorously about anything from mitosis to medieval art. By your insistence on multiple answers to the same question, you slowly convince kids that there is no one right answer. There are as many answers as there are minds in the room, and you're desperately interested in all of them. You will find many examples of initiating questions in this chapter, so for now let's move on to the second basic move an inquiry teacher needs to master—responding to students' remarks.

Move Number 2: Ask Questions to Respond and Follow-Up

Many teachers ask good initiating questions. They know where they want the discussion to go, and they craft a question that could take them there along a scenic route. The problem is that when students offer listless, sloppy, half-baked answers, they accept them. Kids blurt out some fuzzy, quasi-related string of words, ending with a rising tone that functions as a question mark in an otherwise declarative statement. The teacher feigns satisfaction and moves on. End of inquiry. Actually, it's pretty much the end of thinking once kids realize that this is not a precision event. A rough approximation will do.

Let's return to our question about local history. Suppose you ask, "Why do you think people came to live here?" and get the reply, "Maybe they came here because they were scared?" There are a number of possible ways to respond. Some teachers would shoot the kid a puzzled look and move on, as if he'd never spoken. Or supply a rational subtitle for his remarks—"I think Jeremy means people left some pretty dangerous places to settle here because they thought it would be safer." If he didn't mean that initially, he will by the time you're through. Perhaps you'll say "maybe" with a look of serene blankness, all the while thinking, "Jeez, with answers like that, we'll never get through this material!" Reaching the conclusion that this whole questioning idea is a bad one, you launch into an explanation of why people settled in your fair town, and save your questions for a pop quiz.

Whereas, a teacher bent on inquiry would lean in. That's right. You need to get closer so you can find out what that student means. So it's time to ask another good question! Here are some ways you could respond that would push a student to rethink and clarify:

> "That's an interesting idea. Can you tell me more?"
>
> "Can you tell me about the kinds of things that might scare people into leaving their homes and coming here?"
>
> "What kind of things scared people in the past?"
>
> "Why would moving be a good solution if you were scared?"
>
> " Do you know about any of the things that scared people two hundred years ago when our town started?"

All of those questions put Jeremy back in thinking mode. It makes him accountable for what he said.

Follow-up questions generally come in five flavors. They're used to: clarify, expose points of view, probe assumptions, push for reasons or evidence, and probe implications or consequences. That looks like a lot to keep track of, but your gut will point you in the right direction. You can use the following lists to identify follow-up questions that press students to refine their thinking.

Clarification.   Students frequently need help figuring out what they're trying to say. They make statements that are ambiguous, or they lump several different concepts together. Sometimes they blend information that's true with notions that are false, nullifying their statement. Here is an example of a confusing statement with sample questions that you can use to push students to be clear about what they think and say.

Example: Some Indians had these ceremonies where they would burn people after a war or something.

- What do you mean by _____?
- Could you give me an example?
- What is your main point?
- Could you explain that further?
- Could you put that another way?
- Would you say more about that?
- Why do you say that?
- What do you think is the main issue here?
- How does this relate to our discussion (problem, issue)?

Points of View.   Students need help learning to distinguish opinions from fact. The following questions can be used to probe arguments or statements that reflect a student's point of view, but are stated as fact and fail to acknowledge other perspectives.

Example: Having clean air is a good idea but it costs too much money.

- You seem to be approaching this issue from a monetary perspective. Why did you choose that point of view?
- How would other groups of people respond? Why? What would influence them?
- How would you answer the objections that environmentalists would make?
- What might someone who believed _____ think?
- Can/did anyone see this another way?
- What would someone who disagrees say?
- What is an alternative?

Assumptions. Helping your students uncover assumptions in their thinking is like peeling an onion. You just keep exposing layer after layer of ideas until you reach the single, sometimes erroneous thought underlying their statements. It's hard work. You have to be well-rested and tenacious. But this process really sharpens their ability to evaluate ideas presented by writers, politicians, and advertisers. Use the following questions to probe students' thinking when unacknowledged assumptions are embedded in their statements or arguments.

Example: Vouchers are great because then parents can send their kids to any school they want.

- What are you assuming?
- What could we assume instead?
- You seem to be assuming _____. Do I understand you correctly?
- All of your reasoning depends on the idea that _____? Why have you based your thinking on that?
- You seem to be assuming _____. How would you justify this?
- Is it always the case? Why do you think the assumption applies here?
- When wouldn't your statement be true?
- Why would someone make this assumption?

Reasons or Evidence. Teaching students to include reasons or evidence in their statements lifts their dialogue to a more refined and convincing level. It's an excellent way to strengthen the fundamental skills needed for persuasive writing, debate, or public speaking. Use the following questions to prompt students to provide evidence that what they said is credible, or to explain the reasons for a particular belief or statement.

Example: Most of the people who lived in the colonies in the 1770s didn't really care about the revolution.

- Who would be an example of that?
- How do you know?
- Why do you think that is true?
- What led you to that belief?
- What would change your mind?
- What other information do we need?
- Could you explain your reasons to us?
- Is there reason to doubt that evidence?

- Who is in a position to know if that is so?
- What would you say to someone who said _____?
- Can someone else give evidence to support that response?
- How could we find out whether that is true?

Implications and Consequences.   Rigorous thinkers are trained to ask themselves: "And then what?" You can use the following questions to help students thrust their thinking forward in time or through a series of events to hypothesize about the results and analyze the wisdom of their ideas.

Example: If we could just get rid of taxes, we wouldn't have so many poor people. That would be good for our city because we have too many poor and homeless people.

- Tell us more about how that would work.
- When you say _____, are you implying _____?
- But if that happened, what else would happen as a result? Why?
- What effect would that have?
- Would that necessarily happen or only probably happen?
- What is an alternative?

Move Number 3: Insert Information at Key Points

Sometimes eager teachers ask: "If I do inquiry teaching, when do I get to share all the wonderful things I've learned through my own research? Is there a place for telling in an inquiry approach to learning, or do I just ask questions all the time?" Inquiry isn't just a matter of uncovering what your students already know. That's certainly an essential activity because excavating prior knowledge lays a foundation on which to build new ideas. But there comes a point in every discussion where kids need new information to get to the next level. That's where your expert knowledge comes in.

For example, if you're talking about ancient civilizations, your kids may deduce the need for laws, but they could talk all day and never think up the Code of Hammurabi. So you insert critical pieces of information about Hammurabi, including a few intriguing facts. According to Hammurabi's laws, "If fire breaks out in a house, and someone who comes to put it out cast his eye upon the property of the owner of the house, and take the property of the master of the house, he shall be thrown into that self-same fire." That should get their attention! Then point them in the direction of the primary source documents on ancient laws. Start their investigation with a two-pronged question that makes them search and think, such as: What types of laws did Hammurabi write and how are they like our laws? That way you focus their research and indicate the starting point for your next discussion.

So great inquiry teachers ask open-ended questions to launch a discussion and probe student thinking. Building on that discussion, they *teach,* using stories, anecdotes, documents, charts, graphs, photographs, paintings, diaries, and so forth. In this interval, students get more in-depth information that primes them for more questions and thinking.

Another skill of the inquiry teacher is helping students keep track of *what we know so far.* I like to sketch on the board as students talk. These scribbles aren't masterpieces or even intelligible to an outsider, but I've found that even cartoonish images surrounded by words help visual learners stay focused and track the discussion. You can also use lists, phrases, diagrams, or graphs to illustrate the points students make. Then pause periodically to summarize what's been said and identify the parts of the question that are still unresolved. Using this process, you model how good thinkers tackle a question and stick with it until they're satisfied. Your students learn to combine their ideas with remarks from other students, add in the information you provided and their own research "discoveries" to construct a solid body of knowledge and create new ideas. All the while, they're honing their thinking skills.

The Impact of Inquiry on Learning

You may be thinking that inquiry was a great idea in ancient Athens where people like Socrates had time on their hands and servants to tidy up after them. Whereas you're alone on the front lines of the education battle with jumbo-sized helpings of responsibility and little support. Probing questions and long answers require time that you don't have. They take patience, which may also be in short supply. Plus, teachers using the inquiry method must attend to every word students utter, and evaluate both the articulation and the thinking behind it. That's a hell of a lot more work than asking "Who was the fourth president of the United States?"

So why do great teachers use the inquiry method?

The Brain Gym

Did you know that the average teacher speaks 140 words per minute? But the average kid can hear 1,000 words per minute, and youthful brains can process up to 4,000 words per minute! Four thousand! So when you're standing in front of your class in a declarative mode, you're a slow-motion phenomenon in a high-speed world. Even if you're broadcasting at a tongue-twisting rate, a kid's brain has lots of time on its hands. And if you've chosen a topic that holds exactly no interest for your students, you're a silent movie playing for a captive audience. The urge to yell "fire" must be overwhelming.

What's going on behind kids' foreheads during didactic bouts? If you say to your students, "What's the capital of Minnesota?" some of them will acknowledge your intrusion long enough to think "St. Paul," and then stop thinking about you. Their brains return to a topic of their choice, not remotely related to Minnesota. A bunch of other students will hear "What's the capital of Minnesota?" and decide after a nanosecond, "I don't know." But their brains keep on thinking and most of their thoughts are negative: What if he calls on me? I'll look stupid. I should have studied more. Why can't I ever remember anything? Who cares about Minnesota, anyway? I wonder if I can get a hall pass? Either way, it's not a great use of the real estate between their ears.

Inquiry questions catapult kids out of their La-Z-Boys. Faced with a single substantive question that seems to have lots of answers, their brains kick in like the search engine on a computer. All of a sudden they think, "What do I know about this?" Signals go out in every direction. Synapses crackle. The hunt is on, and it looks different in every head. One student is searching for facts while another thinks in pictures. Some dredge up personal experiences, others work from logic, or extrapolate from parallel situations. The point is, they're all on task. One good question can produce 200 cranial hits. Inquiry questions create focus, put the brain in gear and keep it there.

The Owner's Manual

When it comes right down to it, a brain is a pretty good thing to have. It's helpful in school and invaluable in most real-life situations, except maybe on a blind date or talk-radio. But like any really handy appliance, you have to know how to use it. Inquiry takes kids through the owner's manual for their brains. It helps them identify and begin to consciously examine the elements of thought: concepts, evidence, assumptions, implications, consequences, interpretations, conclusions, and points of view. Once they've studied the owner's manual, kids begin to notice the structure of their own thoughts. With a little encouragement, they'll be critiquing the utterances of people around them—their peers, school administrators, coaches, movie stars, and news commentators. And yes, you're likely to take a few friendly barbs, but it's worth it to see your kids running through all their cognitive gears. I like to tape sound bites of politicians or their spinmeisters, and let my kids dissect their utterances for batting practice. With a lot of hard work on your part, you can raise a crop of students who consciously use their brains to find and evaluate information, solve problems, and create new ideas. Ultimately you want them to be firmly in the driver's seat of the learning machine you've built, so that when confronted with a dilemma or a meaty question, they confidently declare "Slide over. I can handle this."

The Thinking Person

So how does it actually work? How do your kids go from dependent muddle-heads to autonomous thinkers? Pause, if you must, to decide if your really want a room full of autonomous thinkers, but then think how much fun it would be to spend every day with several dozen smart people. You'd be the envy of most adults in the business world, universities, or government—need I say more?

When you approach teaching through inquiry, it's like you've put a well-trained mind on speakerphone. You ask a question. That's the inciting incident for the brain. Then your kids make lots of remarks and observations. Their initial responses represent the thoughts that are triggered in the mind in response to your initial question. But here's the skill development: When you ask questions back to probe your students' thinking, you play the role of the inner voice that really good critical thinkers hear when they're working their way through a problem. In other words, you make external and visible the inner process of critical thinking. Eventually your kids internalize the process. Hence, autonomous thinkers.

Training in the inquiry method conditions the brain to raise basic issues, probe beneath the surface of things, and pursue problematic areas of thought. It also helps students:

- Develop sensitivity to clarity, accuracy, and relevance in the thoughts, arguments, and writing of other people.
- Arrive at judgments through their own reasoning.
- Adopt a penetrating and rigorous approach to topics from literature to political science.

Continuous exposure to inquiry questions teaches kids how to think in situations outside of school, to greet life with curiosity and healthy skepticism. It's possible that using the inquiry method may be one of the greatest contributions you can make to individual students and society. Why? Because real life is not a true/false or multiple-choice test. It's a series of critical judgments, from How fast can I drive on rain-slickened streets? to How will I choose between six candidates running for the same office? It's not what your kids read, but what they learn to read into a text and between the lines that makes them thinkers. Inquiry equips kids for life. Can you think of a better way to spend your time?

Wait Time in a Hurried World

By now it should be clear that inquiry teaching is an intensely cerebral activity for teachers and students. You'll need to be well-versed in the subject matter you're exploring with your students—but what great teacher isn't? Your kids need to think. But there's the rub. Thinking takes time. Suppose you ask: What do you think was the hardest thing about being a sailor on a voyage with Christopher Columbus? Suddenly there's a flurry of intracranial activity. Kids are digging, sorting, and evaluating. They're hitting the recall button, then applying the test of historic empathy: What would I hate the most about all those hardships? But that takes time. Different amounts of time for different kids, since even the smartest people process information at varying speeds.

Meanwhile, the room is as quiet as a tomb. Don't panic. And whatever you do, *don't talk*. This will be a real test of your strength, since most teachers suffer from *horror vaccui*. Typically, when teachers ask a question and get nothing in return but several dozen blank stares, they assume that something has gone terribly wrong, and switch to damage control. You know the drill. Talk louder, as if checking the acoustics. Rephrase the question to, "What made the Columbus voyages so difficult?" Now you have two slightly different questions in play, and your students must decide whether they should keep working on the first or shift to the second. Overanxious teachers may blurt out as many as four reiterations of the same question in a continuous string. Confusion abounds. To increase their odds of getting an answer, any answer, they restate the question in an either/or format with answers conveniently embedded within. "Was it the food or the uncertainty that made it so bad?" At this point, sharp students may pick up the scent. "Now we're getting somewhere. That's what she's fishing for." More silence. In a final act of desperation, teachers pounce on a spectacularly inattentive student, or simply answer the question in disgust and shift back to a more restful monologue.

What's going on here? It turns out that teachers, like kids, have been conditioned to the ping-pong approach to classroom dialogues. Researchers studying wait time discovered that when teachers ask a question, they get nervous if they don't hear an answer within three seconds. One. Two. Three. Three seconds? How much thinking can a kid do in three seconds? Or even five? Not much. Nonetheless, once the clock starts ticking, there's precious little time before teachers hijack the thinking process. *They simply can't wait.*

If you want inquiry to work, you must quell the urge to fill the void, because silence is your friend.

How do you develop your wait-muscle? Smoke. That's right. Lean against the chalkboard, assume the most nonchalant pose you can muster, and *visualize* smoking. Not the guilty little nips of people who swear they're trying to quit.

I mean those long, pensive, lung-inflating drags that dyed-in-the-wool tobacco lovers take, after which they squint at a far-off point and exhale in slow motion, loving every moment. Smoke like that while you're waiting, and it will send a message to your students that you have all the time in the world. You're just going to hang out contentedly until they're ready to talk because your only interest is hearing what they *think*.

Smoking is so many light-years from Right-Answerland, your kids may go into shock. And that's the second benefit of smoking. While you're learning to relax, your kids are getting nervous. Silence is a great medium for thinking, but if it goes on too long, they'll begin to feel the pressure. No one's talking. Someone should be talking by now, and it's clear you're not going to crack. Eventually and with great hesitation, a hand goes up. Time to stub out your cigarette and play ball! Haltingly, the first brave soul takes a crack at the Columbus question—"the water got sour after a while and they couldn't drink sea water, so they were pretty thirsty." "Absolutely," you reply, and jot *sour water* on the board.

At this point all the other students relax because you got what you wanted. Except, what's this? You turn, fix them with a look of intense interest, and say, "What else?" A ripple goes through the group. There's another answer? They go back to thinking. And you may need to smoke a little more, until another hand comes up. "They got lost a lot because their maps were bad, so they didn't know if they'd ever get home." Repeat the process, lavishing recognition on this bold thinker, adding *bad maps/lost* to the list. Then ask, "What else?" At this point kids may conclude that you're completely indiscriminate. You accept every answer and dole out commendations. Courage spreads like measles. Eventually you'll convince your kids that you're truly interested in their ideas, not just prospecting for the "right" answer. Then hands will fly up and you'll be too busy to smoke.

Keeping the Brain in Motion

Once you've built up your wait-muscle and grown immune to the occasional bouts of silence, you'll be able to focus on the skills you'll need to master in order to orchestrate inquiry discussions. Think of yourself as a giant synapse in the class's brain. It's your job to connect and redirect all the ideas your kids are spewing out. Another image that works for this is air-traffic controller. In effect, you track the progress of the hunt for answers and send up a flare when kids hit paydirt. But what else?

As the orchestrator of this cerebral jamboree, you need to:

- Encourage your students to slow their thinking down and elaborate on their ideas.

- Stimulate further discussion with probing questions.
- Use the word *wonder* a lot, as in "I *wonder* what you mean by; I *wonder* what that means to you; I *wonder* how that relates to what we already know about; I *wonder* how you could test that idea; I *wonder* if that makes sense to other students."
- State aloud your own personal wonderings about the discussion, sending the clear message that students are expected to listen and think seriously about the whole conversation, not just sit and wait for their turn to speak.
- Translate your students' curiosity into probing questions.
- Model analytic strategies.
- Help students clarify errors in reasoning by formulating questions that they cannot answer except by correcting the faulty reasoning.
- Convey your utmost respect for your students as thinkers.

Planning Inquiry-Based Instruction

Inquiry is not bound to any one subject because it's not about content. It's a way to think about content. Open-ended questions tease kids to wonder, whether you're examining mummification or multiplication. Any part of your curriculum that requires thinking is ripe for inquiry. Any part that doesn't require thinking—well, I'll leave that up to you. Whether you're planning a single lesson or a six-month unit driven by open-ended questions, you'll want to start with some basic considerations.

- What's the big question about this topic?
- What other questions will guide the conversation to its goal?
- What levels of questions should be included—factual, inference, interpretation, transfer, valuing?
- How should questions be sequenced?

The Big Question

The big question captures the goal of your lesson or unit. It unifies all the work that will follow. To identify the big question, ask yourself, What's the point of this lesson? What do I want kids to learn? Then turn that into a question. For example, if I want kids to explore local history from the point when nonnative settlers first arrived, my big question might be: Why do you think people settled in our town in the late 1800s? Through the inquiry process, students should be able to answer the big question knowledgeably, listing or discussing all the factors that prompted people to take up residence in the area.

Once you're clear about your big question, post it, highlight it, publish it. Keep it in front of kids' eyes to unify their thinking and their work. Kids who are raised on big questions learn to evaluate every idea that's presented, every discussion point, every document to see if it helps them toward a big answer. They actively scrutinize information instead of being passive observers of the learning landscape.

Questions Across the Curriculum

Let's look at some questions that could be jumping-off points for inquiry lessons. You can use them as is, or modify them to suit your particular work. I just find it easier to improvise from models than to stare at a blank sheet.

History/Social Science

- Why do you think people invented language? What problems do you think they encountered?
- How do you think people invented the wheel?
- Why do you think people leave their homeland?
- Why do people go exploring?
- What does it take to sustain people in a city?
- What systems need to be invented to make a city work?
- How is city life different from county life? What are the advantages and challenges of each?
- Why do you think some colonists preferred having a king to independence?
- What are the first things you would need to do if you were setting up a new country?
- Who should be allowed to lead our country? Who should be allowed to vote?
- Why might the United States make reparations to Native Americans for treaty violations?
- When might the invasion of another country be justified?
- How is your life different from life during the Civil War?
- What is your reaction to the fact that Thomas Jefferson owned slaves?
- Is slavery ever justified?
- What do you think the government should do about homelessness in our city?

Science

- What do you think computers will be like in the year 2050?
- Why do you think certain birds don't migrate?
- What do you think is the explanation for crop circles?
- What do you think people can do to reduce pollution?
- Do you think product testing on animals is ever justified? Why?
- What problems should science tackle in the next fifty years?
- What would be an effective way to prevent the extinction of certain African mammals?
- What can be done to protect homes from annual flooding?
- What would be a way to reduce traffic accidents during snowstorms?
- What do you know about trees?
- What is similar about ants and bees?
- What kind of shelter could you invent for people living in the desert to protect them from extreme heat and cold?
- What ideas do you have for reducing famine?
- What are some uses for buildings that are going to be demolished?

Literature

- Which poem do you think captured the feeling of being in a battle best? Why?
- What experiences have you had that are similar to the main character?
- If you could meet any character in this book, who would it be and why?
- If you could be any character in this book, who would you be and why?
- How would it change this story if it had been set in the mountains?
- Why do you think the author set this story at sea?
- How does the author let you know what the characters are feeling?
- If you were in this story, how would you have handled the conflict?
- What do you think will happen to the characters after the story ends?
- How would the story be different if the author told it from the bully's point of view?
- If the main character enrolled in our school, do you think you'd become friends?
- What advice would you give the underdog?
- How could you improve this story?

The Arts

- What does that music remind you of in your own life?
- What feelings do you think the composer was trying to convey?
- How would this composition be different if it was played on a piano instead of a violin?
- What images do you see in your mind when you listen to this music?
- What kind of tools might an artist use to make a painting like this?
- Why do artists take photographs?
- Describe what's happening in this painting.
- How are buildings and sculptures similar? Different?
- How is a sculpture different from a painting?
- What textures do you see in this sculpture?
- How would you describe the lines in this painting?
- Why do you think artists paint portraits—pictures of people?
- What patterns can you find in this painting?
- How would you describe what the colors are doing in this painting?
- What do you think gave this artist the idea for this sculpture?
- What story do you think the artist is trying to tell?
- If this sculpture could make sounds, what would you hear?

Math

- What are some ways we can measure the length of the soccer field?
- Why do you think people invented numbers?
- What's the easiest way to add four numbers?
- Why do you think we use commas in big numbers?
- How can you tell this division problem in words?
- How can you show it in pictures?
- What do you notice about the four basic shapes?
- What are some rules you would teach a student just starting to learn the multiplication tables?

An Inquiry-Based Unit: The Rise of Civilization

The year I was teaching humanities in a multiage class of ten-, eleven-, and twelve-year-olds, the focus of our curriculum was ancient civilizations, with a particular focus on the invention of democracy. We would be looking at cities and societies, past and present, starting with life in Mesopotamia about six thousand years ago. Initially I wanted to explore the concept that when people decided to abandon nomadic and agrarian life for permanent settlements that became cities, there were preexisting conditions that allowed that to happen in one place as opposed to another. Specifically, this area was in the Fertile Crescent between the Tigris and Euphrates rivers. In addition to certain environmental conditions, people would have to develop tools and systems that would allow the permanent concentration of a large population in one area. I wanted my students to think their way through the stages from nomad to reading-writing-law-abiding city dweller. It was my goal to pry out of them anything they knew about civilizations by asking a series of strategically sequenced questions.

Here are a few of the big ideas that they raised and fleshed out in those discussions: that there are advantages to living in settlements rather than being nomads; that once people began to live together in large concentrations, they created a demand for certain agencies, systems, and services. New jobs evolved. Institutions sprang up that needed to be housed in structures tailored to a specific purpose, thus they had differentiated architecture—temples, courts, housing, palaces, storage facilities, and markets. The resulting division of labor created free time and a need for entertainment, which begot music, dance, and drama.

The questions I used to guide these discussions were based on my own research and reading. I built each lesson around two or three questions that would prod my kids to think. Only after pumping them dry of any relevant ideas would we plunge into the actual historic materials—books, primary source documents, artifacts, novels, and simulations that revealed the fine details of life in Mesopotamia. The following are the questions I used as a skeleton for our inquiry unit on early civilizations.

- Why might people want to live together in cities or towns rather than being nomads or farmers?
- What conditions would be necessary to support large groups of people living together in a city/town?
- What are the advantages of city living? What are the disadvantages?
- What knowledge or developments would be necessary to build a civilization versus nomadic hunter/gatherer lifestyle?
- How do humans organize their existence when they live together in large numbers?
- What would you consider sufficient evidence to indicate the presence of a city?
- Looking at this Sumerian frieze, what can you infer about their society?

- What jobs might be created in such a society?
- What would have been the main building materials in the Sumerian cities?
- What buildings would they need?
- How would the rise of cities create enemies or conditions for war?
- How would that influence city building and architecture?
- What conditions would stimulate trade?
- Why did the Sumerians need to invent writing?
- What are the challenges in inventing a writing system?
- How would writing change their society or civilization?
- Why would a set of laws like the Code of Hammurabi be necessary?
- What categories of laws would the Sumerians need to have an orderly society?

As you can see, all of these questions stimulate multiple answers, which spawn questions of their own. One or two questions would be enough for a morning's romp in Mesopotamia. I would ask a question followed by What else? What else? In addition to asking questions, I was the note taker or scribe, making visual models on the board to document the ideas and facts we were accumulating. Students kept notes of their own in any format that would help with recall and assist them with their own research projects and assessments. Some made annotated drawings, others favored lists, phrases, or diagrams. Soon we had a board full of notes and sketches representing their collective knowledge. Then we'd flesh out the tantalizing details with slides from the local art museum, replicas of artifacts, floor plans of palaces, cuneiform tablets, read-aloud novels, trade books, and guest speakers.

We hit the jackpot when we discovered a scholar at the local university who was fluent in cuneiform. She spent a morning reading old clay shards and stone etchings to my kids—deeds for houses, wedding contracts, and business deals, all carefully recorded in symbols that resembled bird footprints. This was a primary source document bonanza that let us witness daily life in the Fertile Crescent. Take a look at the text from a rental agreement on a wagon that was used for traveling between Babylonia and Palestine. The contract protects the owner's wagon from being driven the long route along the coast, rather like a mileage limit when you rent a U-Haul truck.

> A wagon from Mannum-balum-Shamash, of Shelibia, Shabilkinum, son of Appani[bi], on a lease for 1 year has hired. As a yearly rental 2/3 of a shekel of silver he will pay. As the first of the rent 1/6 of a shekel of silver he has received. Unto the land of Kittim he shall not drive it.

For the big finish that day, my kids learned to write their own cuneiform messages in damp clay using sharp sticks.

Later in the year we laid the Code of Hammurabi alongside our own municipal codes and marveled at the similarities. We attended city council meetings and monitored local elections to see how far we've strayed from the Greek's invention of democracy. By the end of the year, my students had attended 246 public meetings, testified before the Landmarks Commission, the Pier Restoration Corporation, and the City Council. They dissected an environmental impact study about restoring the breakwater in our bay and trooped into a public meeting with the Army Corps of Engineers with a long list of—you guessed it—questions. The startled corpsmen were clearly unprepared to debate their report line-by-line with thirty citizens too young to vote and too fired up to be intimidated by a six-foot colonel listing ever so slightly to the left from the weight of his medals. That year my kids didn't just learn about democracy. They reinvented it before the wondering eyes of their parents and one very proud teacher. And they did it by mastering the art of asking good questions.

Inquiry and Classroom Culture

If you use the inquiry method consistently, the culture in your classroom slowly but perceptibly shifts. There's no Designated Answerer because kids discover that they're all capable of high-level thinking and together they can create new knowledge. Individual students become the recognized experts on various subjects, so their peers go to them when they need the definitive answer on Edison, or Elizabeth the First, or edible mushrooms. It's a powerful feeling to be an expert, and it gives kids a tiny glimpse of what they can do with their brains. Perhaps the most important development is that your students become experts on the subject of learning. They've learned how to learn. That's a portable skill that will serve them for life.

As you get more comfortable with this back-and-forth rhythm of teaching, your kids will get excited because they realize they're sharing the driver's seat in this mental road trip. They consciously, even viscerally experience themselves learning, and at the same time they have the thrill of teaching. They see the lightbulbs going on in their peers' eyes, and enjoy the heady feeling of being one of the "smart" kids, maybe for the first time in their career. Or they notice the way the topic lurches in a whole new direction when they make an insightful comment. They get a rush of pure adrenaline when they ask a challenging question that hasn't occurred to anyone in the room, including the teacher! When learning looks like this, it's not only a contact sport, it's addicting. Even better than recess or snacks!

Beyond the obvious notion that inquiry discussions strengthen critical thinking, there are plenty of other academic benefits you can reap without any extra effort. Inquiry sharpens speaking and writing skills; it promotes vigorous, motivated reading of adult-level material, as kids pursue their own questions.

> *I cannot teach anybody anything.*
> *I can only make them think.*
> —Socrates

The research center in your room will be the in place to be. Inquiry provides greater access to the curriculum for more students with longer lasting effects. In an inquiry-based classroom, kids no longer *do* school. They don't take deliveries. They create knowledge by thinking together, and that knowledge is more potent than anything found in a textbook.

One fine day, dialogue will break out among your students. They'll shoot questions directly at each other, and for as long as it lasts, you're out of a job. This is the highest compliment you can receive from your kids. Cherish it and then go out and do something really nice for yourself. You're a new-age Socrates, and you didn't even have to sip the hemlock.

Resources

Cecil, Nancy. 1995. *The Art of Inquiry Teaching: Questioning Strategies for K–6 Classrooms.* Manitoba: Peguin Publishers.

Whitin, Phyllis, and David Whitin. 1997. *Inquiry at the Window: Pursuing the Wonders of Learners.* Portsmouth, NH: Heinemann.

Great Teachers Know a Hemingway When They See One

Getting to the Heart of Writing

In This Chapter:

+ What's the Big Idea About Writing?
+ From Craft to Art
+ Getting to the First Draft
+ Everyone's an Editor
+ How to Grow a Writer
+ The Fine Art of Journaling
+ Is There a Hemingway in the House?

Some kids love to write. The verbal/linguistic region of their brain is positively teeming with polysyllables and highly polished phrases snatched from the radio, pilfered from adult conversations, or hoovered up during your last read-aloud session. These kids have an insatiable appetite for paper, as long as there's a pencil nearby. You know who they are—the ones who linger in the room at recess time, pouring intense, secret thoughts into their journals. Or write a class play, even though you're not in the market for one. Truman Capote was like that. He started writing when he was about eight years old, almost as if he had no choice. "Writing was always an obsession with me, quite simply something I had to do." Rachael Carson wrote dozens of tiny doll-sized books, and C. S. Lewis penned and staged elaborate puppet plays, honing his writing skills long before he took Alice on her trek through the looking glass. For kids like this, writing is sport and they're the Olympians.

But many smart kids hate writing. They spend their entire school career held at penpoint. First of all, they're wondering, Why do I have to write, anyway, when the teacher is within spitting distance of my desk? Can't I just tell her what I want to say? For them, writing is just a really, really inefficient way to communicate—slower than talking and far more hazardous. When you speak, nobody notices where you put your commas. Write, and they're after you with a red pencil. And then there's the grueling process of lining up hundreds, even thousands of words in single file. They wonder, Who knows which ones the teacher wants? How can I tell when I'm done? For these kids, writing is just tough, puzzling work.

Nonetheless, the more creative ones manage to turn their writer's block into a sport. First comes the Search and Rescue event. When you say it's writing time, they dive under their tables, as if you just announced a duck-and-cover drill. They're searching for their favorite pencil, which is tragically AWOL and likely to remain so. If found, it's never sharp enough, so several trips to the sharpener are required to remedy the situation. Then the chair needs to be precisely aligned toward some invisible compass point before they can begin, and a drink of water would probably speed the whole process.

When these students finally get a few words on the paper, inevitably they're the wrong ones, so it's time for a brisk round of erasing. Antiwriters employ a full-body approach to the task. They encircle the upended pencil in a death grip, then begin scouring the paper, like a murder suspect removing bloodstains. Soon the tabletop is strewn with bright pink eraser crumbs and you can see light through the freshly scrubbed paper. Next, the crumbs are carefully gathered into a miniature pyramid. For the big finish, the unwriter inhales deeply and expels a small tornado, sending crumbs in all directions. For kinesthetic learners, this is heaven. And cardiovascularly speaking, it's a tour de force. Unfortunately, little or no writing is produced.

Great teachers know only too well that writing is hard work—exhausting for students and massively time-consuming for teachers. But they understand that if students are to make knowledge their own, they must wrestle with facts, struggle with details, and rework raw information into language that reaches their audience. So they give their students safe, effective strategies that will help them become competent writers, and ultimately discover the joy of wordsmithing.

Kids catch on faster if you approach writing in bite-sized pieces. The more you identify the discrete building blocks in the writing process, the greater the possibility for their success. With your help, they'll not only understand why we write, but also glimpse how it looks and feels when writing becomes art.

What's the Big Idea About Writing?

Writing is a brilliant human invention, second only to the wheel or harnessing fire. And yet it's an utterly simple concept. People think and make scribbles to capture their thoughts. They leave the scribbles behind. Later, someone else comes by, looks at the marks, and gets the message. The marks are arbitrary, but everyone is in agreement about what they mean. Communicating by encoding and decoding. Capturing and preserving ideas and information. That's the big idea behind writing.

Your kids can discover their own answer to the question Why do we write? by investigating how it all got started. In 3100 BC, the Sumerians developed a type of writing called *cuneiform*. Around the same time, the Egyptians were working on hieroglyphics. While most people are familiar with the picture-style hieroglyphs, cuneiform "letters" are a real puzzle. To the untrained eye, they look something like bird tracks—elongated wedge-shapes rotated or combined with other wedges, pressed into wet clay or painted on a surface. The Sumerians used cuneiform writing for accounting, to record the first set of written laws known as the Code of Hammurabi, and for espionage. When they wanted to send secret messages between cities, they wrote on the freshly shaved head of a slave, waited for the hair to grow out, and off he went. Upon arrival, he shaved again and had his head examined. Not exactly e-mail but it worked!

Ask your students to imagine for just a moment what their lives would be like without writing. There would be no letters, no newspapers, no comic books— everything would have to be verbal or represented with pictures. Continue by listing the advantages of living in a world where people know how to write.

Codes

To help kids really grasp the notion that writing and reading are actually encoding and decoding, introduce your students to spy language. Let them play with ciphers and codes. You may discover that the very kids who despise writing are expert cryptographers. Soon they'll be swapping elaborate coded messages under your very nose. They just need an intriguing format to put their literacy skills to work. While they're scratching out messages that look like a calculator with a stutter, they'll practice spelling, grammar, and sentence structure. Hook them up with a correspondent, and they'll be translating symbols back to text—in effect, reading in two languages.

Technically, codes are whole words that replace other words. For example, Secret Service agents use code words like *the eagle* or *big bird* to refer to the president. What most of us call codes are really ciphers, where each letter is replaced by another letter or symbol. Both have been around since espionage met writing.

Shift Ciphers

Julius Caesar used shift ciphers to safeguard his dispatches. To build this code, write the alphabet on a line. Now choose a secret number. Suppose it's 5. Put your finger on A and shift over five letters. That would take you to F. Write the alphabet again, beginning under the F. Here's how the code would look:

A B C D E F G H I J K L M N O P Q R S T U V W X Y Z
V W X Y Z A B C D E F G H I J K L M N O P Q R S T U

To encode words, replace each letter in the message with the letter below it. DOG becomes YJB. You can change the secret number anytime. A variation of this is the backward alphabet cipher. Write the alphabet forward, as before, then underneath, write it backward. When you encode, A is Z, B is Y, and Z is A.

Number, Please

Kids can use the same process but assign a number to each letter of the alphabet. The numbers can run in order from 1 to 26, so A is 1, B is 2, and so on. Or they can scramble the numbers like eggs. The coded message looks like a stock market printout. Graphic artists can simply invent their own symbols for each letter for a totally unique-looking code.

From Craft to Art

Writing is not only a tool for practical communication. In the right hands, it's an art—like a painting made of words. A Gauguin instead of a grocery list. When writing makes the leap to art, it's a creative, liberating game with a million pieces. Most important, it has the power to elicit a response from an audience that transcends the content itself. The first time students discover the true power of the pencil, they're exhilarated, and from then on, they're hooked on writing. But first they have to get comfortable with the basic steps that all writers follow: warming up, first drafts, revising, editing, and polishing. The following strategies will help you develop the craftsmanship in your students.

Warming Up

Many of my friends are writers. They get up every day, intent on their literary goals. And they all have their warm-up rituals. Some rise at dawn; others can't drag themselves out of bed until the morning talk shows have yielded to the soap operas. Some go out for coffee. A few hit the gym. Some can't think until they've showered; others lounge in their pajamas, reading the headlines. The classifieds. Anything to avoid the computer. I can count on one finger the number who just sit down and dive into their scribbling with a relish. When Ernest Hemingway was asked what was the most frightening thing he'd ever encountered, he replied, "A blank sheet of paper." So if you want your kids to become writers—real writers—not just short-order wordsmiths, you need a fistful of warm-up activities to prime the pump.

From Your Lips to Their Pens

I'm sure you know the research about reading aloud to kids. It's the greatest predictor that kids will become readers. Kids who are read to, read. So you should read aloud to your students everyday—that goes without saying. But you can double or triple the horsepower of your read-aloud sessions if you make your book selections with the "art of writing" in mind. Search for literature that's rich with visual imagery, emotional content, or a surprising use of words. If you chose literature related to your social studies or science topics, you add another layer of learning in the same amount of time.

Now teach your students to listen for the writer at work. Before you start reading, tell them to listen for excellent sentences or unusual words, and ask them to picture the story in their heads as you read. When I was studying history with my students, I read aloud from many novels written for adults, including books about Queen Elizabeth I, the fall of Constantinople, and the Civil War because the authors captured the intimate details of life in the past like no textbook ever written. My kids hung on every vivid detail about LBT—life before television. When you finish reading these excerpts, ask:

- What pictures did you see in your head?
- What words did the author use to make those pictures?
- What was your favorite part? Why?
- What was a great word that you heard? A great phrase?

Here's why kids get better at writing by listening to you read aloud: They hear new words in context, so their vocabulary grows. They internalize the tricks that writers play with sentences: compound, dependent clauses, adjectival excess, sentence fragments, and words that can stand completely alone. They discover the uses of dialogue to sharpen their characters and add drama. They learn about the different forms of literature. When it's working well, they get lost in a book. That's the art of it.

Listen and Draw

To help your students grasp the picture-making power of words, let them draw pictures that capture what they're seeing in their heads as you read aloud. They can make simple sketches, line drawings, stick figures, maps, even abstract lines and shapes that capture emotions, sound, or action. Any visual equivalent of the narrative will do. Pass out scrap paper or have your students make a Listening Journal that they can add to all year. Read vivid material, then ask students:

What did you see in your mind?

What words did the author use to make that picture for you?

When students cite a passage that made a picture for them, reread the relevant words, phrases, or sentences while they hold up their drawings. Finally, ask them to write some of the words the author used around the edge of their picture, to make a border or frame connecting the words and their images.

Hand Writing

Hand Writing is a warm-up that captures youthful imagination and a trove of rich vocabulary, in one fell swoop. You can use this activity when you're getting ready to write about any topic—science, history, literature, or current events. Suppose you want your students to write about the amazing rainstorm that drenched your city overnight. Simply ask students to picture the storm, and write one word with their finger *on the palm of their hand* that describes the lightning (clouds, puddles, thunder). Since the word is invisible there are no worries about spelling or penmanship.

Now here comes the fun. Have kids hold up their hands for you to see. You scan their invisible words, and respond with comments like, "That's a great word! Would you read it to us?" or "I love that word! Tell everybody what you wrote." Once your students grasp the imaginary nature of this game, they'll probably feel brave enough to scribble more sophisticated words that are a part of their listening and speaking vocabulary, but haven't made it into their writing yet.

Your job is easy. Exclaim over their words and write them on the board. Then tell students to erase their hands and write a new word to describe something else about the storm—for example, what they like to do best on a rainy night. Repeat the reading-and-praising process. In no time, students will be staring at a wealth of words about the topic, clustered by category. Now they're ready to go. They know the words they want to use. They don't have to fumble for spelling, and I doubt you'll hear anyone say, "I don't know what to write."

Hand Writing is very powerful for kinesthetic learners, who crave tactile stimulation and learn better when they can use larger muscles and nerve endings, along with their cerebellum. It also helps visual-spatial learners to see related words organized in clumps, which later turn into paragraphs. And most important, all kids can participate with a 100 percent guarantee of being successful. Hand Writing has never been so much fun!

Skinny to Steroids

This is an audience participation warm-up that emphasizes adjectives and adverbs, the rich embroidery of the writer's art. You simply challenge students to transform minimalist sentences into something more. Some kids get so excited that this simple warm-up becomes a cardiovascular event.

Just write a mind-bogglingly simple sentence on the board. Subject and verb will do. Try something like: *The cat eats.* Leave big spaces between words. Then ask students: Does the sentence tell what the cat looks like? Do you know what it's eating? Or where? Or why? What words you could add to make the sentence tell us more about this cat? At first, you'll get suggestions like *black.* Stick that in front of *cat,* and reread the sentence aloud. Continue asking for suggestions. Squeeze words in, put them on stilts above the sentence, and hook them on from below. In no time, you'll have a sentence on steroids.

The beauty of Skinny to Steroids is that it's a stand-alone activity. You can do it in two minutes. Perfect for those scraps of time before the bell rings, while stragglers are getting to their seats, or to rouse groggy brains first thing in the morning. Once you've modeled the process with the whole group, you can use it in small groups. Give the same skinny sentence to several groups, giving them three to five minutes to work, then have them read their steroid versions aloud for all to applaud.

Empty Your Head

Writers like to play with lots of ideas before they close in on the actual writing process. Kid writers have lots of ideas, too, but faced with a writing assignment, they sometimes go blank. Empty Your Head helps them discover how much information they have inside their heads, rather than staring mutely at a pristine sheet of lined paper and feeling dumb. This simple process gets all the ideas out on the table with no fussing, so you can use it to prime kids for writing about an historic event, a character in a read-aloud book, a holiday, a science experiment, or a creative topic. It can be done as a whole- or small-group activity or let your students work individually.

Start with the outline of a head—either on the board or chart paper for group work, or give each student a paper with the outline of a head. Now ask them to empty their heads by writing all the words that come to mind about the designated topic. That's all. They just keep writing until nothing else comes out. When they're done, ask them to count their words and circle the most interesting ones.

You can take this a step farther by visually linking words that are related. Give students a set of crayons and tell them to review all their words, choose one and draw a line from it to all the other words that "go with it." For example, if the topic is frogs, students might link *skin—green—shiny—bumpy—spots*. Then they change crayons and link another set of words.

This exercise reinforces the idea that while all the words on their Empty Your Head paper are related to the major topic, the linked words belong close together in rich sentences or paragraphs. It really helps visual/spatial and kinesthetic learners use their strengths to see how ideas need to be organized before they start writing.

Annotated Drawing

Annotated Drawing is similar to Empty Your Head, but it plays on the strength of visual learners who think in pictures. To warm up for writing, let them record their ideas with sketches. If the topic is winter they might sketch snow, rain, birds migrating, kids skating or skiing. Then have them go back and surround each sketch with a halo of words that elaborate on it. The picture of snow might have *blizzard, drifts, snowplow, snow day, fort,* and *frostbite.* The final product resembles a thought diagram that can be used as a starting point for constructing sentences, paragraphs, or a longer piece of writing.

Sequence

One of the concepts young writers need to grasp is that there are many ways to make a paragraph, but some ways are definitely better than others. They can't just jot down the first thing that comes to mind and call it a paragraph. They have to think about which idea should come first, next, and next. Sequence is the element that makes writing make sense.

Students need to practice sequencing ideas before they start a draft, otherwise their erasers will be doing most of the work. Here's a cut-and-tape approach to constructing a paragraph that's sequence savvy.

- Start with a cluster of related ideas from the Empty Your Head activity.
- Give each student a strip of paper. Tell them to choose one word from the Head and write a sentence on the strip using that word.
- Then cluster the students in small groups or work as a class to sequence the sentences until they make sense. They can arrange their sentence

strips on a tabletop, the rug, or in a pocket chart. Encourage them to keep reading their sentences aloud to see if they make sense.

- When they're satisfied with the sequence of their sentences, they can tape their strips to a piece of paper in order. Display the compositions, read them aloud, and ask students to talk about the sequences that work well.

This activity helps visual/spatial and kinesthetic students who learn best when they can see and manipulate ideas, because they can physically shift the sentences from place to place, actually building a paragraph strip by strip. This is also an effective way for students to translate their research notes into sentences and ultimately a coherent paragraph or report.

Writers' Hats

Many writers and many, many visual artists have favorite items of clothing that they wear to put themselves into a creative frame of mind. Artists cherish shirts that reek of turpentine or paint-spattered shoes. Writers favor fishing or baseball hats. So you may want to encourage your students to bring in a favorite hat to wear whenever they write. Visitors to your room may think they've wandered into a costume party, but never mind that. Hats can block out visual distractions and focus young writers on the world of ideas inside their hat. Being playful about writing also eases anxiety in reluctant writers, and announces that this is a special time of day, when creativity and individualism rule.

Getting to the First Draft

When you ask some kids to write a paragraph, essay, or report, they can't get to their pencils fast enough. Ask others and you get a marathon stare. The blank paper or computer monitor waits, and waits, for a first sentence and then the hundreds, even thousands of words that must follow. Faced with such a daunting task, some smart kids just freeze. When prodded, they reluctantly confess, "I don't know what to say."

Actually, they do know what to say. If you threw away their pencil, they would babble on for hours. But writing is not like talking, where words flow automatically, logically, and seemingly without effort. Writing is a vastly complex enterprise involving hundreds of decisions, even for a simple science report about *Why Worms Make Lousy Pets*.

While you may be focused on your long-range goals like topic sentence, details, and closing sentence, kid-writers experience writing as a word-by-word process. The moment they put a word on paper, they're confronted with What comes next? And next? And next? In the face of this seemingly endless parade of words, they're expected to survey their thoughts, sort the big ones from the small or totally irrelevant, and then mentally sequence all that material so that what they commit to paper is coherent and maybe even interesting. And while they're at it, let's not forget those capital letters and periods!

Presented with such a tall order, reluctant writers usually resort to one of two strategies. The first is the deer-in-the-headlights. They gaze from you and to the virgin paper and back again, hoping that one or the other will disappear. The other strategy—Write anything! Ideas tumble onto the paper like stream-of-consciousness at high tide. The final product often resembles James Joyce's *Ulysses,* and it's just about as easy to read.

What's going on here? In both cases, students are suffering from overload. Picture a bumper car inside their heads. It careens from one idea or detail to another, visiting many aspects of the topic in no particular order. This is useful for brainstorming, but disastrous when kids are poised to write a first draft. One student is daunted by all the choices and shuts down. The other compulsively records every new thought and calls it a paragraph. Both need help.

Juggling Jell-O

Even with a whole lot of warming up, constructing a story, essay, or report is complicated work. With lots of good ideas come lots of decisions, and there's no right answer. Move one sentence and the whole composition comes apart. It's like juggling Jell-O. If kids are trying to do it all mentally, they can get very frustrated. So how can you help your students get to a working first draft without the agony? They need to discover that:

- Writing is a way of thinking—if you can think about a topic, you're on your way to writing.
- Writing is a process, and most of the steps in the process don't look anything like the final product.

Adults who are helping young writers need a couple discoveries of their own:

- Many smart kids who struggle with writing are weaker in linguistic intelligence, but have great strengths in visual/spatial and kinesthetic intelligence.
- Kids can harness those intelligences to break through writer's block, whether they're working on a journal entry, essay, or research paper.

Here's a process that allows novice and reluctant writers to shape some pretty solid writing.

1. Dump the paper, pencil, and computer. Get a big sheet of paper and some colored marking pens. If you're out of giant-sized paper, use a

page from the classified or stock market section of the newspaper. And don't insist that kids sit at a table to write. They can hang their papers on a wall and stand, or spread out on a floor and sprawl. Kinesthetic learners do better when they can move around.

2. Now pose a question—the first of many. "What's one idea that belongs in your first draft?" It doesn't have to be the main idea, or the first. Just an idea. Let's return to the topic of frogs. The ideas might be: habitat, food, eggs, or types. Kids pick a pen, write the idea in big letters, and circle it.

3. Ask again, "What's another idea?" Change pens and write. Repeat the process until the main ideas are all spread out on the paper, like colored targets. It's a visual table of contents for the first draft of the essay, story, or report.

4. Now kids flesh out their ideas by focusing on one circle at a time. Ask, "What are some things you know about this idea?" They jot down words, phrases, or sentence fragments in the same color. These jottings furnish the details of a paragraph. Move from circle to circle, until a web of words surrounds each idea. This color coding helps visual learners see each paragraph as a cluster of related words and ideas.

5. If you're working on developing rich language, go back and brainstorm adjectives for some of the phrases. This mapping process can go on for days, until students have excavated all the usable, rich, and unique ideas about the topic.

6. Now it's time to structure the writing. Ask: Which idea comes first? Which next? Where's the big finish? Kids love Post-its, so give your reluctant writers a bunch of these sticky tabs and tell them to number them starting at one. Then they stick the tabs on the colored targets, identifying the sequence of the first draft. When that's done, kids have a color-coded map of the task and lots of words to launch the writing. At this point, they know what to "say."

7. Now here's another trick to keep them from getting stuck: Kids don't have to start with the first paragraph first. They can choose the idea that's most appealing or fully developed, and write that paragraph first. The success of getting started will get the juices flowing, so the rest will be easier to tackle. And since this is first draft, they can literally cut and paste paragraphs together once they are completed. This is just like the cut-and-paste function on any computer, but it's done with paper and tape.

8. Don't let them get hung up on the opening sentence. It's a tough one for all writers. Sometimes it's written last. Just encourage them to work piece by piece until they have a first draft.

9. Take breaks. Writing is strenuous mental work. Kids need to get away from the first draft and do something physical. Later they can reread it with fresh eyes and have some fun editing and polishing.

10. Help students do a self-assessment. Ask, "Find the sentence that you think is your best, and read it aloud to a partner. What's the most interesting part of the whole piece? Why? What part was easiest to write?" And don't forget to heap on the praise. Writers crave it. Kids thrive on it.

Everyone's an Editor

Many kids are so excited by the completion of a healthy first draft that you'd think they'd won a Pulitzer. And it is a big accomplishment. So imagine their surprise when the teacher suggests that there's more to be done. In a blinding flash they understand why it's called the *first* draft. The disappointment can be crushing.

Single-drafters are a pretty determined group. They trudge or rush from the top line to bottom and then hang up their pencils. But they'll never discover the art of writing unless you can break through the one-draft mind-set. First, let's look at some reasons for their resistance.

1. I just want to be done. It's good enough.
2. There's nothing more to say. I'm bored with it.
3. Quantity not quality. She said one page and she got it.
4. Less is less. The less I write, the less I have to correct.

It's a real challenge to help students escape this utterly pragmatic approach and discover the pleasures of writing. One way is to introduce editing and revising as a game.

Editor-in-Chief

When we ask kids to edit and revise their own writing, they often come up with exactly zero changes. They simply don't see any errors. And there's an undeniable logic in that. After all, if they knew it was a mistake, they wouldn't have made it in the first place. They need some target practice with finding common errors, but it works best if they start with someone else's writing.

- First, give students a copy of one flawed paragraph. It should have errors in grammar, punctuation, and/or capitalization. At the top of the paper write the number of errors that can be found in the paragraph. That's the target.

- You can write the paragraph yourself or copy a section of text from a social studies book, primary source document, or novel, and add the errors. That way students are plowing through relevant content and good writing while they sharpen their revising skills—two or three birds with one activity. You get way more mileage out of this activity than from grammar worksheets with isolated sentences.

- Now, since we know it's easier to spot what you're actively looking for, tell your editors that in this hunt, they're just looking for three basic kinds of errors:

Ins	Things the writer needs to put in—punctuation, missing words, word endings.
Outs	Things the writer needs to throw out—extra punctuation or confusing words.
Others	Other forms of words (spelling of homonyms), other forms of letters (capital or lowercase), other punctuation.

- Then the hunt is on. Give your students a set amount of time to find and mark the errors with colored pens or pencils. If you have a kitchen timer, set it. Kids love a race, even if it's just against a clock. For kids who enjoy puzzles, this activity is a lot of fun. It will warm the cockles of your heart to see antiwriters doggedly searching for that last error and cheering when they find it. Be sure to provide lots of praise for getting close to the target.

Run-on Sentences

Once kids build up some momentum in their writing, there's a real reluctance to stop, as if they'll lose their train of thought and find themselves in limbo between sentences. Hence, run-on sentences. Here are two ways to help kids spot this problem in their own work. They can go through their writing and underline every *and,* then read their piece aloud to hear if the *ands* can be replaced with a punctuation mark. Another method is a breathing technique. They read their piece of writing aloud, inhaling only at the beginning of each sentence. If they have to go a long time between breaths, they begin to "feel" the length of their sentences and question their punctuation.

Polishing

When writers go back over their work, weeding out dull words and inserting spicier equivalents, it's called *polishing.* To help your kids understand polishing, give them a dull rock and some water, cooking oil, hand cream, or furniture wax. Have them look closely at the rock, polish it, and look again. Talk about the rock before and after. They should note that they can see more shapes, lines, or colors. Explain that writers polish their work by adding details so that readers can see their ideas more clearly.

You can use any piece of writing to model polishing, but you might want to go back to the paragraph that you used for the Editor-in-Chief exercise. Choose one sentence and model how you can add words like they did in the Skinny-to-Steriods exercise, and/or replace dull words with shiny ones to polish it. Reread the improved version. Then let students work in pairs on polishing other sentences in the paragraph. Have them read the improved parts aloud to show the difference. By the time they're finished, they're staring at a paper that is a marked-up mess, but glistening with shiny prose.

You'll need to do this exercise quite a few times, but in the process kids learn that a marked-up paper is a sign of victory over dull writing. Instead of cringing at red marks on their writing, they begin to associate marking up their own draft with feeling smart. That's how you break through their resistance and lure them toward the idea that there's more to writing than just pouring out an idea. There's polishing an idea with words so rich and precise that it glows in the dark.

Thesaurus

Once kids embrace the notion of polishing, you get the thrill of taking them for their first ride in a thesaurus. They're usually astonished to discover this power tool for wordsmiths, and wonder why adults have been hoarding the secret for so long. Life after *Roget* will never be the same in your classroom.

For a start, give your kids a word and see how many equivalents they can think of without assistance. List all their ideas. Then show them how to use a thesaurus, and see how the list grows. The first time I trotted out a thesaurus, I was teaching my kids about domestic architecture. I challenged them to see how many words they could find for shelter. Sixty-four! Overnight, they became thesaurus junkies. Every time I turned around they were mainlining *Roget*. Your kids will, too. Inevitably, there's some overreaching, and you end up reading drafts that sound like they were written by twelfth-century monks. But that's how kid-writers stretch, experiment, and eventually refine their efforts.

Once your students know their way around the thesaurus, encourage them to use it to energize verbs. Using more precise verbs is one of the surest ways to improve their writing. For example:

Hurt → poke, slap, tease. Eat → gobble, nibble, slurp. Laugh → chuckle, howl, giggle.

Challenge them to banish tired words like *sad, glad, mad, happy* in favor of more vivid emotional renderings.

If your classroom is connected to the Internet, you may want to check out the visual thesaurus created by the graphic artists at Plumb Design (www.visualthesaurus.com/online/index.html). Their Visual Thesaurus explores the relationships between words and their meanings and displays them as spatial maps that move like constellations crossing the night sky. Up to fourteen different relationships can be displayed. The target word appears in the middle of the display with the meanings displayed as circles connected to the word. Words with the same meaning are displayed and connected with solid lines. It's a little complicated but very interesting once you get the hang of it. This may be the device that gets visual/spatial or kinesthetic kids hooked on revising and polishing.

Highlighting Improvements

Kids love yellow hightlighters. If you don't believe me, leave one in plain sight and turn your back. When you turn around again, it's gone! So use kids' passion for these pens to encourage rewriting. This simple technique is another way to link pleasure to revising first drafts. As your kids are revising and editing, pass out the yellow markers and tell them to highlight every place where they make a change, whether they're correcting punctuation or beefing up verbs. At the end of the session, have them count the yellow marks. The more yellow the better. Then do some visual, aerobic graphing. Ask students to stand and hold up their papers if they have one to five yellow highlights. Next five to ten. Of course, the person with the largest number is seen as the high-status highlighter. Robust revising becomes a very positive experience. That was your goal. Bravo!

How to Grow a Writer

Growing writers is delicate work. The first challenge is presented by the process of writing itself. Writers sit and stare, but they're working. They agonize over a single word for half an hour, but they're working. So their industry is nearly invisible until they get the perfect combination of words on the paper. The trick for you is to know if your students are growing imperceptibly or simply vegetating.

The second challenge is that writing makes people—adults and kids—feel vulnerable in ways that mathematics never will. Writing is creative work. When you critique writing, you're up close and personal. So proceed with caution if your goal is to raise a crop of competent, confident writers.

Techniques for Giving Feedback and Input

Hemingway said that writers "need the legs for it," as if they were prizefighters in the ring. And that's a good image. The opponent is an idea that bobs and weaves, until the writer finally wrestles it to the ground. Professional writers go through dozens of drafts before they're satisfied. That takes stamina—legs.

Encouragement is the most powerful way to give your kids the legs they need to struggle with the complex process of sequencing ideas, sharpening sentences, selecting just the right verb, and ultimately finding their unique voice. Encouragement keeps them engaged when they want to give up—all writers want to give up at some point. Your comments should highlight what kids are doing well and point them in the direction of more growth.

There's a Jewel

A simple practice for giving feedback is to amble around the room while your kids are writing and notice what they're doing well. Point to a word, phrase, or sentence, and say "There's a jewel." "That's exquisite." Use words like *dramatic, musical, touching, emotional, surprising, amusing, puzzling, unexpected, intriguing, curious, brilliant, unique, impressive, clear, insightful, picturesque, vivid, sharp, graphic, amazing,* and *inspiring.* In the process, you model the power of rich, specific words. You're a walking thesaurus of encouragement.

Focus on the Gold

Before you approach another a set of student essays or stories with correcting in mind, I'd like you to think about the 49ers. The Gold Rush guys. They spent their days sluicing sludge, but their eyes had a single focus—flecks of gold. So I recommend that the marks you put on student papers should help kids focus on the gold in their work. I know this runs counter to how most of us were taught, and how we were taught to teach. But consider this: Using the traditional red-pencil approach, you mark everything that's wrong. You're spending lots of time telling/showing kids what not to do. When they get their papers back, their eyes immediately focus on the negative. More powerful by far is giving input through positive remarks and examples. As often as possible, find the gold within the students' work—a phrase, sentence, or section that is done so well that it becomes their new standard as they continue to work. Underline exceptional phrases, write *great image, excellent verb, very visual,* in the margins. That way kids don't spend their time staring at the sludge, but continually sharpen their eyes to spot the flecks of gold.

Self-Praise

One goal of feedback and input is to train students to independently recognize their successes and multiply them. Your ideas are essential, but always encourage students to identify their best—best word, best sentence, best image in any piece of writing they produce. As a group you can agree on a symbol, such as a star, that means "best." At the end of each writing session, have students take a minute to scan for their best and mark it. Have them turn to a neighbor and quickly share their star power. If you have one-to-one story conferences with students, always ask, "What part do you like best and why?"

Advanced Praise For

Writers get better at their craft from listening to good writing. They gain confidence when people clap and cheer. So having your kids read their writing aloud is another way to grow writers. Unfortunately, some of your best writers—loaded with linguistic and intrapersonal intelligence—may be very shy. They roar like a lion on paper, but they're meek as lambs when it comes to performance. Other kids are good writers, but lack confidence in their work, so they're too unsure to risk reading aloud.

Here's a way to encourage kids to share their work with the class. The technique is called Advanced Praise For. Set the kids up in pairs for this activity because it feels relatively private and safe. Kids read their work to a partner, then listen to the partner's work. Give them time to talk about what they liked, or point out a particularly good word or sentence.

Now here's the trick. When they're finished with Pair Share, you ask: Who heard a great piece of writing, a great poem, a great story? Hands will fly up all over the room. Call on students and say: Whose great writing did you hear? They will identify another student and say what they liked about the piece. Those comments are exactly like Advanced Praise For—the lavish remarks you see on the back of a book jacket. Before you ever read the book, you know that a lot of other people liked it. The power of this technique is that shy or unsure writers are encouraged to read aloud because they already have peer approval. And the class is set up to like their work, so the risk factor is greatly reduced. Encourage clapping. That helps, too. Eventually closet-writers gain courage and may even get hooked on the applause.

Authors' Hour

Once your students discover the joy of producing good writing, they'll want and deserve an audience. Here's how I dealt with a bonanza of great writing in my class. At the beginning of each week, I'd put the heading Authors' Hour in the upper left-hand side of the chalkboard. During the week students would write their names under the heading in a growing list until Thursday afternoon, when we'd all settle down around my overstuffed chair, and listen to the latest batch of writing they'd produced. Poems, science fiction, short stories, plays, chapters from emerging novels.

At first we would be done in twenty minutes. By the end of the year, authors' hour stretched to ninety minutes of rich, confident writing. Three students wrote medieval-type poems in a single voice, calling themselves The Three Widows. Another student regularly recruited four or five others to read his disjointed by unfailingly humorous plays. Two jocks became wildly popular for their poems—one going on to win several contests in poetry journals. It was the single greatest activity I discovered for motivating personal writing. You can use the same format with younger students who can share poems, journal entries, and short stories.

Am I a Writer Now?

It's important to connect kids to the idea that the work they're doing is exactly what grown up writers do—not some empty school exercise that bears no relation to a career in writing. It's also very motivating for kids to begin to think of themselves as writers—not just students who are writing. To help them grasp that concept, read aloud stories about what famous writers did when they were kids. A delightful introduction to the writer's life is *The Abaracadabra Kid* (1996) in which Sid Fleischman tells how he went from reluctant reader to Newbery Award–winning author. It's a lively tale with lots of tips on how to get started in the writing game. Another lovely book is *A Grain of Wheat* (1985) by Clyde Bulla, in which he describes his childhood on a Missouri farm and how he decided to become a writer. Kids who are serious writers may want to take the publishing plunge. If getting into print is their dream, try *The Young Writer's Guide to Getting Published* (2001) by Kathy Henderson. It has over 150 listings of publishers for authors from eight to eighteen years old.

The Fine Art of Journaling

Some kids are elated by the sight of a brand new journal, each of the 100-plus pristine pages waiting eagerly for the scratch of a pen. Others are completely defeated. They know with a certainty that approaches a natural law that they will run out of ideas long before they run out of pages. Rather than entertain the idea of becoming mediocre journalists, they search for strategies to foil the enthusiastic teacher who offered them the small blank book, as if it were a chocolate.

Here are some strategies kids use to deal with journalphobia:

1. *How much do I have to write?* If the answer is one page, they begin scrawling a simple message in three-inch-high letters, calculating exactly the number of gigantic words it will take to fill the page.

2. *How many sentences?* Again there is a mental calculation so rapid it would put an IRS agent to shame. Five sentences. Three words each. Piece of cake! So begins an entry of such simplicity, it would make Hemingway seem verbose. *I like pets. I have three. One is a dog. One's a cat. One's a rat.* You asked for five sentences, you got 'em.

3. *Anyone seen my journal?* Truly ingenious journalphobics will simply lose the damn thing. When you announce it's journal time, they begin to prospect in their desks. Coming up with nothing, they riffle through their backpacks until the entire contents are spread over an area the size of a basketball court. Eventually, you announce that "time's up," and they quietly celebrate the failure of another search party.

Despite the determined resistance your students may generate, journals are an amazing tool for growing young writers. You just need some strategies of your own.

The Value of Journals

It's hard to overestimate the value of keeping a journal. Every entry, scribbled, read, and reread, is an opportunity for students' mental, emotional, social, and artistic growth.

- A journal is a sounding board. Unloading in a journal helps kids get through the rough spots in life when they're feeling cranky, unloved, intolerant, or stupid.

- A journal is an outlet. Writing to express normal bouts of anger, hope, fear, or jealousy keeps emotions from getting buried too deep to reach. Using capital letters, exclamation points, and lots of adjectives is a way to yell without disturbing the peace.

- A journal can be a room of one's own where kids go to explore their private thoughts and eccentricities without scrutiny or censorship.

- A journal is a safe place to fantasize about fame and fortune without risking rejection.

- Journals can be laboratories for emerging writers. Their earliest entries may be the seeds for novels, short stories, poems, or autobiographies.

Do-It-Yourself Journals

When journals were first introduced into elementary schools, the goal was to personalize writing, to make it more like the real thing and less like an empty exercise. Unfortunately, the journaling process became so standardized that in many classrooms all kids were issued the same journal, they wrote to the same prompt at the same time every day, on demand. "Take out your journal" has become as familiar as "take out your math book."

You can repersonalize the practice of journaling simply by having your kids make their own journals. This is a lot easier than it sounds because the journal I'm thinking of is just a front and back cover made from recycled paper, a few pages inside, and a clip. That's it.

A few more details: The cover can be made up of magazine advertisements, colored paper, posters, cardboard, cereal boxes, or heavy wrapping paper. It could even be a couple of baseball cards clipped together. Forget about rectangles and eight-by-eleven-inch paper. Journals can be palm-sized, since many kids love tiny anythings. How about a circle or triangle? The more unusual and personal, the better.

The clip is really the most important part because it allows kids to control the number of pages in the journal. Reluctant writers might decide to have only two pages to begin with. No threat there. So they sandwich the pages between the covers, apply the clip, and start writing. Then one of two things will happen. Either they will fill up the whole journal and happily announce, "It's full. I'm finished." (This may be the first time these kids have ever finished a journal or any assignment for that matter. So celebrate!) Or, they'll *need* more pages—even *want* more pages! This is a huge breakthrough because for once they have more ideas than pages. That's a great place to be with reluctant writers. You may have students who create a new journal every week, but again, keep your eye on the prize. They're writing. That was your goal. Bravo!

More Journal Formats

There are lots of other journal formats that you can use to encourage your kids to record their daily observations and road test ideas that could grow into larger writing projects. You may end up with a dozen different formats in the same class. In fact, letting kids explore options helps them accommodate their learning style or the level of sophistication in their writing. Some may insist on having lined paper. Others are happy with blank pages. And it really doesn't have to be writing paper at all. Index cards can be a perfect medium for a journal, especially for a kid who is a visual or kinesthetic learner and wants to take apart, spread out, and reorganize the pages periodically—to see the whole in one glance. The following are suggestions for more journal formats.

Calendar Journals. Every December and January local businesses give away wall calendars as advertising. Since most teachers, out of necessity, are experts at cajoling, it's fairly easy to collect a set of these for your class. A calendar is an easy way to introduce young kids to journaling. The daily boxes are the journal space. Each one will hold a few words, a microscopic sentence, or a tiny drawing about the day. This is a very visual way to teach the days of the week and the months. It also helps kids look forward to upcoming events and begin to understand that they can save the highlights of their day or week through writing. At the end of the year, put the whole calendar in a box or envelope for safekeeping with the child's name and the date on the outside. You can also use desk calendars or daybooks for the same purpose. If you aren't doing journals in your class, pass this idea on to parents. Journals are a lovely way for parents and kids to catch up on the events of the day.

Jump-Start Journals. The hardest part of writing is often getting started. For kids who really have difficulty with journaling, you can jump-start the process with some teasers that help them focus. Make a plain journal with a dozen pages—no more. Write prompts that are really sentence fragments at the top of each page. The sentence starters could include:

I wish

My favorite

I love it when

I hate it when

The best thing about

When I grow up

Tomorrow

If only

Never, never, never

In the middle of the night

If only my dog could

If only my mother would

Next time I see a

Reluctant writers can flip from page to page until they find a sentence starter to match their mood. Some children need prompts for a long time. Others find a prompt that really speaks to them, and run with it, extending their entry for pages and pages.

Sneaking a Peek: A Bookshelf of Other Kids' Diaries

One of the challenges of keeping a journal or diary when you're young is that the same things happen day after day. Kids get frustrated when their journal entries look like they came out of a copy machine—*I went to school. Math class was terrible. Nora wouldn't sit with me at lunch because she's acting stuck-up again.* So they abandon the writing and slouch around, longing for excitement. In retrospect, they might be having some adventures that would look great on a page. They just need to see a few good models of other kids' journals. A trip to the library is in order.

There are hundreds of wonderful diaries, mostly in the fiction section because very few kids sit still long enough to document their lives. Fictional journals are often lively and humorous, giving readers a chance to witness other kids surviving familiar problems. A delightful example is *Heads or Tails: Stories from the 6th Grade* (1995) by Jack Gantos. It's perfect for kids who are nervous about the approach of middle school.

Many diaries have the added bonus of capturing another time and place, so kids witness the daily hardships of the Civil War or lumber along the Oregon Trail through mesmerizing first-person accounts. Using these as read-aloud selections builds knowledge about your history-social science topics. As you read, your kids are transported to another era, and absorb content information almost osmotically. Try any of the following:

- *Diary of a Drummer Boy* by Marlene Brill records the adventures of a boy who joins the Union army and ends up fighting in the Civil War.
- *Birdie's Lighthouse* by Deborah Hopkinson is the diary of a 10-year-old in 1855 who lives with her family in a lighthouse on an island.
- *When Will This Cruel War Be Over: Diary of Emma Simpson* by Barry Denenberg records the life of a 14-year-old girl during the Civil War.
- *Winter of the Red Snow* by Kristiana Gregory is the Revolutionary War diary of Abigail Stewart.
- *Journey to The New World: The Diary of Remember Patience Whipple* by Kathryn Lasky recounts the adventures of 12-year-old Mem, traveling on the Mayflower in 1620 and living in Plymouth, Massachusetts.
- *Dreams in a Golden Country: The Diary of Zipporah Feldman, Jewish Immigrant Girl* by Kathryn Lasky.
- *A Picture of Freedom: The Diary of Clotee, a Slave Girl* by Patricia McKissack.
- *I Thought My Soul Would Rise and Fly: Diary of Patsy, a Freed Girl* by Joyce Hansen.

The Real Thing

Nonfiction journals connect readers with real kids who recorded their lives, often during times of war or great hardship. The classic in this category is *Diary of a Young Girl* by Anne Frank. Others titles to look for:

- *Zlata's Diary* by Zlata Filipovic, about life in war-torn Sarejevo.
- *The Diary of Latoya Hunter: My First Year in Junior High* by Latoya Hunter.
- *Children in the Holocaust and World War II* edited by Laurel Holliday contains secret diaries of children.

Is There a Hemingway in the House?

Some kids won't pick up a pencil except to exercise their imagination. They chafe at the confines of nonfiction writing, which they see as simply juggling facts into logical order. What they love is the rich freedom of escaping into a world of their own making. Some like to write the type of nonsense that made Dr. Seuss famous. Other kids have strong novelistic tendencies. Their heads are teeming with interesting characters and dramatic events. A few write fiction to work out personal problems beyond the confines of their journals. When kids get into the fiction game, they're intuitively playing by the same rules as Mark Twain, Roald Dahl, and Ernest Hemingway. Fiction relies on five elements—character, plot, setting, conflict, and resolution. You can help your students incorporate these elements into their writing by asking some simple questions as they begin to plan their stories or revise first drafts.

Character

Who's going to be in your story?

What does he/she look like?

What does he like to do?

Setting

Where does your character live?

Where will the story happen?

Will your character go anyplace else?

Plot

What's going to happen in the story?

What happens first? Next?

What else might happen to your character?

Conflict

Does your character have any problems?

Does he/she have friends or enemies? Who are they?

Does anyone get hurt, lost, in trouble, or need help in the story?

Resolution

How does the story end?

How did the characters solve their problems?

Building Dialogue Skills

If you leave kids alone with a pencil and the front page of the newspaper, suddenly it's mustache season. Every face is sporting facial hair, glasses, cigars, or dark windows where the front teeth used to be. Within minutes, everyone's in disguise. So give that editorial impulse a nudge with this simple dialogue-building exercise. Give each student a page from the newspaper that has photographs of people. Ask them to look closely at the pictures and think about what the people in the pictures might be saying. Show them how to make speech bubbles and they're off—creating dialogue to go with the images. This is a deceptively simple activity, but let's look at the skills it builds.

- *Picture reading.* Kids really have to look at the picture to determine the setting, the action, and the participants. We ask them to do this all the time in reading groups.
- *Predicting.* What might that person say in this situation?
- *Creating.* Composing dialogue and using punctuation.

This activity costs exactly nothing since so many towns have free throwaway papers. Or, ask people on your staff to recycle their papers for a week, and you'll have lots of material for pumping up the volume on dialogue skills.

A Final Word of Encouragement

You don't have to be a great writer or even enjoy the process of writing to be a great writing teacher. You know when a writer has done his or her job well. You find yourself laughing aloud and trying to suppress a lunatic grin. Or you lunge for a pencil because you just have to write down a priceless sentence or quote. When writers are at their best, you look

> *If you would be a reader, read: if a writer, write.*
> —Epictetus

up from a wonderful novel and are shocked to find yourself in your own house in the twenty-first century. So you know a Hemingway when you see one, and the chances are you will discover more and more of them in your very own classroom as you hone your encouraging skills.

Resources

Calkins, Lucy. 1983. *Lessons from a Child.* Portsmouth, NH: Heinemann.

Hambleton, Vicki, and Cathleen Greenwood. 2001. *So You Want to Be a Writer? How to Write, Get Published, and Maybe Make It Big!* Hillsboro, OR: Beyond Words.

New Zealand Ministry of Education. 1992. *Dancing with the Pen: The Learner as a Writer.* Katonah, NY: Richard C. Owen.

SECRET #7

Great Teachers Are Escape Artists

Exploring the World Beyond

In This Chapter:

American students aren't famous for their geographic knowledge. Hell, 14 percent of American adults can't even find the United States on a map! The closest many students get to learning about the real world is a weekly visit to the school library, where *The National Geographic* continues to be a hit among preadolescent boys—bare-breasted women in foreign climes being the major draw. Occasional forays into current events provide slipping glimpses of distant lands and global issues, but on the whole American students are oblivious to the growing consensus that all the people on Earth are part of a single community with shared economic and environmental concerns. Our kids struggle to understand complex notions about economics, politics, culture, and the environment, while elaborate demonstrations are underway right outside their classroom door. Human problems are created and solved. History's being made.

Occasionally, a few intrepid adults and children escape the thrall of the classroom to discover life and learning in the world beyond. In Tucson, they called one such adventure *Elote Projecto*—the Lot Project.

The Lot Project

Thirty elementary school children crowded into the Tucson, Arizona, City Council chambers, and took their seats. But this was not your usual let's-go-to-city-hall outing. These kids were on the agenda. They meant business and the city fathers listened. In speech after speech, in Spanish and English, these fifth-grade students talked about the economy, ecology, zoning, and property values, subjects near and dear to politicians' hearts, but rarely included in the elementary curriculum. Their request—would the council members donate a city-owned, trash-strewn lot to the school district for educational purposes?

How did a group of ten-year-olds end up making real estate deals with the city council? The year was 1992. Ochoa School was at the bottom of the heap in standardized achievement, yet the principal, teachers, and parents knew their kids were smart. "In the newspaper every year, they say that Ochoa or the schools on the southside are the lowest," said Virginia Licea, whose youngest daughter, Elizabeth, was in first grade at Ochoa. "Those tests are not measuring the knowledge of our children. They are degrading our children."

Enter Dr. Paul Heckman, a man determined to expose all the ways that these students were smart. Dr. Heckman was the lead researcher in the Education and Community Change Project (ECC). He was convinced that the students at Ochoa had knowledge, abilities, and interests that could provide the starting point for some important learning opportunities, so he urged the teachers to put down their textbooks just long enough to discover what fascinated their kids. One teacher decided to take a leap of faith, which is how she and her kids ended up wandering in the neighborhood, inventorying trash-strewn lots, liquor stores, and abandoned houses that were havens for criminals.

It could have been a misery marathon, but instead of being discouraged, they'd found a cause. Students and adults in the community joined forces for a clean-up day, but soon after, the trash was as plentiful as ever. That's when the students decided that the only way to make progress was to adopt the lot and make it an extension of their classroom. "I invited my kids to write speeches to present to the Tucson City Council, pointing out that we should have the lot for educational purposes," reported Linda Ketcham. "That was on a Friday. On the following Monday, ten students returned to school with diagrams and speeches." Hence, the trip to city hall and their successful bid for the lot.

In the months following the meeting, these economically poor students of color and their teachers made plans to transform the lot into a laboratory for botany, biology, architecture, and environmental rehabilitation. Some students measured the lot to estimate the cost of fencing, some studied the soil and identified plants that might grow in the hard desert earth, while others worked on budgets. Their vision was to create a small urban park and wildlife center.

In the process, the students learned to write persuasive speeches and thank-you letters, draw maps, plan gardens, and design signage. They also struggled with the social reality of their neighborhood. Local businesses donated the vegetation and drip irrigation system that allowed them to plant twenty-one trees on the site in a single year. But the water system was vandalized repeatedly, so students sharpened their communication and outreach skills. They created fliers and distributed them from door to door, asking neighbors to watch for suspicious activity.

Elote became an outdoor classroom, where students spent up to 25 percent of their time. In the process, they raised their academic achievement levels, mastered sophisticated community-organizing techniques, and learned what it takes to participate successfully in the political process.

Dr. Heckman contends that this learning-by-doing method can improve children's abilities in basic skills such as reading, writing, math, and science. "What we're doing is having children go out in the real world and do something about it and learn from that activity. We're trying to have them engage in the game of being a scientist or a mathematician or an historian."

What did the Ochoa students make of their experiences on the lot project? Dr. Viki Montera was one of the researchers who facilitated the construction group of the Lot Project. When she asked her students to write about their year on the project, she received written comments and annotated drawings, in Spanish and English, in which students consistently expressed their satisfaction with the project and their own learning.

> I liked everything because I did what I wanted to do and I got to write a lot. I did almost all my work and I didn't miss a day of the Lot project.

> I liked everything I did in the Lot group. I liked the ditch a lot. I liked how they cleaned the lot. It is not messed up like it was before with a lot of bottles. I would try to come on time to our group.

> I liked working with other people and teachers and I liked the lot project because I think I learned a lot of things, especially about designing before building, but I didn't like that we had to stop working because of school stopping.

Ten years after the Lot Project began Ochoa Elementary continues to struggle with low achievement on standardized test scores. If you log on to their website you will find the statement—*Ochoa is a community that comes together for children.* And this is indubitably so. They have full-day kindergartens, preschool for four-year-olds, a welcoming babies program, literacy assistance, reading tutors, a full-time music teacher, breakfast, lunch, and summer feeding programs. But this is also a school that can point with pride to the era when its students and teachers came together for the community.

What's the Big Idea About Your Community as Classroom?

Great teachers like the ones at the heart of the Ochoa project recognize the unlimited potential of their communities as textbook and laboratory. Uptown, downtown, huddled with city officials, or distributing food at a local shelter, students have the opportunity to confront complex issues in the flesh. Even the simplest community outing can provide a treasure-trove of shared experiences to dissect and discuss back in the classroom. When community explorations raise concerns and lead students to ask questions like: Why are there no parks on the poor side town? Why are there so many liquor stores in our neighborhood? Why are the beautiful old buildings being torn down? Why are taxes spent on street furniture but not on schools? authentic research follows. Indifferent students with a limited record of academic success often thrive when their work is connected to a real context that they know well—their own environment. Seized by the novelty or urgency of their personal projects, they are transformed from consumers to producers of knowledge.

If you're intrigued by the thought of community-based learning, but doubt that you could forsake the test-driven world of school for any length of time and still retain your job, here's the ammunition you need to strengthen your resolve. There are at least eight reasons community-based learning is regarded as a highly effective strategy for engaging a wide spectrum of students—from free-range to the honor rollers. Dust off your great expectations and read on.

1. *Community-based projects put kids in the driver's seat.* Explorations in the community begin as mysteries. At first there are only questions. Can we save an old building from the bulldozers? Can we sponsor legislation about feeding the homeless? The more you allow your students to pursue their questions and concerns, the more ownership they feel for the work, which is why many community adventures turn into crusades.

2. *Community-based projects are academically and socially rigorous.* Dragging thirty kids around a city block or hustling them onto a public bus may not look like learning, but community-based curriculums are usually more challenging than many classroom-bound programs. In addition to grappling with content,

students must master a broad array of performance-based skills—like debating with developers, navigating bureaucracies, and synthesizing sophisticated data for presentation to peers, parents, and community leaders. These skills are road tested in real-life encounters in the adult world. When kids address the Town Council or the Coastal Commission, they're expected to be poised and articulate and to base their arguments on facts—just like everybody else. You hold your own or fail. Nobody talks about grade level.

3. *Community-based learning requires different ways of knowing.* Community-based learning is brain-friendly. All nine intelligences are activated as kids explore and attempt to root out the stories in their community. Authentic projects, such as changing zoning laws around school sites to reduce the number of liquor stores, need thinkers, talkers, and writers, analysts, provocateurs, and diplomats. Every kid has a chance to excel.

4. *Community-based learning is active.* If you decide to abandon your classroom for the adventures of the street, get yourself some comfortable shoes, a bucket of bus tokens, and a first-aid kit. The kit's for you, so stock it with whatever keeps you going—aspirin, protein bars, espresso shots. Your class is liable to look like a back room at the Smithsonian, with construction materials, artifacts, tape recorders, videocams, journals, transcriptions of interviews, and computer downloads jostling each other for workspace. It's life in the fast lane, cognitively speaking, and for a pure adrenaline buzz, this kind of teaching is way better than caffeine.

5. *Teaching and learning are shared.* Community-based projects will keep you busy, but you won't be the font of knowledge from which dazzled students drink—great teachers have never coveted that role. Instead, your kids will be co-teaching the curriculum as it evolves. With a bit of guidance, students organize themselves into work groups with a clear purpose, creating a pool of talent with drive. All kids find roles that make them indispensable, as researchers, writers, model designers, or video editors. As they work side by side, everyone gets smarter.

6. *Life and learning are fused.* Community-based learning catapults kids into a world that they usually only glimpse on television or from the window of a car or bus. They experience a direct and powerful connection between their work as students and their community, as when the kids at Ochoa School struggled to reclaim a piece of land in a neighborhood with a history of neglect. They learned to write letters, craft petitions, and speak in public—high-level academic skills targeted at changing the landscape of their community.

7. *Student work has meaning in the world beyond.* One of the reasons students drop out, physically or just mentally, is that they don't think school means any-

thing to anyone except the teacher. And some teachers are so robotized by the relentless sameness of the job that even they don't seem to care. Taken from either point of view, it's hard to imagine getting yourself all in a lather, or even investing an earnest effort in, say, your 197th spelling test. It simply doesn't matter. Community-based learning, however, has meaning precisely because of its flesh-and-bloodiness. It's urgent. When students work alongside community members to change legislation affecting homeless families or boycott purveyors of imitation guns, they get direct feedback about the value of their work and their personal power to effect change. That tells students that they aren't just renters, or nonvoters, or invisible by virtue of their age. They're high-status contributors. Kids don't drop out when school delivers a message like that.

8. *Projects take on a life of their own.* It's a rare teacher who can tell you precisely when a community-based project began. A kid pops up with an intriguing question. The headlines in the newspaper are arresting. There's a momentary outrage in the community, dismissed by all but a handful of concerned citizens, who happen to be your students. Next thing you know, you're in the thick of it, and life in your classroom will never be the same. A single project may unfold over an entire year, as students assess their progress, refine strategies, and ask, "What do we do now?" This organic approach to learning provides a model for creative and productive adult lives.

What Is a Community Anyway?

If you're going to use the community as your classroom, it helps to have a working definition of your new daytime address. The word *community* suffers from overuse, but the actual concept of community can be as elusive and endangered as the spotted owl, especially if you're teaching in a metropolis. A good way to get your kids focused is to simply inquire about their notions of community.

- What do you think community means?
- Is it just the physical space and built environment?
- Is it everyone living within certain boundaries?
- Are there several different communities within our town?
- What does it take to belong to one of them?
- Who lives in your community? Who doesn't? Why?
- Who has demographic data about our community? How do we get it?

From the very moment you ask *how can we learn more*, you're on your way to a great adventure. The following sections can help your students get smarter through focused wandering, mapping, documenting discoveries, and uncovering local history. Enjoy!

Escape Artists: Tips for Exploring Your Community

Most cities, towns, and even little hamlets have an official city website. Log on to yours and take your students on a virtual field trip. There's usually a menu or search function to help students explore their town online. For example, the website for my town lists: street closures due to construction, the latest budget news, a public meeting on building a skatepark (this would be a perfect meeting for students to attend), disaster preparedness, a full calendar of community events, tree removal plans, and news on Coastal Clean-Up Day. If you don't have Internet access in your classroom, download and print out the website content at home and bring it in for research material or scoop up an armload of your local newspaper. That's another great way to keep your finger on the daily pulse of the city.

Investigating Your Neighborhood

Virtual trips are great for a rainy day, but if you really want to give your kids a visceral experience of the complex human machine that is their community, you need to go exploring. Nothing can take the place of the real thing, so pencil in time for walking trips in the immediate neighborhood or more extensive explorations on the bus or subway. Field trips are essential information-gathering excursions that establish a common learning experience—all students have the same information at the same time. They also send a strong message that there are many ways to learn about a subject. Anything from a close inspection of a construction site to a guided tour of the community garden can be research. Some students learn more on a twenty-minute walk than during a whole morning squirming in their desks.

Rules of the Road.   Before you leave on any community trip, take time to plan for success. Think about and discuss these questions with your kids:

1. *Why are we going?* Every student should be able to explain the purpose of the trip. This distinguishes your trip from recess or simply hanging out, and gives students a focus from the minute you depart.
2. *Where are we going?* Take the trip by yourself beforehand, noting how long it takes, including time to stop, discuss, and collect data. An idyllic walk can become a punishment if you have to force march your kids back to school just before dismissal.
3. *How will we gather information?* Decide if you want to collect data during the trip through notes, sketches in a journal, photos, or video recordings. Or you may want to wander and observe, then debrief and record when you return to campus.

4. *What about permission?* Consult your administrator when you're planning any trip and then get parent or guardian permission in writing. Before leaving give the school office your route and estimated time of return. Take a cell phone for emergencies.

5. *How will they be safe?* Be very explicit about safety rules and any specific hazards that you noticed on your scouting expedition. Take plenty of adults, but make sure they understand that you need them to help supervise all the kids, not play mommy-and-me or socialize with other parents while you try to keep thirty kids safe.

Before and After Maps.   Before you go out into the community, ask your kids to draw a map of the school and the surrounding area, just using the images in their heads. This is a freehand creation that can be aerial, symbolic, narrative, or realistic. As a warm-up, ask your students to think of things in the community that are important to them: the school, relatives' and friends' houses, a favorite store, a park, a pond, a movie theatre, or a bike trail. Encourage them to show the roads or pathways they use to get to these places. Some may annotate their maps with words and symbols but that isn't necessary at this point. When students are finished, display the maps so students can identify similar features, and appreciate the uniqueness of the mental maps we all carry around in our heads. Use this activity to assess how much your kids know about maps and their community. Observe what's included on their maps, the level of detail, and their general familiarity with cartographic conventions. Have them draw a second map when they return, to highlight their discoveries or simply add more details to their original map.

Scavenger Hunt.   One way to help students focus on details during a first trip in the community is to turn it into a Scavenger Hunt. Make a list of things students should look for as they are walking or gazing out the window of the bus. Include fire and police stations, fire hydrants, libraries, clinics, banks, mailboxes, bookstores, parking signs, and anything else you want them to notice. You could have a theme for your hunt, such as things our taxes pay for, public safety items, social service venues, or recreation opportunities. With a checklist and pencil in hand, kids spend their time visually scouring their environment for data, instead of prospecting under a bus bench for small change.

Tablecloth Topography.   After a community walk, let your students solidify their discoveries by making three-dimensional models of the territory they covered. In this activity students re-create the topography of the town using recycled materials. Clear off a large table and cover it with a tablecloth—that's the actual surface of the land. Gather up objects in the room that will help them map out where they went and what they saw. If your town is nestled in a valley, kids can stuff books, towels, or boxes under the tablecloth to make the hills. Ribbon or yarn can be streets, streams, or rivers. Recycled items such as tissue boxes, milk cartons, foam containers, or small blocks can represent buildings or bridges. This activity promotes visual and spatial thinking along with recall, decision making, and lots of conversation.

Paper Bag Mapping. Have your students choose a building or landmark that they saw on their trip. Working from memory, photos, or their journal sketches, ask them to draw doors, windows, and signs on a paper bag to represent that structure. Then push back the tables and let them arrange their bag buildings to make a model of the town. They may want to grid off the streets with chalk or tape to get their bearings. Lots of thinking goes into the process, and your visual, spatial, and kinesthetic learners should really excel in this activity. If the bags tip over, put a paint bottle or block inside. When you're done, pin the bags onto a bulletin board to create a relief map of the town or reuse them to work out urban planning problems. For example, your kids can redesign your city putting schools near parks for shared green space, or relocating businesses to decrease traffic problems. They can solve some sophisticated urban problems with one set of bag buildings.

A Day in the Life of City Furniture. After a community exploration, have your kids imagine that they are a bus bench, streetlight, trashcan, stop sign, or billboard. Encourage them to describe what they see, feel, smell, and hear all day and night. Remind them that these objects overhear lots of conversation fragments as pedestrians pass by. Incorporating these snippets of dialogue will add life to their writing and give them a chance to practice using quotation marks.

Capturing Epiphanies—Documenting Discoveries

Once you and your kids hit the streets, they'll be flooded with visual impressions and raw data. It will take time to process all of it into a coherent picture of your community. In the meantime, you need to have systems to help different types of learners hang on to their discoveries. Think about the various intelligences—visual, verbal, mathematical, interpersonal, and musical. Now consider a wide range of documentary tools to accommodate those learners, including the following.

Community Explorer's Journal

Journals have long been popular with artists, naturalists, explorers, and inventors as a place to record their observations and experiences. We know what troubled Thoreau and how Darwin felt when he was at sea for months because they were journal keepers. They used words, sketches, equations, and diagrams to record their ideas.

The Community Explorer's Journal is not just another "writing assignment." It's a place to capture images and ideas about the things they see in the community. The entries will be fragmentary—notes about smells, bits of dialogue, funny signs, strange people, words mixed with sketches, and printed material like bus transfers. Anything that helps students vividly recall the time, place, and events once they get back to your classroom, where they can connect their personal experiences on field explorations with a deeper understanding of community issues and their role as citizens.

Since journals are personal, they should look unique. Instead of buying a crate of commercial journals, let your kids design their own. Journals have one simple requirement—space to write or draw. Beyond that they can be any size or shape. The cover can be made of cardboard, cloth, tin, or wood. Give your kids a few days' notice about the journal-making project, and encourage them to bring in any materials they want to create their Community Explorer's Journal. Provide plain or lined paper for the inner pages, scissors, glue, string, staples, and a pile of old magazines. Talk a bit about the creative possibilities and then let them go. You may end up with journals shaped like bridges or rivers, covered with bark or tire treads, a foot long or the size of a postage stamp. It's all part of the adventure.

While we're on the subject of adventures, introduce your kids to the ultimate explorers, Lewis and Clark, by reading sections of their journals, or log on to Lewis and Clark Rediscovery Project (http://rediscovery.ed.uidaho.edu/). All of the stories, data reports, images, artwork, and maps on this website were contributed by teachers and their students to provide glimpses of life along the historic and present day Lewis and Clark Trail.

Photography

Cameras are another way to document your community investigations. With a digital camera and a computer, the possibilities are almost limitless. However, you may want to get disposable cameras because they can be pretty thoroughly manhandled and still take decent pictures. Ration the number of shots kids can take, write on the outside of the box to keep track of who's shooting what, and then you just toss the whole thing in a mailbox. Photos make great conversation starters or visuals for presentations. They can also be used as a starting point for drawings or murals. Glue a photograph on the center of a piece of paper and let students complete the image beyond the photo by filling in the surrounding area. For example, if you start with a photo of people disembarking from a bus, kids may add street signs, the road, traffic, exhaust, and stop lights. Somehow, the photo acts like the first piece in a puzzle and kids eagerly fill in the rest. The combination of photography and handmade art is fascinating.

Videotaping

Videotaping is another way to capitalize on the skills of visual learners. With a few technical lessons and a sturdy neck strap, your kids can explore the world of the documentary filmmaker while collecting community data. They can gather footage of a congested intersection, a trash-strewn vacant lot, a dangerous alley near school, or an old building that needs restoration. Back in class they can play the film over and over to study the images in depth. The footage can provide evidence at meetings, and make a visual statement of a problem for presentations to city council, or bolster a petition drive or grant proposal.

Students can do on-camera commentaries out in the community like news reporters working on location. Put together a team of visual, verbal, and interpersonal learners for this type of work. Show their footage to other classes as a peer-teaching project. Making tapes like this requires kids to develop language skills, including organizing ideas and sequencing images, writing scripts, and speaking clearly.

Experience Charts

You can document field experiences with young children by being their scribe. Take a tape recorder along on your walks and stop periodically to record characteristic sounds and your students' observations. When you get back to your classroom, replay the tape and ask them to "empty their heads." That means they talk about anything that captured their attention or raised questions. Record their remarks on big charts as quickly and graphically as possible. Use a mixture of words, symbols, and sketches. Nonreaders can follow right along and everyone will be more attentive if you illustrate their remarks. Don't worry if you can't draw well. Neither can they. Stick with simple lines that capture the essence of an idea, and add a splash of color. For example, if you saw a fire engine, draw a long rectangle, add two wheels and put a ladder on the side. With a bit of red, you're in business. Act confident and your kids will understand that this is just symbolic language—not art. Add words next to the drawings to reinforce the idea that words are another way to represent objects or ideas. Pictures help nonreaders access the charts for later conversations or project work and build their sight vocabulary.

Where in the World? Getting Smarter About Mapping

I'm not sure why maps fascinate kids, but they do. Maybe it's the sight of their whole world shrunk down to the size of a bath mat. Maybe it's the way maps raise questions like, Where does grandma live? How about Uncle Richard? Why are some words on the map so small? Why are some countries so big? The best way for kids to learn about maps is to wallow on them. Tables are good workspaces but sprawling on the floor also suits serious finger-travelers. Throw in a magnifying glass, rulers, marking pens, and they'll create their own lesson plan.

Maps Aplenty

Scavenging for maps is easy because we're a map-loving country. Let's start with the freebies: maps at theme parks, car rental counters, train stations, bus stops, in airline magazines, and in the telephone book. Drop by your local historic society, Chamber of Commerce, or the tourist information center for more maps of your area. For a small fee, try the auto club and gas stations. Don't forget maps of the ocean floor, the surface of the moon, and the galaxies beyond.

Uncertain, Texas, and Other Place Names

Avid map-readers discover city names that seem to be lifted from a novel or comic book. *Aromatic Creek, Frostburg, Purgatory Peak, Yum Yum, Ding Dong,* and *Welcome.* I swear—they're for real. The index of an atlas is a great place for kids to find unusual place names. Visit a used bookstore for inexpensive old atlases. They don't have to be current because you're just looking for names, not planning a road trip. See if you can find *American Place Names* by George R. Stewart, which tells the stories behind the names. Tesnus, in Tennessee, is "sunset" spelled backward. And how do streets get their names? Go to www.potifos.com/streetname, where your kids can discover the story behind avenues, lanes, and roads.

Cartography 101: First Attempts at Drawing Maps

There are always a few kids in every class who freak out if you ask them to draw anything—including maps. Here's a way to help your kids get comfortable with cartography. Lure them with a dollop of shaving cream, and soon they'll forget all about their phobias. Squirt a shot of shaving foam on each table, and let your kids smear it around until they've created a silky, fragrant writing surface on which to practice drawing maps. If you want to guide them through the process, ask them to show you all the different ways to draw streets—grid, parallel, radiating from a plaza or circle, following the curves of the landscape. Have them erase by smearing, and then start over. Ask: What if you put a park or a lake right in the middle of your city because you want your town to have a beautiful center? Now how would you arrange the streets? Ask: What else do you want to put on your city map? Where would you put the houses, schools, fire department? Using this no-risk format allows kids to loosen up and experiment without worrying about laboriously erasing mistakes. Kinesthetic kids will be ecstatic. Perfectionists are liberated because it's impossible to get it wrong. Everybody loves this slippery activity and when all is said and done, your kids will have clean hands and desks. How often does that happen?

What Can a Map Tell Us?

One Saturday morning I was listening to *This American Life* about a man who mapped the shadows of trees on his street, pumpkins on porches at Halloween, and underground electrical lines. It was a revelation about the endless possibilities for creative cartography. Divide your kids into teams of two or three. Give each team a map of the school and have them brainstorm the unusual things—seen and unseen—that they could show on their map. For example, they might want to map:

- Sounds
- Smells
- Trash cans and litter
- Paths where people walk
- Kids playing or clustered in groups
- Signage
- Greenery

Take a walk around the school so each team can observe and map, using invented symbols to indicate the data collected—dots, *x*s, *o*s, letters, colored areas, and hatch marks. Back in class, have them draw a legend on their map explaining their symbols. Display all the maps and let your kids wander, look, discuss, and make observations. Then talk about what they noticed. Compare and contrast the symbols on all the maps. Where do the symbols overlap? Why? What's their theory about that? Have your students brainstorm ideas for other things they could map on the campus or in the neighborhood. Compile the maps into a book called All Kinds of Maps.

There's No Place Like Home—Getting Smarter Using Local Maps

Map reading is a challenge. Even the simplest map has hundreds of words and numbers, plus symbols and colors, all of which need to be deciphered. When you kids first look at your own city map, it may seem like they're staring at the backside of Mars. They can't find one recognizable element in this sea of information. Don't intervene. Just let their eyes swim for a while. They're fine-tuning their visual discrimination skills, and eventually someone will sing out, "I found my street!" Several kids who live in the same neighborhood will flock to see the discovery. That's good. Once they have their bearings, more discoveries will follow. Step back and let the learning happen.

After they're comfortable navigating around your city map, it's time to push their thinking by asking a series of questions that combine observation and critical thinking. Here's a starter list.

- Can you locate the boundaries of our city? What do you notice about the shape of the city?
- What natural landforms do you see in our city—bluffs, islands, valleys, hills?
- What pattern was used to design our town? Grid? Natural contours? Central square? Riverfront strip?
- Are the city blocks long or short? What is the effect of long versus short?
- What are the major streets? Which way do they run? Why do you think that's the case?
- Which streets are wide? Which are narrow? Why?
- Is our town foot-friendly? Can people walk easily and safely to the places they need?
- Where are the public gathering places?
- What transportation systems are indicated on the map?
- Does the map give clues about which neighborhoods are more prosperous?

Mapping Change

Try to get your hands on some older maps of your town, so your kids can study new and old maps side-by-side to see how times have changed. Ask: What's the same? What's not? Is your town larger or smaller? Where did it grow? Why? While you're on the subject of community change, don't miss the chance to read aloud the classic story, *The Little House* by Virginia Burton (Houghton Mifflin, 1978). It chronicles the changes that engulf a small house as the open countryside is devoured by a city. In the end, the house is rescued, refurbished, and carted back out to the country. Two other great titles are *Wump World* (1974) and *Farewell to Shady Glade* (1981) by Bill Peet. Both books deal with the changes in familiar environments and how people and animals are displaced. Visit the website of the Landscape Change Project (http://geology.uvm.edu /landscape/highschools.html) where you can examine the work of K–16 students in Vermont who are contributing to an online archive of historical and modern photos of the Vermont landscape in order to document change.

Down Memory Lane—Discovering the Used-to-Be Community

Somewhere in town, maybe squeezed in a storefront or tucked in the basement of city hall, you have a historic society—and that's a lot more fun than it sounds! The one in my town has a stiff-spined schoolmarm who scolds naughty visitors and a Pioneers' picnic with carriage rides, antique cars, and storytellers. Your historic society is a gateway to places that used to be and little-known local landmarks. The docents and enthusiasts who run it may lead tours of historic homes or publish a brochure for self-guided adventures so you can meander around town to find the original stagecoach depot or the first film studio.

Community Lifespan

As soon as you begin to talk about your community in historic terms, kids are challenged by the idea that for hundreds, even thousands of years, people have been born, labored, and died in the very spot where they go to school or play soccer. The town of Deerfield, Massachusetts, is surrounded by fields that have been under continuous cultivation for 10,000 years!

A simple time line can help your kids visualize continuity and change in your town. I used a ream of old-style computer printer paper to make one continuous time line about thirty feet long and one foot wide, but butcher paper or kitchen shelf paper will work. Mark off the decades and centuries, then post it above your chalkboard. At first it will be empty, except for a marker on the date when your town was founded. Each time your kids uncover an important event or person in the town's history, they can make a picture, glue it on the time line, and add some words of explanation. The time line helps visual and spatial learners grasp the sequence and patterns of events over time. This progressive project can grow all year.

First Nations

Who were the Native Americans who lived in your area before your town was established? How did they live? What did they eat? What were their beliefs and culture? When did they leave the area and why? Are any of their descendants still living in the area? If you can find a tribal descendant, invite that person to meet with your students and share artifacts and stories.

The Founding Fathers and Mothers

Investigate who started your community. Where did they come from? Why? What was it about this location that attracted them? Students should think about access to fresh water, fertile soil, mountains for protection, rivers or the sea for transportation. Ask:

- What was our community like in the past?
- How has it changed?
- How has it stayed the same?
- What was the racial and ethnic makeup of our community in the past? How has it changed? What caused the changes?
- If the founders of our town could see it today, what do you think would surprise them?

Use the photo archives of your historic society, library, or city hall to learn more about the founders. Look for journals or oral histories, and check with other local agencies to discover archival material about city history.

Living Archives

If you want vivid, personal details about community history, locate people who've been around for a long time. Try retirement homes, senior citizens' clubs, the Rotary or Elks Club, and the volunteers at the local historic society. Invite these "living archives" to share stories and artifacts from their childhood and life in your town. If they have photos, scrapbooks, maps, or newspapers, ask if you can make copies or scan them into your computer to build your own archives. Have your students prepare a list of questions in advance and think about ways to accurately record the answers. You can also arrange to meet people at landmarks or go to the local retirement home to interview residents about their experiences living in your town. If you want to delve deeply into individual stories, your students could write biographies of the people they meet.

Historic Buildings—Learning Through Landmarks

Wandering in a well-built city can be one of the transporting delights of community-based learning. Spying a distant steeple, entering a colonial tavern, running your hands over the Baroque surface of a cast-iron warehouse—these are sensory experiences that simply cannot be captured on the pages of a textbook. The built environment is a brick-and-mortar history book if your kids learn how to read it.

Learning to Look

The first challenge from the built environment is to get kids to actually look at buildings. That may sound obvious, but buildings are such a constant in our lives, that we often fail to notice more than the doorknob as we pass in and out. Your kids will start to take notice of the architecture around them as soon as you start asking questions.

- Why do you think this was built?
- How was it built? Why did the builders use those materials?
- Who was the architect? Did he/she design other buildings in town?
- What was it originally used for? Has that changed?
- Who lived or worked here?
- Has the outside or inside been physically altered? How can you tell?
- Should an old building be preserved and protected?
- How might it be used in the future?

Once you start looking at buildings, kids will begin to pick out the types that they prefer. Encourage them to generate a list of adjectives to describe the characteristics of buildings that appeal to them: curving, plain, textured, tall, fancy, austere, open, sleek, chunky, squat, elegant, slender, or airy. Help them learn the names of the architectural elements: columns, porch, turret, gables, cornices, attic, pavilion, eaves, brackets, cupola, shingles, siding, portico, and pediment, just for a start. Make a list and add to it each time your kids identify a new element. Then go to the website Architeacher: Historic Preservation Education (www.architeacher.org/historic/historic-main.html), and click on the section about architectural styles. Your kids can see a beautiful slide show of American buildings from a humble log cabin to a Georgian mansion, with excellent text that puts the buildings in their historic and social contexts. You can also log on to the The Center for the Study of Art and Architecture at www.architeacher.org for more ideas about community planning, teaching tips, and model programs.

If there's an architect in your neighborhood, ask him or her to lead a walk in the community. If you and your kids are fond of old buildings, log on to the National Trust for Historic Preservation (www.nationaltrust.org). The goal of the Trust is to prevent historic buildings and neighborhoods from being torn down or allowed to deteriorate. The Trust website is full of educational opportunities, including how to help a building become a landmark. My kids spent six months arm wrestling with developers and Toys-R-Us to save a turn-of-the-century building in our town. By the end of the year these ten-year-olds were familiar faces at city meetings and experts in the politics of preservation. I was never prouder to be a teacher.

No-Fault Architectural Drawings

If you have students who are convinced they can't draw, even art-phobic and proud of it, drawing buildings is a great place to go to battle with their neurosis and win. *You* can teach your kids to draw all kinds of buildings, even if you yourself can't paint a wavy line with a wet mop. Here's the secret: Apply the same strategy that you've learned throughout this book–task analysis and good questions—to drawing. After that, it's all cheerleading.

To start, give your kids a clipboard with low-grade paper and a pencil. Now ask them: Can you draw a square? How about a circle? A little triangle? A straight line? Diagonal line? They will all succeed and feel pretty relaxed, so you're off to a good start. Now you tell them, That's all you'll need to know to draw any building we'll see in our community. But today we're just going to draw interesting doors and windows. Setting such a specific topic narrows their visual focus so they really pay attention to details, and it's simple, so their confidence grows.

Grab your clipboards—just a piece of cardboard and a large clip—and head down the street. You're just collecting sketches of doors and windows, so stop in front of the first interesting building you see and have students look— just look. Encourage them to use words to describe the shapes they see and then draw. This approach helps verbal kids strengthen their visual skills.

Guide your kids to notice that a door is sitting snuggly inside a frame. The same goes for windows. Have them count how many lines they'll need to draw around the door to indicate the frame and threshold. Go on collecting down the street. Exclaim over unique examples. Praise efforts, excellent lines, good observations. On another day, repeat the process, just looking at rooftops. Your kids will discover a clutter of interesting stuff—chimneys, TV antennae, vents, shingles, rain gutters, downspouts, and decorative plasterwork. Or, focus on steps, porches, siding, and sidewalks. After each trip, post *all* the drawings in your classroom and let your kids study them. They'll begin to appreciate the rich details, even in a simple building, and recognize the drawing styles of their peers.

When your students are feeling confident, let them choose a piece of a building and really try to include all the details: doorbells, mailboxes, building numbers, windows or peepholes in the door, door handles, latches, and keyholes. At this point, their eyes will be as sharp as their pencils, so your job is to be the encourager. If your kids are art enthusiasts, come back to the room and let them add color with watercolor washes, marking pens, or colored pencils. Post all of the drawings in the room, not just the ones that look like they were spit out of a computer.

Deep Mapping

Deep maps are documents that combine place, people, and events over time. They're like a visual, tactile biography of your community, revealing elements of geography and history, as well as social, cultural, and personal information about the characters featured in your town's story.

To get a mental image of a deep map, imagine a map of your town as a webpage. All over the map are buttons or links. Each time you activate a button, you learn more about a specific aspect of your town—in effect, you go deeper. Then you return to the surface again with greater understanding, touch another button, and dive for information again. That's the basic notion of a deep map.

What can students put on a deep map? While traditional maps show roads, boundaries, place names, water features, mountains, monuments, and attractions, deep maps should peek beneath the surface of the town to reveal:

- What used to be in a certain location and why it disappeared. This can include plants, forests, animals, natural and manmade features.
- Who settled here and why—accident, wagon broke down, resources, or expansion.
- Who lives here, who used to be here, and what happened to them (biography).
- The sounds, smells, and feel of a place.
- The evolution of architecture and the built environment.
- What kind of commerce developed and why.
- The ethnic and cultural influxes and influences.
- Influential leaders, outlaws, artists, and inventors.

- The impact of people on the location—pollution, depletion, or destruction of resources.
- Myths, stories, and legends that have been passed down about your town.

The sources of information for deep maps are the very ones that your students have used throughout this investigation of your community: primary source documents, historical fiction, experts on local history, artifacts, old local maps, town directories and newspaper archives, cemeteries, local holidays and celebrations, old timers, plus all the information they've stored in their Community Explorer's Journal.

The range of materials students can use to create their deep maps is almost limitless: student artwork—drawings, paintings, sketches, photographs, or Xerox copies of old documents; natural materials such as leaves, soil, flowers, shells, stones; documents or records like sections of old maps layered to show change in one particular area, newspaper articles, excerpts from diaries, logs, public documents or journals, and sound recordings.

Formats for Deep Maps

Designing a deep map is very creative. The physical map itself can be artistic and imaginative or precise and scientific. It can reveal all at a glance, or create rabbit holes down which you plunge to learn more about a certain place. At the same time it's a huge organizational task that requires skills in sequencing, logic, and symbolic language. You can suggest any of the following formats or let your kids come up with their own versions.

Lift Tab Map. This is the nonelectronic version of the buttons and links on a website. Kids start with a map of your community. They attach tabs at strategic points on the map. When viewers lift the tab, they find information about that site. For example, if you have a pier in town, the tab at that site might reveal pictures of all the other piers that been built and destroyed in that same spot. Tabs can indicate the birthplace of famous citizens. Lifting them uncovers an old portrait, significant accomplishments, or a photo of a headstone. The tab can actually be like the cover of a small book, with layers of pages below.

Pocket Map. This is a great format if you have lots of documents and photographs that you want viewers to examine on their own. Start with a map of the community. Attach paper pockets to key locations and write the topic on the outside. For example, one pocket might say *City Hall* and contain pictures of your city hall over the decades or centuries. It might have a copy of a newspaper article of the fire that destroyed City Hall, or pictures of antiwar demonstrators on the steps. Heavy mailing envelopes make sturdy pockets that can take the wear and tear of lots of visitors. The pockets can hold pictures, text, and artifacts, anything that provides deeper information about the person, place, or event indicated on the front of the pocket.

Biographical Map. If you have kids who learn history through stories about people, they might want to make a deep map that focuses only on the people in your community—past and present. Starting with a map of the community, they would identify significant locations in the lives of the famous and infamous, then draw, write, or collage information onto the map to create biographies of the town fathers and mothers, local musicians, artists, inventors, writers, athletes, and legislators. This project may overlap with family histories and genealogy.

Slot Map. This deep map format is excellent if your students have collected a significant number of bulky artifacts that tell the story of your community. Instead of starting with a flat map, get those slotted cardboard boxes that look like a multitier inbox, or have your kids construct them out of cardboard. Put a tray or shallow box like a drawer in each slot. Label each shelf with one of the big topics in your community's history—battles, famous people, industry, the Gold Rush, natural disasters. Or organize the information by eras. For example, the top slot could be the current decade or half century, with each descending slot going back in time—sort of like an archaeological dig. Visitors to these deep maps pull out the tray to discover more about a certain community topic.

Box Map. This format is a fan-folded map mounted in a box, like a cigar box. The outside of the box can be covered with old photos of your community. The map itself is a long piece of paper folded like a fan that fits in the box. The last section of the map is glued to the bottom of the box. As you pull the map out, each fold reveals a different topic, period in time, person, landmark, or major event in your community. When the map is folded back into place, the box represents the totality of local history.

Becoming an Expert

Once your class has spent a fair amount of time getting smarter about the community, it's time for each student to zero in on a single intriguing aspect of your community and become an expert. Research explodes as kids pursue their passion and develop a niche of expert knowledge. Eventually they will present their projects to others, so that everyone gets smarter about the many subtopics of your community. Here are some potential ideas for expert research projects:

- Bridges
- Lighthouse or pier
- Historic buildings or neighborhoods
- One particular building—the tallest, the oldest
- Amusement parks
- Famous people in your community
- Specific ethnic or cultural groups
- Founders of the town
- My family's history in this town
- Water and power systems
- Famous storms and natural disasters in our town
- Manufacturing and business
- Our town during various wars
- Native Americans who lived here before the town was established
- The oldest newspaper
- Firsts in town history
- Our town in the seventeenth, eighteenth, or nineteenth century
- Pastimes in times past—what did adults and kids do for fun?
- Local artists, writers, or musicians
- Regional architecture
- One-room schools

Culminations—Sharing Expert Knowledge with the Community

As your kids focus on becoming experts, remind them that this isn't research for research's sake—not like those painful papers we used to write in college and share with exactly no one. Becoming an expert is a means to an end, and the end is sharing expertise with peers, parents, and community members. There are lots of ways to showcase your student-experts. The following are a few suggestions.

Local History Fair

Having a History Fair is like staging a teach-in. You set a date, reserve a big space like the school library or auditorium, and invite every person even remotely connected to your projects or interested in the topics. The living resources you consulted will be on the top of the guest list. Then call or write every city official and district bigwig. Send invitations over to the local retirement villages and the Chamber of Commerce. Invite the librarians who helped out, and of course, other classes in your school. The more, the better. These aren't just guests or an audience. They are going to interact with your kids, and through their questions challenge your students to think at very sophisticated levels. On the day of the event, your kids set up their spaces, like vendors at a convention, but instead of hawking products, their pushing ideas. Their own. They can set up models and do demonstrations, or stage reenactments, perform plays, do readings, or give musical performances. I had kids who structured their presentation like a game show and participants were questioned about local history, often with hysterical results. This type of culmination/assessment is so exhilarating that students usually end the day by asking when they can do it again. You'll end the day thrilled with the quantity and quality of student learning that's on display.

Historic Newspapers

Your kids can synthesize and share their research by publishing a fictional newspaper about your community that might have been written decades or centuries ago. A wonderful model of this approach to history is the *Chronicle* series of books published in 1989 by Ecam Publishers. They're out of print now, but try finding them through your local library or a used bookstore. Believe me, they're worth the hunt. The premise of Chronicle was simple: What if a newspaper reporter had been on the spot and witnessed the big stories in history—like the building of the pyramids? What would history look like if it were as accessible and fresh as the front page of your newspaper? So pitch the same idea to your kids, except they're covering the history of your community. What would the headlines have said on the day of the historic earthquake? Or when English people showed up for the first time? Visual kids can design print advertisements and use old photographs for illustrations. The archives of your library or historic society will have some old newspapers on microfilm that you can use as reference material. Students may want to publish newspaper editions from different periods in your community's history, or to document a series of major events. Try to find a way to make lots of copies and distribute them to other classes studying local history.

Mobile Minimuseum

This is the Ringling Brothers approach to culminations. Like any good circus, you take your show on the road, serving up exciting bits of community history in lots of venues. Consider having your students design a mobile exhibit to teach about your town's history or present your students' point of view on a current issue—such as development, pollution, or the condition of the parks in town. It needs to be easy to assemble and transport and fairly durable. When the minimuseum is ready, set it up in your school or at the PTA meetings, take it to the Board of Education, to the local library, or even to the shopping center. Send flyers to churches, retirement homes, recreation centers, the historic society, the chamber of commerce, asking them to host the minimuseum. Offer to have your students make presentations to accompany the exhibits. You'll attract more people if you scan in old photos of community families, like the display in the visitor's center at Ellis Island. Have a reception for your students and their guests at one of the locations. Be sure to contact the media and issue a press release.

Design a Brochure

Another way for students to distill their research into a useful product is to have them design a brochure for your community—one that would attract visitors to your town and teach the locals about their history. It can contain demographic data, lists of services and businesses, recreation opportunities, and points of interest. Students can use historic photographs mixed with their own drawings to illustrate their writing. Distribute the brochure to other students and families. Drop some off at the local library or the visitor's center.

How Does Our Community Need Us?

While your students are busy investigating the interesting nooks and crannies of your community, they will inevitably stumble across some very dark corners. They'll see homeless people, witness the conditions in which some older people live, or discover that some neighborhoods are shabbier and more dangerous than anything they have seen on television. Students in other schools lack books, playground equipment, or even a playground. The poorest area of town has a microlibrary that's open three days a week—no nights—while a capacious, well-stocked, well-lit library is open seven days a week in a better zip

> *In Chicago I began my practice of urban tourism, which continues to this day. I wandered everywhere, walking for hours—took buses to the end of the line, just to see where they would go— prowled around strange neighborhoods —and studied maps of the city.*
> —Daniel Pinkwater,
> *Chicago Days, Hoboken Nights*

code. There's more than enough inequity and need to go around, and children clearly see the unfairness that is invisible to many adults.

Remember how I mentioned at the beginning of the chapter that sometimes community adventures turn into crusades? Well, this is how it happens. One day your kids stumble across a problem and they just can't get it out of their minds. First they want to know why adults haven't fixed it, and after hearing few good reasons, they usually decide to take the matter into their own hands. Now you're in the realm of truly authentic learning. Crusading requires a very specific set of skills, so if you find yourself being dragged down this path by a group of idealistic kids—all kids are idealistic when they find the right cause—you'll need to get smarter about social justice education. Check out Chapter 10 for more ideas. You could end up in the history books!

Resources

Books

Heckman, Paul. 1996. *The Courage to Change: Stories from Successful School Reform.* Thousand Oaks, CA: Corwin.
Macaulay, David. 1980. *Unbuilding.* Boston: Houghton Mifflin.
———. *Skyscraper.* Boston: Houghton Mifflin.
———. 1983. *City: A Story of Roman Planning and Construction.* Boston: Houghton Mifflin.
———. 1998. *The New Way Things Work.* Boston: Houghton Mifflin.
Weitz, David. 1975. *My Backyard History Book.* Boston: Little, Brown.

Online Resources

Community Maps Project
Joint project between University of Florida art students and local elementary school children to create community maps: http://nersp.nerdc.ufl.edu/%7Erol1851/community/maps_project.html

EarthIsland Institute: Borneo Project
Community-based mapping of traditional village land in the rainforest of Sarawak, East Malaysia: www.earthisland.org/borneo/ourwork/mapping.html

ESRI's Community Atlas
Teachers and students work to develop descriptions and maps of their community. The resulting projects can be searched and viewed through: www.esri.com/industries/k-12/atlas/

Green Maps for Healthy Cities and Sustainable Communities
In particular, look at the children's projects at www.greenmap.com

Nature Mapping

A program with the goal of making communities and individuals aware of their natural resources and offering tools to monitor these resources. Check out their workshops and maps of the predicted distributions of various species at: www.fish.washington.edu/naturemapping/index.html

Common Ground

The home page of Common Ground—the inspirational source of over a thousand maps celebrating the distinctiveness of place—can be found at: www.commonground.org.uk/

SECRET #8

Great Teachers Are Gossipmongers

Putting the Social Back in Social Studies

In This Chapter:
- What's the Big Idea About History?
- Meet Bill Coate
- Tools of the Trade
- How to Make Documents Talk About History
- How to Make Images Talk About History
- How to Make Objects Talk About History
- How to Make Buildings Talk About History
- How to Make Books Talk About History
- Encouraging Investigative Independence
- You Were There—Historic Simulations
- Authentic Assessments in History

History is supposed to be a story well told. At least that's what the educational frameworks say. So why is it that when it's history time in many classrooms across America, students feel like they've wandered into a game show and chosen the wrong category? The teacher peppers them with one-liners, all of which require numeric answers—1066, 1776, 1812, 1929. Where's the story? Or, she reviews the list of Top Ten Treaties. No one's pulse races. Although battles seem more promising—action, carnage, winners, and losers—they usually read like the diary of a real-estate broker—who got how much property and where the losers decamped to sulk.

Sulk is probably too strong a word. History instruction—and some instructors—seem to be lavishly underemotional. Entire cultures are annihilated through bacterial warfare; amazing libraries are reduced to ash, taking with them intimate knowledge of the Roman world; utopian communities are crushed, totalitarian leaders elevated. No outcry. Not even a sigh. "It's a good day to die" comes as close to an emotional revelation as you're likely to get, then it's . . . "turn to the last page of the chapter and answer the questions." *Not* a story well told.

And while we're on the subject, whose story is it anyway? If you casually flip through an elementary history book, you'd think we were descended from a race of hermaphrodites. Or perhaps human cloning has secretly been around for centuries, with one powerful man after another quietly stockpiling his DNA to create duplicates for the next big event.

Something is clearly missing. Try women and children.

If you're not talking about females of all stripes—queens, female spies, surgeons, chemists, engineers, painters, stagecoach drivers, and architects, you're practicing censorship. Your kids need to meet Mary Moore, an African American who invented a painkiller in 1799. And don't forget Sarah Bradlee Fulton, the mother of the Boston Tea Party, who delivered dispatches through enemy lines. Why was her contribution less notable than Paul Revere's?

It can be a real revelation to ten-year-olds to discover that while they're still trying to figure out where they left their homework and fighting over who gets the remote control, their peers in times past were participating in the big events of history. Most Pony Express riders were kids. The poster advertising jobs said, "Riders wanted . . . Orphans preferred." Eighteen-year-old Jennie Curtis delivered a speech that galvanized striking railroad workers in Chicago in 1884. Wouldn't you love to read that speech? So would your kids.

What's the Big Idea About History?

Great teachers know the big idea about history is that it's a story about people—what they did and why they did it. It's full of daredevils, dunderheads, and scoundrels—the stuff of gossip. What could be more riveting than to casually mention to a group of oh-so-cool fifth graders that there were whispers of cannibalism in Jamestown? "They say a man salted his wife and packed her in a trunk for winter. Who knows?" I'd put money down that your kids will spend the rest of the day scouring their colonial documents for evidence of man-eaters. Or, you can share in a confidential tone that First Lady Eleanor Roosevelt carried a loaded revolver. The same thing that draws people into the movie theatres attracts kids to history. Kids love blood, and getting scared or grossed out. If you doubt that, just start a discussion about the Black Plague with your students. You'll have to throw them out of the room when the bell rings.

Why then, with all the stories about maniacs, masterminds, and feats of raw courage just ripe for the picking, do so many kids still leave school ignorant of the bliss to be found wandering through the middle ages in the company of a knight, or viewing the Renaissance through the eyes of Leonardo da Vinci? If you ask, these unfortunates swear that they "hate history." They're wrong. They just hate the way it's taught.

So here's your challenge: How can your kids get to know dead people? A time machine would be perfect—jump in, fire it up, and in no time you're on medieval soil or crushed in a crowded Atlanta street, marching for civil rights.

Let's assume that your standard history textbook is a less-than-fascinating vehicle for time travel. It probably has some good pictures and an atlas that can be read with very youthful eyes. It's certainly a resource. But if you want to do full-blooded history, you'll need to transport your kids back to the scene of the crime so they can discover what really happened, and who did it. How did life in another time look, sound, and smell? What were people writing about? Who were the superstars? You need to make dead people talk.

Meet Bill Coate

Here's the first thing I loved about Bill Coate: His idea of a great field trip is to take his kids to a graveyard, followed by junkets to the coroner, tax assessor, and newspaper morgue—any place they can track down dead people. In another life, Bill might have been a gumshoe—he even has a Dick Tracy–style hat. But he's a fifth-grade teacher, and a great one, at that.

Cruising graveyards has become an academic tradition for Bill. Early in the year, he takes his kids to the local cemetery in Madera. They wander among the headstones, reading and speculating until they find an intriguing grave. If the stone is fancy and the epitaph tantalizing, Bill announces, "Let's dig 'im up!" and the adventure begins.

The town of Madera claims only twelve square miles, just four off-ramps, in the center of the two-hundred-mile-long central valley of California. The area is flat farmland; the town is a one-story affair that appears to have escaped the influence of urban planners. Motels shoulder gas stations. Railroad tracks bisect the city. The elementary school has a generous playfield circled by portable classrooms in an unremarkable neighborhood.

It's not Boston or Philadelphia or even Sacramento. But it's history-rich territory for Bill Coate, a man who gleefully proclaims that he has "always been a resident of the past." As a child he tirelessly poked around the swamps of Florida discovering evidence of Native American tribes, "Eventually my mother made me surrender my treasures to the local historic society." But that didn't dampen his interest in all things old. When his family vacationed in a small town in Georgia, he passed his days exploring a Civil War–era train station and pestering the locals to find someone who could tell him more.

Bill has spent much of his adult life in similar pursuits—coaxing crumbling documents and remote locations to reveal their secrets. His current passion is Madera, a place where many losers in the Gold Rush lottery went to tend their disappointment. They became grocers, dryland farmers, laundrymen, or stagecoach drivers, building the historic foundation of Madera that Bill and his students are uncovering and restoring, one story at a time.

Bill's students will forever think of history as a contact sport. They don't sit back and wait for information to come their way—they make house calls. And like good detectives, they've learned to monitor their hunches, follow their nose, ask and ask and ask.

How It All Got Started

In 1984, Bill took his class out for some *al fresco* academics. While exploring along the banks of the Chowchilla River they came upon three old graves, all bearing the last name Minturn. Only one had an epitaph: "Her Children Shall Arise and Call Her Blessed." Bill and his kids were intrigued. Who was Abby West Minturn? This was even better than a Civil War depot. These were real people, right in their own backyard.

So Bill and his kids began to snoop. No one in town remembered a Minturn family and the name didn't even ring a bell at the local historical or genealogical societies. The Minturns had been erased from local memory. The way Bill saw it, "the town was suffering from a case of historical amnesia." So Bill and his kids embraced Abby Minturn like a long-lost relative. They became Minturn magnets, scouring the town for anything remotely connected to Abby and her kids. The Minturn mystery became the central feature of their days and occupied them after school and on weekends, too.

Soon they were regulars in offices around town that rarely saw a child, much less a gaggle of twelve-year-olds intent on examining obituaries and titles to land. Slowly they began to resurrect a struggling family, transplanted from New England, plagued by suicide, sudden death, and the harsh realities of frontier living. But the challenge was to turn a pile of raw data into a story that would awaken in its readers the same curiosity and awe that Bill and his kids felt standing on the banks of a river, staring at three tiny graves.

Enter Irving Stone

That's when Bill's longtime colleague Tom Andrews made a connection with the novelist Irving Stone. Suddenly Bill and his kids were sharing their adventures with the novelist who brought Michelangelo, Vincent Van Gogh, and Sigmund Freud to life for millions of readers. They'd discovered their common passion. In Irving Stone, Bill found a mentor, a writing coach, and a friend. Stone was fascinated with a band of preadolescents who shared his inexhaustible appetite for the past. For four years, until his death, Stone wrote, visited, advised, and encouraged Bill's students as they struggled to master the art of researching and writing historical fiction. Early on he made a suggestion that became an epiphany for Bill and his kids. Shift the voice to first person. (The first draft of the Minturn Chronicles was in third person.) With this single suggestion, Bill found the form that would become the hallmark of an entire library of student-authored books, all written as fictional historic diaries. The result of this unique collaboration was dubbed The Madera Method: Learning Through Research.

The Madera Method

The Madera Method is an immersion approach to history. Walking into Bill Coate's room is like stepping into a time machine. The walls are swathed in large black-and-white photos—who's who in Madera history, the top ten historic buildings, the 1904 fire, a general store, agricultural workers, and families on carriage excursions to nearby Yosemite. There's a floor-to-ceiling bulletin board of the pioneer who is the current target of their research. The computers that line one wall are hooked in to electronic archives. A microfilm machine stands at the ready for studying a century of material from the local newspaper. A paper time line runs around the walls to display the information students unearth about people, events, inventions, natural disasters, and any other developments that shaped the lives of the Madera pioneers.

Bill is clearly in his element as his students tackle the life and death of Yee Chung. He hunches over on his stool, then springs up and gestures emphatically to a photograph. His voice drops to a conspiratorial level, ". . . and this is the kicker . . . he had two wives."

On this morning there was a special treat—a 120-year-old handwritten diary in a wooden box. This was so definitively *the real thing* that we could smell the decaying leather cover as soon as the box was opened. In small, neat, vinelike handwriting that was as perfect as a computer-generated text, there were entries about Christmas and sick children and horses and the price of dry goods. I was mesmerized. One group of Bill's students will be publishing an annotated version of this diary before it is lovingly returned via wagon train to the hometown of the settler who wrote it.

Yes, there's a trip by wagon train. This is not a Disneyesque outing. First the students study old diaries, letters, and maps. Then they head out into the hills for six days to retrace part of a pioneer journey. They eat, sleep, walk, and dodge rainstorms, all of which helps them develop historic empathy for the people who settled in Madera. They cook their own food, gather wood, feed and water the animals, and learn to drive the mule-drawn wagons. Throughout the journey, the kids keep journals that are ultimately published as "Tales of the Trail."

The goal of the Madera Method program is to teach students reading, writing, and history through researching historical projects, then publishing their works. Bill and his kids live the experience together as local history detectives. They begin as curiosity seekers, hone their research skills, and culminate each year by publishing a new volume that makes a significant contribution to the historic knowledge of their community. In the process they strengthen their skills in grammar, history, anthropology, economics, research, critical thinking, and cultural awareness.

Bill has a following among history-loving teachers and generously shares his unique approach with anyone who's interested. Thanks to his dedication and the Internet, you and your students can learn the Madera Method—step-by-step from headstone to bound book—simply by logging on to (http://sunsite.Berkeley.edu/MaderaMethod) and clicking through this amazing resource.

Madera-Style Social Justice

Occasionally, Bill and his kids get more than they bargained for—a good story and the opportunity to right a wrong, even if it's a very old one. If there's a hint of injustice, the mere whiff of something unfair, Bill says, "That's like saying sick 'em to a dog." Such was the story with the Borden Cemetery. Bill and his kids found seven headstones in a neglected field four miles outside of town. The single clue they could glean from the weed-choked plot was Chinese characters etched in the stones. Bill scanned the area for informants and spied the Madera Irrigation District right across the road. "Let's go over and ask who owns this field," he suggested. The response they got at the water headquarters—nervous, furtive, half-answers—told him they were on to something, and the hunt was on.

By this time, Bill's students were old hands at riffling public records. They headed for the tax office, the title office, and the newspaper morgue. "That's not a cemetery," was the response at the tax assessor's office. "Well, somebody ought to tell the people who are buried there!" was Bill's response. Eventually, their investigations turned up the forgotten Chinese community of Madera—and a big problem. The cemetery was on private land. The taxes hadn't been paid for some years, so the land was schedule for a quiet sale. The last trace of the Chinese immigrants who came to California during the Gold Rush and stayed to build the railroad and work the ranches would be wiped off the face of Madera.

"My kids were hooked. They were determined to save the cemetery, so they decided to raise money to pay the back taxes. But we were foiled again—the county informed us that we would not be allowed to pay the taxes." Here's where Bill Coate, detective, turns social justice crusader—and a brilliant one at that. If the cemetery was doomed to destruction, then at the very least, his kids would hold a Ceremony of Remembrance to honor the long-dead people they had resurrected through their investigations. And while they were at it, why not invite some honored guests—like the Secretary of State March Fong Eu and the Chinese Consul General? On the day of the ceremony, with the land still slated for sale, twelve important people were ushered to seats under a white canopy facing the graves. Bill's students presented all their research, bringing the extinct Chinese community of Madera back to life, including the seven who rested at their feet. At the end of the ceremony, the students asked the twelve guests to act as an informal jury. "How would you vote as citizens of our community? Should this sacred ground be designated an historic site?" As the CNN cameras whirred, each and every citizen cast a *yes* vote, including the representative from the irrigation district.

The rest, as they say, is history. The Borden Chinese Cemetery is an historic site with an impressive granite stone marking the entrance. The students published *Forgotten Field, Forgotten People* to share their research with the community. It is the most definitive study of the Chinese experience in Madera County, all because some nosey kids and their teacher wouldn't give up. For nearly twenty years now, Bill Coates and his kids have kept company with a small, rural town going about its business, but through their passion and intense scrutiny, they're creating a portal through which the citizens of Madera can experience its rich and lively past. Each year they capture a piece of the ebb and flow of small human dramas, one pioneer at a time. Irving Stone expressed the importance of their quiet enterprise in the preface he wrote for the books published by the Madera students. It reads,

> This is the greatest adventure of mankind: to find something that was never known before or understood. Each new piece of knowledge does not need to have a specific or functional use, at least not at the moment. It is a sufficient triumph that we have learned something and proved it by documentation, that had been formerly part of the darkness.

Tools of the Trade

I have a hunch that few of us are wagon-train material. I'm such a wimp, I take emergency rations on a two-hour plane ride. But you don't have to saddle up or even cruise graveyards to give your kids a brush with history. They can rub elbows with people in the past by examining authentic objects and original texts. Introduce them to the things that people painted, built, scratched in a diary, or proclaimed on a stage long, long ago. Let them get close enough to interrogate historic figures and relive famous events using the tools of working historians, including:

- Primary source documents
- Visual images
- Artifacts
- Literature
- Architecture

These items are powerful eyewitnesses to history. But witnesses are only useful if you can make them talk. Your job is to stoke the inquisition in your classroom. Teach your kids to get the story out of historic sources by asking *who, what, where, when, why,* and *how* questions, especially, *How do we know?*

How to Make Documents Talk About History

Primary Sources as Historic Evidence

Primary source documents are firsthand accounts that were created by people who took part in or witnessed an event. They include texts, documents, and first-person accounts. Secondary sources are books and documents created by people who did not witness or take part in the events but who have used primary and secondary sources to investigate the subject.

Text Documents.   Primary source text documents include items such as public records, birth and death records, census reports, church records, newspapers, treaties, legal documents, government documents, accounts books or ledgers, ships' logs, cartoons, city directories, and business papers. Examples would be the *Declaration of Independence,* the Constitution of the Iroquois nation, a plantation ledger, or the Code of Hammurabi, the earliest known written legal code, composed about 1780 BCE in Babylon. The Code lays out the basis of both criminal and civil law, and defines procedures for commerce and trade. Many of the laws have a contemporary ring, despite being nearly four thousand years old. For example:

> If a judge try a case, reach a decision, and present his judgment in writing; if later error shall appear in his decision, and it be through his own fault, then he shall pay twelve times the fine set by him in the case, and he shall be publicly removed from the judge's bench, and never again shall he sit there to render judgment.

Your kids can get primary source documents to talk about history by asking questions such as:

- What is it?
- Who wrote it?
- When and where was it written?
- Why was this written?
- Who is the story or information about?
- Who was the intended audience?
- What do the words say? What do they mean?
- What do I wonder about this document?
- What guesses can I make from this (inferences)?
- What biases might the writer have?
- Who else knows about this event?

It used to be that you had to break into the local archives after hours or bribe an historian to get your hands on certain primary source documents. Now they're as accessible as fast food. Most textbooks have snippets of them, but the full texts are available all over the Internet. For one-stop shopping, go to www.uidaho.edu/special collections/Other.Repositories.html for a listing of over 5,300 websites describing holdings of manuscripts, archives, rare books, historical photographs, and other primary sources for the research.

First-Person Documents. First-person accounts are powerful texts because their personal details create a sense of you-are-thereness that wipes out the 300 or even 3,000 years that separate writer and reader. Seemingly familiar words are used in a way that twangs in a twenty-first-century ear, capturing our attention. You can time-travel simply by turning a page. First-person accounts include: diaries, eyewitness accounts, autobiographies, travel narratives, interviews, correspondence, journals, radio and television broadcasts. Examples would be Edward R. Murrow's radio broadcasts during the blitz of London, Pliny the Younger's account of the eruption of Vesuvius, and the travels of Marco Polo.

To sample the lure of first-person documents, turn to any page in *Roughing It* by Mark Twain, a hilarious but information-packed account of Twain's trip west to dig for wealth in the rocks of Nevada. Instead, he found fame and fortune as a writer and entertainer. The following section describes sleeping in a stagecoach filled with mail as it presses through the darkness over rough terrain.

We began to get into country, now, threaded here and there with little streams. These had high, steep banks on each side, and every time we flew down one bank and scrambled up the other, our party inside got mixed somewhat. First we would all be down in a pile at the forward end of the stage, nearly in a sitting posture, and in a second we would shoot to the other end, and stand on our heads. And we would sprawl and kick, too, and ward off ends and corners of mail-bags that came lumbering over us and about us; and as the dust rose from the tumult, we would all sneeze in chorus, and the majority of us would grumble, and probably say some hasty thing, like: "Take your elbow out of my ribs!—can't you quit crowding?". . . Still, all things considered, it was a very comfortable night.

Firsthand accounts of any period in history are so plentiful, the hardest part will be choosing which ones to use. When you find the one that's perfect for your kids, guide them through their interrogations so that they learn to extract every morsel of information from the text using curiosity and critical-thinking skills. Your kids can get first-person accounts to talk about history by asking questions such as:

- What is it?
- Who wrote it?
- When and where was it written?
- Why was this written?
- Who is the story or information about?
- What's unusual about the language?
- What do I wonder about this document?
- What guesses can I make from this?
- What biases might the writer have?
- How does this information fit with my understanding of this time period or event?

How to Make Images Talk About History

Paintings and Photographs as Historic Evidence

Pictures are perfect tools for getting to the past—fast. They provide a window through which your kids discover how people dressed, married, and were buried in other cultures and times. They can study the details of Gothic cathedral construction, or Egyptian reed boats. Historic visual documents include photographs, paintings, portraits, documentary films, etchings, and maps.

Learning to Look. Most young kids have 20/20 vision—a cause of constant envy in teachers with aging eyes. Nonetheless, many of them are visually challenged when it comes to looking at a *still* image. And I say, blame television! Television relies on a bull's eye format. All the important images are right in the center of the screen. They move every three or four seconds, and when they aren't moving, they make noise, so the viewer receives a constant flow of prompts about where to look in order to extract information from the screen. Television is an extremely low-effort event.

Fast-forward to the classroom. You present your kids with a black-and-white photograph. They're stumped. Take the famous Margaret Bourke-White photograph of the 1937 Bread Line during the Louisville flood (view it at www.masters-of-photography.com/B/bourke-white/b-w_living_full.html). The image doesn't move or make noise. It has important information in all four corners, background and fore. This is tough. At first kids lock on to the biggest, most central image—the car—and figure they've looked at everything. They think they're done, bring on the next picture. That's your clue that they don't really know how to look. So teach them how, simply by asking open-ended questions like these:

- What do you see? What else? What else?
- Who do you think these people are? What gave you that clue?
- What do you think they're doing? What made you think that?
- What are they holding? Why do you think they're carrying those items?
- What is the weather like? How can you tell?
- What does the mood of the group seem to be? What makes you think that?
- What's in the background?
- What's the message?
- What do you think the photographer was trying to tell us with this picture?

Be sure to solicit multiple answers to each question—there is no one right answer in this type of inquiry investigation. Before you know it, they'll be picking details out of the image like a school nurse going after nits. That's how you teach kids to look. To learn more about techniques for using open-ended questioning, see Chapter 5.

Here are more questions that will help your kids make a visual document give up its secrets about history:

- What is this?
- Who made it?
- When was it made?
- What's going on in the picture?

- Who do you think the story is about?
- When do you think these events happened? How can you tell?
- Where did they happen? What clues are in the picture?
- Why do you think they happened?
- What might be important about this?
- What was the creator trying to say?
- Who is still alive who might know about this event or these people?
- How is life in this image different from now?

Using visual images to explore history is surprising to kids. They expect pictures during art time—if you still have art time—but not during history/social science. More important, pictures open the door wide for students who have keen visual intelligence. They're also a boon for students with reading disabilities and second-language learners, allowing them to use their eyes and brain to access information directly, vaulting over the language barriers. Analyzing paintings, etchings, drawings, and photographs can be more effective than reading aloud to students who are weak in auditory processing. These visual time machines rev up motivation, lower defenses, and accelerate the research process.

Sources of Images

Your school or district may no longer have bins of large art prints that used to be standard fare for classrooms, so where can you go for images that function as primary source documents for history lessons? Many art and natural history museums have libraries that lend slides to teachers for a nominal fee—something like five dollars a week for fifty slides. Their collections typically include slides of paintings, medieval manuscripts, buildings, monuments, sculptures, and even prehistoric tools and ritual objects. If you can beg or borrow a slide projector, the visual world, historically speaking, is yours. The historic society or city hall archives may sell inexpensive copies of historic photos. My local library has an online catalogue with thousands of photographs that can be printed for fifty cents apiece. For less that the cost of a Happy Meal, I had pictures of every roller coaster on the pier since the turn of the century. Other sources of images include:

- Postcards for small-group work
- Old calendars
- Cut up used art and history books
- Copies of etchings and black-and-white photos
- Internet archives to download and print
- Parents, grandparents, and colleagues

How to Make Objects Talk About History

Artifacts as Historic Evidence

We tend to be very text-oriented when we investigate the history of Western civilizations. But the best information about some cultures is found in artifacts—clothing, gravestones, coins, tools, and musical instruments. This is particularly true when studying the early history of North America, when the continent was thick with Native American tribes. Our most tangible connection to these people is through their handicrafts—a beaded-blanket from the Osage tribe, Kwakiutl masks, buffalo robes, and weapons.

Examining artifacts is a highly effective instructional strategy because it appeals to kinesthetic, visual, and spatial learners. They gather information with their hands and eyes, noting shape, size, texture, weight, and materials. The most puzzling artifacts, like the crank for a Model T or a shoebutton hook, force kids to scrutinize, wonder, and speculate. That's the lure. That's the work.

To sharpen your students' observation skills and give them some batting practice with identifying artifacts, bring in some odd objects such as: apple corer, garlic press, coal burning iron, industrial bobbin, potato masher, ice cream mould, teaball, shoe last, sausage maker, or any other unfamiliar objects you may have cluttering up your garage or kitchen drawers. Put each object on a separate table and have small groups of students circulate from table to table to examine each object. Then have each group tell what they thought the object was and how they arrived at their conclusion. Compare and contrast ideas before you reveal the objects' actual purpose. Encourage students to bring in unusual objects from home to continue honing their skills.

Here are some questions your kids can ask when they want to make an artifact talk about history:

- What is this item?
- When was it made?
- Where was it made?
- Where was it found?
- What else could it be or mean?
- What does this item remind me of?
- What does it make me wonder?
- What is important about this item?
- What is unique or unusual about this?

Sources of Artifacts

You can launch an amazing discussion with a few authentic artifacts or reproductions. Passing around a hunk of buffalo skin and a deer hide drum can be the highlight of your lesson if you're trying to establish the link between Native Americans and animals, so it's worth it to track down some three-dimensional materials for your research table. Our Natural History Museum has a lending library of stuffed animals, rock collections, antique bowls, weapons, and textile samples. The more delicate items are in plastic boxes, so kids can look to their hearts' content without harming the specimens. Other sources for artifacts include:

- Artifact reproduction companies
- Local historic society
- Antique stores
- Secondhand and thrift shops
- Garage and tag sales
- Internet swaps and sales
- Parents, grandparents, and colleagues

How to Make Buildings Talk About History

Architecture as Historic Evidence

Discovering the brick-and-mortar history in your community can be as simple as taking a walk through the neighborhood and sketching the leaded windows, Dutch doors, and stone foundations. Or, it can be as elaborate as passing through the gates of a restored village like Sturbridge, Williamsburg, New Paltz, or Deerfield and entering another century, complete with historic interpreters. What can kids learn about the past through architecture? How tall people were. The types of building materials that were common and their sources. How public and private space was divided and decorated. Who lived where in town. How the size of structures relates to status. The number and kind of religions represented by historic churches. For more ideas about looking at and drawing architecture, see Chapter 7 and read the section on historic buildings.

Here are some questions your kids can ask to learn more about history by looking at buildings:

- Who built this?
- When was it built?
- Why was it built?

- For whom was it built? Who else has lived here or used this building?
- Was it always used for the same purpose? What is it used for now?
- Was it always in this place or was it moved?
- Is this how it looked originally or has it shrunk or grown?
- How is this building different from structures that are built now?
- How is it the same? Why?
- What about the gardens and landscaping?
- Does it have outbuildings and how are they used?
- Why do some stone walls look different from others?
- What do the patterns in the bricks mean?
- What can we learn about the people who made or used this building by looking at the size, shape, doors and windows, materials, decoration, and location?

Other Sources of Information About Historic Buildings

There are heroes in your town, usually members of the Landmarks Commission or the Historic Conservancy, determined to preserve and protect historic landmarks. They're eager to give your kids the Preservation 101 tour in the hopes of breeding a new generation of activists who will go to bat for elderly buildings. Your local historic society should have a list of the oldest or most significant structures in town and possibly self-guided walking tours complete with maps, dates, and stories. Just ask. If you want to play with the big boys in preservation, log on the website of the National Register for Historic Preservation (www.nationaltrust.org) to learn about nationwide preservation efforts, along with information about American architecture.

How to Make Books Talk About History

Literature as Historic Evidence

Most great teachers are experts at using literature to teach about history. They choose class sets like *My Brother Sam Is Dead* (1977) or *Roll of Thunder, Hear My Cry* (1976) because reading historic fiction doubles your history time while giving your kids the pleasure of devouring a really good book. And research shows that kids learn factual information more readily and retain it longer if it's embedded in a narrative format.

Another reason literature belongs in your history program is that some time periods, cultures, or groups of people are not well represented in the visual arts or artifacts. African American slaves rarely appeared in paintings or photographs, and their material culture was sparse. But they did pass down songs, folktales, and stories along with a collection of narratives recorded after the Civil War, which are unsurpassed for capturing the daily lives of slaves.

There's also a vast store of knowledge hidden in historic fiction for adults. It makes superb read-aloud material—not whole chapters, just passages selected for their descriptive power. For example, *A Durable Fire* (1990) by Virginia Bernhard is an amazing evocation of the first winter in Jamestown, also known as the Starving Time. Your kids will pick up so many details of daily life and catch the emotional tone of this near-catastrophic time just listening to you read, it will be as if you dumped them in a snowdrift outside of the stockade. At the same time, you're developing their ears for good literature while feeding them a high-calorie diet of history, history, history.

Time Machine Books

A lesser-known but fascinating way to hook kids on history is to read time travel books—an underrated genre to be sure. Most of these stories open with a couple of curious kids who accidentally unlock the secret to time travel and escape to another century. They joust with knights, rescue maidens, and learn to adjust to life without TV. When they return to the present, they know a lot about history and have a new appreciation for home and family.

Some Time Machine Titles

Middle Ages and Renaissance

Max and Me and the Time Machine by Gery Greer. 1983. New York: HarperCollins.

Stranger in the Mist by Paul McCusker. 1996. Colorado: Lion Publishers.

The Kid Who Got Zapped Through Time by Deborah Scott. 1997. New York: Avon.

A Griffon's Nest by Betty Levin. 1975. New York: Simon & Schuster.

A Connecticut Yankee in King Arthur's Court by Mark Twain. 1889.

Trolley to Yesterday by John Bellairs. 1989. New York: Dial Books.

American History

The Edison Mystery by Dan Gutman. 2001. New York: Simon & Schuster Books for Young Readers.

Qwerty Stevens, Stuck in Time with Benjamin Franklin by Dan Gutman. 2002. New York: Simon & Schuster Books for Young Readers.

Three Rivers Crossing by Robert Lytle. 2000. Spring Lake, MI: River Road.

Happily Ever After by Anna Quindlen. 1997. New York: Viking.

The Humpbacked Fluteplayer by Sharman Russell. 1994. New York: A. A. Knopf.

Vision Quest by Pamela Service. 1989. New York: Atheneum.

Civil War

A Boy Called Girl by Belinda Hurmence. 1982. New York: Clarion.

The Root Cellar by Janet Lunn. 1985. New York: Puffin.

Window in Time by Karen Weinberg. 1991. Shippensburg, PA: White Mane.

Nineteenth Century

Time Out by Helen Cresswell. 1990. New York: McMillan.

The Ghost in the Mirror by John Bellairs. 1994. New York: Penguin.

The Switching Well by Peni Griffin. 1993. New York: Simon & Schuster.

Roughing It on the Oregon Trail by Diane Stanley. 2000. New York: HarperCollins.

The Orphan of Ellis Island by Elvira Woodruff. 1997. New York: Scholastic.

Biography

There are countless biographies that can take your kids to any period in history without a passport. Just ask a good children's librarian and soon your arms will be sagging with great titles. Here's one book you simply mustn't miss. It's *We Were There, Too: Young People in U. S. History* by Phillip Hoose (Farrar, Straus & Giroux, 2001). This unique book tells the role that young people played in our history, from the boys who sailed with Columbus to today's young activists. Based largely on primary sources—first-person accounts, journals, and interviews—it highlights the fascinating stories of more than seventy young people from diverse cultures. The author, Phil Hoose, is a warm and gentle man who truly loves kids and history.

Encouraging Investigative Independence

Now that you've glimpsed the broad range of items that contribute to a deep, sustained investigation of the past, you're probably wondering where you're going to put all that stuff? How do you encourage investigative independence, so that kids reach for an effective range of resources when they're on the trail of an ancestor or an answer? You need a Research Center. It's a place where kids go when they have questions. It could be a corner of the room, a foot-locker, or a set of bookshelves, as long as the materials are organized and readily available. The collection will grow over time, especially if your kids know that you welcome their contributions. What should you put at the Research Center?

City directories and phone books

Maps, globes, and atlases

Chronicle of the world and Chronicle of America

Prints and postcards

Farmer's almanac

Sears Roebuck reproduction catalogue

Picture books, novels, biographies, and autobiographies

Time lines

World, U.S., and local history books

Artifacts and reproductions

CD-Roms

Videos

Remember, the Research Center is not an assignment. It's not off-limits until history time. It's the spontaneous answer to the impulse, "I wonder. . . ." If you're a great teacher, the path between your students and the center will be well worn by the end of the year.

You Were There—Historic Simulations

My students were in love with Marco Polo and his million stories. They could practically feel the grit in their teeth as they read about highwaymen attacking Marco's caravan during a sandstorm. They were mesmerized by the notion of a human kite. What they couldn't understand was the big deal about spices. Who would pay a year's wages for a tiny bag of pepper? How did simple traders parlay a camel ride across Asia into a fortune? They were asking important questions that involved geography, economics, opportunity, middlemen, and supply-and-demand. I wanted a simple, graphic answer. So I devised a silk route simulation called the Prices of Spices.

It really was quite simple. First my kids located all the major cities between Venice and Bejing on their medieval maps and we listed them on the board in east-to-west order. With our route set, kids volunteered to be the traders in each city, and I gave them a few minutes to prepare. Some made city signs or placards announcing—*Spices Bought and Sold Here*. Andrew, a brilliant, quiet student, dove into the coat closet and emerged turbaned in a purple sweatshirt, looking like something out of the Three Kings.

I gave each group a bundle of paper currency and launched the simulation by giving a small tin box of pepper to the residents of Beijing. They traveled to the next city and sold the tin. Those traders ventured west until they found the next group of eager buyers, then negotiated a price and returned home. The Venice-bound pepper moved from city to city, and each time the price rose as traders tried to cover their expenses and make a profit. After each transaction, I recorded the going price on the board. At the end of its journey, the price of pepper had skyrocketed. The discussion that followed was more illuminating than Chinese fireworks.

Simulations are staged replications of an event that allow students to understand the event or concept by having an experience similar to the people who went through it. The simulations can be as elaborate as Bill Coate's wagon train trips or as simple as passing a tin of pepper. In the process kids exercise critical-thinking and interpersonal skills—all in a real-life historic context. If you're tempted to dismiss simulations as too time-consuming, bear in mind that a well-constructed simulation has the potential to authentically integrate reading, writing, oral language, and sometimes math, science, and the visual and performing arts. That's a lot of skill development for your Beijing buck.

A great teacher and writer Max Fischer has created books of simulations that you can consult for more ideas, or just make up your own simulations wherever you get to a contentious moment in history. You could stage a demonstration supporting and opposing voting rights for women; dramatize the unfair taxation of Chinese gold miners in the 1850s; re-create the trial of Susan B. Anthony for voting illegally. Kids will beg for more.

Authentic Assessments in History

If you subscribe to the notion that there are different ways of knowing, then it follows that there should be different ways of showing. What's the point of immersing kids in paintings, artifacts, and historic novels if you're going to turn around and give a multiple-choice test to see what they've learned? It just doesn't make sense. That's why you simply must consider authentic assessments. With just a little imagination, you can dream up a half dozen tasks so your students can show you what they know.

Authentic assessments should mirror your teaching activities. Bill Coate's approach is a perfect example. All year long his kids dissect primary documents in pursuit of their pioneer. Would it make sense for him to present them with 100 questions on an objective test to confirm that they've been learning? No.

It would just put them off. Instead, he urges his students to show everything they know by writing fictional diaries, crammed with details about the person and the times. If you were using photographs to track the changes in your community, an authentic assessment would challenge students to produce a portfolio of then-and-now photographs documenting historic sites and explain how they've changed over time.

The best assessments demonstrate mastery and produce new knowledge. They're also much more public than pencil-and-paper tests. Students present their findings to parents, peers, and knowledgeable community members through demonstrations, performances, or products, testing themselves and teaching others at the same time.

Authentic assessments are potentially more equitable in accommodating learning styles and acknowledging multiple ways of demonstrating competence. The following are ideas for authentic assessments in history.

Debates

Debates give students a chance to take a thorny historic issue—votes for women, Manifest Destiny, reservations for Native Americans—and apply their knowledge in a dynamic format that requires specific historic knowledge along with the ability to speak clearly and logically. Debates also strengthen persuasive-writing skills. One of the great social benefits of debating is that students discover that there are two sides to most issues. They learn to respect their opponents and to let them have their say without interrupting. A lot of adults could use these skills!

Learning Fairs

Learning fairs look like a swapmeet or a farmers' market for ideas. They function like a teach-in. After your kids become experts by researching a specific area, they set up booths and teach anyone who walks by—students, community members, or adult experts. At my school we staged a Medieval Faire, Colonial Fair, Babylonian Fair, and Early Santa Monica Fair. These marathons were the highlight of the year for students and families.

Renaissance Dinner Party

After my kids had staged several learning fairs, we began prospecting for a new format to culminate our Renaissance unit. Since we had taken a biographical, who's-who-in-the-fifteenth-century approach, I wondered what it would have been like to have all the Renaissance luminaries around the same table. The conversation should be fantastic. My kids found a menu from a dinner party given by Leonardo da Vinci—pasta, bread, and grapes. We transformed the room with murals, ivy, velvet drapery, and candles. On the day of the event, students arrived dressed as the person they had researched, prepared to converse, debate, even quarrel *in character* to convey all they knew about the Renaissance. Queen Elizabeth presided over our table and the Pope made a surprise entrance, bursting out of the coat closet in a flurry of red robes. Historically speaking, it was the best party I ever attended!

Readings and Dramatic Performances

Students with strength in creative writing can adapt historic information into their own literary forms—poems, short stories, ballads, or plays. Their assessment would be a performance of their work with an interactive session at the end during which their audience can ask questions about the historic content and comment on the performances as original literary offerings.

Re-creating the Past with Models

This is a great activity for kids who process ideas best when their hands are busy. Building models of historic ships, bridges, forts, war machines, buildings, or entire cities motivates them to scrutinize primary source documents for details about construction, materials, function, and decoration. Adding a cast of characters—models of people—encourages more research. The process and the product draw on specific historical knowledge with the bonus that the work itself is both creative and aesthetic.

Murals and Quilts

Murals allow students to depict people, places, and events in history visually, incorporating details from their research. Simple murals can be sketched on butcher paper, then completed with tempera, watercolor, or acrylic paint and marking pens for the fine details. Or students can create a history quilt using a series of images organized around a central event or theme. A slavery quilt could show scenes of Africa, the Middle Passage, New World auctions, and life on a plantation. A quilt can depict changes over a period of time, such as images of Native American tribes living on the plains, herds of buffalo, then the settlements and the railway. A biographical quilt can show key events from the life of one person, such as Ben Franklin. Paper quilts are the easiest and most economical to make, and kids can use pens to write a narrative on the squares or around the border.

Short Stories

Students with a flair for fiction can create a series of short stories to share their historic research. They can create a cast of characters and follow them through the Revolutionary War or on a wagon train headed west. To assess the student, you would focus on the accuracy of details about the physical, political, and social worlds; the students' ability to capture the mood of the time; and their use of the characters' thoughts and comments to reveal the impact of events in the world around them.

Picture Books for Younger Kids

One way that students who like to write and draw can synthesize what they've learned is to make a picture book for younger students. Condensing a story into its essential elements is a difficult task. Kids must sift through all their research to find and sequence the most important and compelling events on which to build their story. Illustrations can fill in more of the details. Students should read their books to appropriate audiences and check for comprehension and appreciation, as a way of assessing their effectiveness.

Oral History Videotapes or Audiotapes

Tape recorders and video cameras can be excellent assessment tools, especially for students who have difficulty writing. Instead of writing a report, students can go electronic, talking about their topic, showing artifacts, going on location, interviewing people as sources of information, and visiting buildings or battlefields to bring their research to life. Plan screening times for the videos with a question-and-answer session after, during which students can elaborate on their presentation, talk about what was left on the cutting room floor, and respond to suggestions from the audience. This kind of give-and-take stretches verbal and social skills, and gives novice filmmakers a chance to teach other students about film and history.

Kid-to-Kid Publishing

Occasionally students will dive into an area of history and find very few resource books—none written for kids. This is particularly true in the case of local history, unless you live in a huge, well-documented city like New York or Washington, DC. Even then, the history books for kids are likely to take a more superficial, city-as-theme-park approach. When my students were studying local history, as many third-grade students do, the one and only children's book on Santa Monica had been published in 1934. After months of research in the library and at the Historic Society, and through interviewing local historians, they decided it was time for a new edition of city history for kids. They wrote and published *From Villages to Verandas: A Multicultural History of Santa Monica*, ninety-eight pages of little-known facts, interviews, and illustrations. Their most original contribution to local history was the chapter examining segregation in Santa Monica and a discussion of contemporary racial issues. We proudly distributed copies to all the school libraries and they've become a staple for kids and teachers who are curious about our city's past.

What Do They Get Out of It?

If you love history the way Bill Coate and I do, you don't need a reason to teach kids about the past. You get it. But if anyone ever asks how an intimate knowledge of fifteenth-century life helps kids function and succeed in the twenty-first century, trot these ideas out and watch them sit up and take notice. Learning to investigate history is a powerful way for students to sharpen their critical-thinking skills, and to make meaning of the links between the physical and social world. They recognize cycles of human behavior and can think analytically about how people change and improve. What can we learn from people who lived long ago and what do we owe to the people who will follow after us? Studying historic events makes kids better consumers of contemporary life. They have ideas about how leaders should behave and the role of citizens in any government. Finally, they get to meet people who are still fascinating though they have long since passed from this world.

> *Most of us spend too much time on the last twenty-four hours and too little time on the last six thousand years.*
> —Will Durant

Resources

Books

Fischer, Max. 1993. *American History Simulations*. Westminster, CA: Teacher Created Materials, Inc.

———. 1995. *Geography Simulations*. Westminster, CA: Teacher Created Materials, Inc.

———. 1995. *World History Simulations*. Westminster, CA: Teacher Created Materials, Inc.

———. 1997. *Ancient History Simulations*. Westminster, CA: Teacher Created Materials, Inc.

———. 2002. *Medieval Simulations*. Westminster, CA: Teacher Created Materials, Inc.

Kent, Peter. 1996. *A Slice Through a City*. London: The Millbrook Press.

Detailed cross-sections show a European city from the Stone Age to the twentieth century, including the structures that are raised and torn down, the people who inhabit the city, and an accumulating underground collection of artifacts.

Leon, Vicki. *The Uppity Women* series. York Beach, ME: Conari.

Macaulay, David. 1973. *Cathedral.* Boston: Houghton Mifflin.

————. 1975. *Pyramid.* Boston: Houghton Mifflin.

————. 1982. *Castle.* Boston: Houghton Mifflin.

————. 1983. *City.* Boston: Houghton Mifflin.

Online Resources

Archiving Early America

The main focus of this website is primary source material from eighteenth-century America—all displayed digitally. A unique array of original newspapers, maps, and writings come to life on the screen just as they appeared to people living more than 200 years ago. www.earlyamerica.com

Digital History

Huge site with major section on children in history including their journals and diaries. www.digitalhistory.uh.edu

Education World History Sites Review

This site rates hundreds of history websites for content, aesthetics, organization, and general usefulness to teachers. www.education-world.com/awards/past/topics/history.shtml

History Wired

This site offers a virtual tour of a large collection of objects from the Smithsonian's National Museum of American History. http://historywired.si.edu/index.html

Immigration: Stories of Yesterday and Today

This site includes virtual tours, biographies, and lessons about how immigrants from all over the world traveled to the United States to build new lives. http://teacher.scholastic.com/immigrat/index.htm

Virtual Jamestown

Site contains an interactive segment, maps and images, court records, labor contracts for indentured servants, public records, letters, firsthand accounts, and virtual panoramas of Jamestown based on the paintings of John White. www.iath.virginia.edu/vcdh/jamestown

SECRET #9

Great Teachers Are Drama Queens

Using the Arts as a Second Language

In This Chapter:
- What's the Big Idea About the Arts?
- The Brain, Learning, and the Arts
- Helping Students Learn Through Drama
- Helping Students Learning Through Movement
- Helping Students Learning Through Music
- Helping Students Learning Through Art
- Recognition
- When All Is Said and Done

There was once a starving artist who found the reality of garret living less romantic than the myth, so he took a job teaching junior high special education students in the South Bronx. That alone speaks to his desperation. At the time—the 1980s—special education was not the jewel in the crown of New York City's school system. The job was rough. The kids were rougher. School hadn't worked for them so far, and they doubted that anyone—Tim Rollins included—could reverse that dismal trend. Learning was the last thing on anyone's mind.

Perhaps from naïveté, perhaps inspiration, Tim Rollins tackled literature. Big books. Serious books. The wallflowers of the public library. As you can imagine, *The Red Badge of Courage* and *Moby Dick* weren't exactly on these kids' reading list. But Rollins used art to help them "hear" the messages embedded in great literature. He'd read. They'd draw. They all talked. Pretty soon he couldn't get rid of them at lunchtime, and when the dismissal bell rang, they showed exactly no enthusiasm for sprinting out the door. They were willfully and persistently interested in whatever it was that Tim Rollins was doing.

So this artist-turned-teacher devised another survival strategy. He created an after-school arts program funded by the National Endowment for the Arts. He called it the Art of Knowledge Workshop. The kids who literally ate, drank, and slept art in his studio called themselves KOS—Kids of Survival.

Off campus, out of the shadow of school, the reading continued—Langston Hughes, George Orwell, Malcolm X. You wouldn't call it reading in the traditional sense—it was more like literary cannibalism. Rollins and his kids dissected, ingested, and ruminated. They underlined and argued as preparation for creating an artistic response that amounted to literary criticism.

But their art making took a quantum leap the day that one kid graffitied the pages of a book in Rollins' personal collection—a mistake that sparked a whole new vision of art as language. Rollins dismantled their latest book club selection, and glued the pages onto a canvas, forming a soft gray grid. Then they painted on the deconstructed text. Rollins' inspiration became the signature of KOS, and a learning phenomenon was born.

Since then, Tim Rollins and the KOS have re-created this process across the country, modeling the power of art as a language finely tuned to the topics of literature and life. Starting with a single literary work, such as *The Frogs, Prometheus Bound, Dracula,* or *Amerika,* Rollins works intensely with kids who never owned a library card, and never cared to—until he showed up. His process feels like a multiple intelligence assault on the target text. Students listen, read along, and talk. They look at slides, listen to music, and try to get a feel for the social and historic context of the author. Then they go to work, creating hundreds of drawings to process their thoughts. Finally, the images are synthesized into a unified visual response that speaks in a voice as unique and dynamic as the writing that inspired it, dazzling creators and spectators alike with its content, emotion, and social significance.

Nonreaders and schoolphobics turned into literary critics and museum-quality artists. Not bad for a starving artist in search of a day job.

What's the Big Idea About the Arts?

Great teachers know that there's one huge reason to embed music, drama, movement, and the visual arts in every aspect of their curriculum: The arts are ways of knowing. They're systems for making and expressing meaning that give kids an alternative way to probe and discuss school subjects. For example, if you are studying the Civil War, you might launch your studies by having your students study the heart-wrenching photographs of Mathew Brady, examine recruitment posters for the Confederate army, and listen to Civil War songs. The resulting discussion may include references to the overblown claims in the poster compared to the ragged, shoeless soldiers. Your students may sense the hope and pride in the lyrics, which is totally absent in the desperate expressions of the young recruits. They'll probably wonder if the lyricist and poster designer ever saw action on a battlefield, and what they would have made of Brady's photographs.

The benefits of having the arts in your curriculum are so numerous that it boggles the mind to see how thoroughly they've been eradicated from many school systems. Consider for a moment, the Top Ten reasons for embedding music, drama, the visual arts, and movement into your day.

The Arts

1. Provide a universal language that transcends race, culture, and time.
2. Give students a way to communicate without speaking or writing.
3. Offer alternative ways to present content material, so all students can learn.
4. Activate multiple intelligences to help students learn in different ways.
5. Promote active learning.
6. Create opportunities for self-expression using mind and body.
7. Develop higher-order thinking skills of analysis, synthesis, evaluation, and problem solving.
8. Are essential tools for constructing alternative assessments.
9. Build our awareness and appreciation of other cultures.
10. Bring a sense of adventure, spontaneity, and joy to learning in your class.

The arts are stealth strategies for learning. They lure indifferent students into trying, and shine a spotlight on kids who have spent their entire school careers on the academic fringe. When schools include the arts, they also achieve:

- Improved academic test scores
- Improved school attendance, fewer dropouts, and increased graduation rates
- Reduced discipline problems
- Improved school climate and teacher renewal
- Greater awareness of art careers among students
- Improved quality of life for all students, not just for the elite or the talented

Now let me be clear. When I talk about including art in your classroom, I don't mean you-get-to-draw-on-Friday-if-you're-good art. I'm not talking about art appreciation, which treats the arts as rarified objects or special events. Then it's back to business as usual—which is to say a high-calorie diet of art-free academics. No. I'm talking about the physical act of working in an art form, which activates large, highly specialized regions of the brain; art used as another voice with which kids communicate their unique ideas about their work in your room. The arts are tools for active connecting, not passive spectating, and a superb medium for thinking and expression. As such, they should be a daily occurrence in your classroom.

The Brain, Learning, and the Arts

In the not-too-distant past, art and scholarship were thought to be antithetical. People would say, "She's very artistic," as if referring to another species. There were smart people, not-so-smart people, and artists. Happily, in 1983 Howard Gardner put a serious crimp in that point of view with his theory of multiple intelligences. Four of the seven original intelligences he identified—fully half of the working brain—are focused on the arts. Visual, kinesthetic, musical, and verbal intelligence provide us with painters, sculptors, printmakers, photographers, graphic designers, Web designers, dancers, mimes, composers, conductors, tuba-jockeys, DJs, playwrights, novelists, screenwriters, directors, and actors. Each is as smart in his or her own way as a biochemist or accountant.

As a great teacher, your challenge is to get smarter about recognizing those arts-based intelligences in your kids and then put them to work for you. Suppose you see a child hunched over a math paper, doing something that looks improbably industrious. Upon closer inspection you discover it's not the math that fascinates him after all. He's etching tiny geometric embellishments around the perimeter of his page. You could blow your cool and sentence him to eraser duty, or recognize that you have a visual-spatial learner on your hands, and help him devise ways to use art to understand math concepts. Or you may have a perpetual hummer or tapper in your class, and the vocalizing intensifies whenever you pass out written assignments. Those are actually clues to musical intelligence, not attempts to drive you insane.

Chapter 3 takes a concise look at all nine of the intelligences that Howard Gardner described. Now let's spend some time exploring strategies and activities that capitalize on all the ways your kids are art-smart.

Helping Students Learn Through Drama

When some teachers hear the word *drama*, they imagine a red-bewigged child screeching, "Tuh-mah-ruh, tuh-mah-ruh, I luv yuh, tuh-mah-ruh. . . ." It makes them want to pounce on the ibuprofen. Too often drama just means the headache and hassle of a school play, which can consume more time and effort than a Broadway extravaganza. Relax. This section is not about staging *The Wizard of Oz* one more time. The goal is to help you discover ways to use drama as a tool for learning and assessment. In this case, drama means physical movement, vocal action, and mental concentration. No screeching.

If your kids are anywhere near average, they watch approximately forty hours of television a week, during which they've unconsciously absorbed basic notions about character, dialogue, plot, conflict, and setting, along with the lyrics to forty-seven annoying commercials. So they already know a lot about drama. You can harness that knowledge to achieve your classroom goals, using strategies as simple as pantomime or improvisation, which allow kinesthetic kids to translate curricular ideas into actions. Smart but unresponsive students are often galvanized by a more theatrical approach to learning that has built-in opportunities for action, creativity, and emotional expression. They get to act out instead of act up, and all of you reap the benefits.

The Two Best Things About Putting Drama in Your Curriculum

1. Drama brings stories to life, enriching literature, poetry, history, and social science.
2. Drama is a vehicle to convey ideas and emotions, strengthening oral and written expression, thinking, and social skills.

I'm from Missouri

Most teachers read aloud. Really good teachers do so daily, and they incorporate comprehension checks to make sure their kids are tuned in. They'll usually ask something like: Tell me how the main character felt when he saw his fishing boat sink. The problem with this approach is that it's slow. Only one kid at a time can reply. The others are in suspended animation—unless they're unraveling a sweater cuff or prospecting for lint to pass the time during pauses in the story.

Show Me is an alternative approach to comprehension checks that lets your kids move, gesture, and make faces to show you what they understand about a text or a story. You tap directly into kinesthetic and spatial intelligence, and all your kids can respond at once. That includes your second-language learners, who can demonstrate their receptive language levels without ever saying a word. *Show Me* is simple. Just say something like, "Show me what Frog did when he discovered he'd lost his button." Appropriate student responses would be holding their heads, pacing up and down, wringing hands, scanning the ground, making a worried or sad face. Kids move, mime, gesture, and mug—all dramatic skills—with the single purpose of showing what they know.

It's so much fun that they return to listening with increased focus, waiting for the next round. Repeat these "show me" pauses throughout the reading. Here are some other examples:

- Show how the main character felt when . . .
- Show what the boy did when he saw the bear.
- Show what grandma did when the swarm of bees flew across the yard.
- Show how the weather changed from morning to night on the day of the storm.
- Show me how you think the judge looked during Jake's testimony. What about the jury?

This brand of drama is spontaneous and takes a matter of seconds because all of your kids get to be active and creative at the same time. But they're focused on your learning goals, not on performance for its own sake. At the end of the story, work together to develop a list of verbs that describe their actions. Post the list as part of your word bank.

Karaoke Without the Music

People seem to either love or hate karaoke. The enthusiasts—some would say exhibitionists—can't get enough of the physical and emotional satisfaction that comes from performing a song really well, without the performance anxiety. With lyrics at the ready, and a great back-up band, they can just focus on belting out a tune that can dent the back wall.

That's the appeal of Readers Theatre, too. Kids get to portray the characters in a story, without the terror of memorizing and promptly forgetting their lines, because they have a script in hand and lots of time to sharpen their read-aloud skills. Some forms of Readers Theatre are very spare—two or more readers simply stand or sit in a semicircle, holding their scripts and reading aloud. But if you want to capitalize on multiple intelligences, encourage your kids to add simple props and gestures. That way kinesthetic and visual kids get more involved in creating their characters. These elaborations also give the audience visual and kinetic clues to help them follow the story, rather than just watching the equivalent of a radio play.

Now here's a way to transform a singsong recitation into a blood and gutsy, literary event: Choose a great script. Then really zero in on the dramatic quality of the reading. Help your kids crawl inside their characters' minds by asking them to think about how their characters feel in the story. Elicit words like *frustrated, angry, depressed, stuck-up, terrified*. Then ask: How does your body feel when you experience that emotion? How would your voice sound?

Help kids get in touch with the visceral, emotional subtext of the story resonating in them, so they can project that into their reading. Preparing for that type of performance forces kids to scour the text. They need to discover the author's purpose for telling the story, the overall mood, and the particular traits of their character. That requires repeated readings, so kids go way beyond decoding, to comprehension and interpretation. As a bonus, they internalize complex sentence structures and the sound of well-crafted prose, so their writing gets a boost.

Nurturing actors is one element in a successful Readers Theatre project, but don't overlook the powerful learning that can result when kids take on the role of acting coach. Every class has kids with great interpersonal skills. Enlist them to listen as the "readers" practice their lines and give them feedback. Coaching looks easy, but it takes a lot of concentration to do it well. Coaches must focus on the content and delivery, and then articulate their observations in a clear and diplomatic manner. To ensure the coaches' effectiveness, teach them how to make suggestions using phrases like: Maybe you could try. . . ? It was really good when you. . . . I liked the part where you. . . . What if you said it this way?

Adding physicality, vocal expression, and emotions to a piece of literature through Readers Theatre zaps the characters, dialogue, and action from two-dimensional scribbles trapped on a flat page, to three-dimensional images with shape, size, and guts. Kids think: Oh, that's what the story looks like. This trains students to visualize other texts on their own. When they develop the habit of "seeing" text as pictures in their heads, comprehension and retention soar.

Say What?

Dramatizing ideas creates an excellent foundation for writing assignments because drama creates images that can be translated into prose or dialogue. *Say What?* is a dramatic technique that helps kids learn to write dialogue—a crucial element missing from so many student compositions. Here's the process for *Say What?* Describe a simple scenario to your students, such as: A girl brings home a stray cat and tries to convince her mom to let her keep it. Ask volunteers to act out the scene, emphasizing what the characters say as well as their gestures and actions. This activity taps into verbal, spatial, kinesthetic, and interpersonal intelligences. Encourage whining, begging, and emphatic retorts. Have some fun. Then have all your students write their impressions of the scene, using quotation marks to highlight the dialogue. Here are some scenarios for starters:

- Two kids are playing checkers. One accuses the other of cheating and they argue.

- A child tries to convince a parent to let him watch just one more TV show before bed.
- A student forgets her homework and tries to explain to the teacher.
- A kid hates his lunch and tries to trade up for more interesting food.
- Three kids are going to the movies together but they can't agree on a film.
- A student tries to convince a friend to join a soccer team, but the other is afraid of looking like a fool in public.

The goal of these exchanges is for students to practice spontaneous dialogue, and then incorporate it in their writing. Use Pair Share to give all students a chance to read their scenes and get feedback.

Helping Students Learn Through Movement

You'll notice this section is not called Dance. I'm deliberately avoiding the word because I don't want to scare away the two-left-feet crowd prematurely. And *dance* paints a very specific picture—music, a choreographer, and precise steps that one must learn, practice, and perform. It suggests expertise. Some can. Some can't. But movement is as elemental as breathing, so it can be incorporated into your learning routine with very little experience and big rewards.

You may be thinking, "You want me to encourage movement? Are you nuts?" Right. Planning for movement could seem insane or at the very least redundant, since many teachers spend large chunks of the day trying to bribe or rein their students into a nonkinetic state. But there's a lot of learning that can be coaxed from a twitching tangle of arms and legs, and you don't have to be related to Baryshnikov to pull it off. This section will give you ideas on using movement to stimulate intelligence and academic performance. Tap shoes are optional.

Movement is divided into two big categories: *locomotor* and *nonlocomotor* or *axial*. Locomotor is movement that covers yardage. To run, hop, gallop, slide, skip (either forward or backward) is locomotion. Axial movement means that the body stays in one place but bends, twists, stretches, or swings in space. As a purely physical activity, movement improves strength, flexibility, balance, coordination, and reflexes. Plus, when kids move they burn calories, which is no small accomplishment in a society where childhood obesity, high cholesterol, and heart disease are major health concerns.

But the mental gains are even more impressive than the muscle tone. Even the simplest experiments in movement require kids to do motor planning, invent moves, observe themselves, and make decisions. They work by trial and error, using kinesthetic intelligence to create patterns in space. When kids dabble in choreography, especially with a partner or group, they use spatial intelligence to coordinate their bodies and relate through gestures. In its most advanced form, movement taps into interpersonal and intrapersonal intelligence to communicate ideas, tell a story, or express emotions.

The Two Best Things About Putting Movement in Your Curriculum

1. Movement lets students explore ideas about time, space, energy, lines, and shapes, which helps them understand geometry, art, architecture, engineering, physics, and athletics.

2. Movement lets students express ideas and emotions with their bodies, which helps them understand concepts about psychology, history, and literature.

Galloping Grammar

There are some kids who can talk intelligently for days, but struggle mightily when it's time to put words on paper. Their first drafts are a torrent of syllables, with nary a capital letter, comma, or period in sight. And forget about spacing—you can't even wedge a dime between most of their words, so the whole page reads like the Rosetta Stone. No matter how many times you talk about periods and capitals, no matter how many times they parrot back the rules, it's not happening. Clearly their ears are not the portal for your message.

So help these kids learn punctuation and spacing with their muscles, joints, and sinews. Here's the basic strategy. Students say a sentence out loud and simultaneously make a movement to go with each word or punctuation mark. Try to picture this. They start with their arms high in the air to show that the sentence starts with a capital letter. Then they take one long pace for each word, so they can feel the separateness. Add a clap for even more emphasis. They pause to stand on one foot for commas, and end by jumping with both feet together to make the period. Challenge your kids to invent movements for question marks and exclamation points. Encourage improvisation for the best results.

Take Your Thesaurus for a Walk

Kids can learn about synonyms and the nuances of language through movement, too, while exploring the wonders of a thesaurus. Start with a word like *walk*—overused to the point of exhaustion. Help your kids discover all the other ways they can describe ambulation by introducing them to Roget and the delights of a neon vocabulary. List all the words they find that could mean *walk*—*saunter, amble, stomp, tip-toe, sneak, waddle, limp, lurch, shuffle, stagger, toddle, jog, dart,* and *wander.* Then ask them to act out each word. It will be a challenge for kids to modify their motions to express the subtle differences between these verbs, but here's where your kinesthetic kids shine, and you'll probably have some great laughs in the process. What's the effect of hearing, seeing, and acting out unfamiliar words? Your students will inevitably upgrade their written expression, if only for the fun of inventing a sentence for *lurch* or *saunter.* You can use this process to bury lifeless words like *mad, sad,* and *glad,* replacing them with *furious, delighted, ecstatic, depressed, frustrated, jealous,* and *shocked.* Using juicy words is one of the true delights of the writer's craft. Movement can speed this epiphany.

Dynamic Science

Many concepts in science have motion at their core, but they fail to capture kinesthetic and spatial kids' attention because we insist on reducing science to a lifeless paragraph in a text. You can restore the dynamic element to science simply by having students demonstrate through movement their understanding of concepts such as atomic structure, the three stages of matter, heliotropism, molecular response to heat and cold, or the rotation of the planets around the sun.

Scarf Dancing

This is a very quiet approach to expressive movement that stimulates spatial intelligence. Give your kids a scarf to hold as they move. This simple prop lets them see the lines and shapes their bodies create, like dragging sparklers through the darkness on the Fourth of July. Scarf dancing is also a great way to help visual and kinesthetic kids learn the alphabet, review phonics, or practice handwriting. Picture this. Instead of asking your kids to write capital B on blank paper for the umpteenth time, or write the letter that sounds like *m-m-m-m,* give them scarves, space them around the room, and go to it. When you say "Draw a capital B," they reach and sway and suck in oxygen, all the while staring at sinuous lines in the air. Large muscles participate in the task, activating muscle memory. It's fun, so kids try harder and longer. What could be bad about this? If you don't have scarves, visit your local thrift store where they have boxes of them very cheap.

Nickel and Dime Tap Shoes

I remember my first tap shoes—huge, armored, and black patent leather. I graffitied the back patio for weeks with my earnest efforts. It didn't matter that

I wasn't particularly good. Shirley Temple, Fred Astaire, and I had something in common: noisy feet. That's what kids like about tap dancing—the noise. Tapping is supremely kinesthetic. Intense sensations arrive through the joints and muscles, amplified by a range of sharp, scratchy sounds.

If you love to dance, here's a great way to share your passion with your kids. Start a tap dance academy right in your room. No tap shoes? No problem! Kids just need an old pair of shoes, some coins, and white glue. That's it. Let them figure out the arrangement of coins on the soles, and once the glue really dries, they're ready to go. The playground makes a perfect stage to strut their stuff.

But there's more. My colleague, Lisa Bartoli, discovered a way to help her kids master their multiplication tables without all the drudgery. They pull on their tap shoes and head out to the playground, where they march while calling out the number sequences—2, 4, 6, 8 and back down again, until they have driven the multiplication patterns into their brains through their feet. Then her kids invented tap dances to accompany chanting the times tables—"Two times three is six"—stomp, twirl. They're the champion multipliers in the school, and probably the only kids you'll ever meet who think of multiplication and smile.

Helping Students Learn Through Music

One of the greatest discoveries of infancy is the power to make noise. First there's the myriad of mouth sounds babies produce. When grip and coordination improve, they graduate to smacking the table with anything in their reach. The sudden sharp rap of a spoon delights them. That's why they do it over and over until parents want to scream.

Finding, creating, and using sounds intrigues kids of all ages. They drag sticks along fences, smack tree trunks, and delight in pounding almost any hollow object. The rip of Velcro shoe fasteners has been known to reach symphonic levels in primary classrooms, especially at rug time.

Since teachers spend a fair amount of time trying to quell the natural symphony that kids generate even when they're trying to be quiet, you may think it wise to skip this section. And there are plenty of reasons why you can't do music—no instruments, no tape recorders, no time, can't carry a tune in a bucket. But music making helps kids develop mentally and emotionally. When they attack a tin drum, jiggle a tambourine, or wheeze into a harmonica, they're exploring melody, harmony, rhythm, and tone and the patterns that form the structure of math. Music can help kids who struggle with language express intense emotions or moods. Using instruments as simple as a kazoo or a metal pot and spoon, you can convince inventive, active students that your classroom is the place where they can be seen and heard.

The Two Best Things About Putting Music in Your Curriculum

1. Music brings the sounds of other eras and cultures into your classroom, enlivening history, anthropology, social science, and multicultural studies.
2. Music is a vehicle for creative invention, expression, and performance.

Can't Even Play the Radio

You don't have to have an ounce of musical intelligence to tap into the benefits of music in your classroom, and apparently the benefits are significant. In one school, teachers added background music to a study hall and found that it contributed to substantial growth in reading comprehension. Another school found that playing music reduced inappropriate behavior on school buses, and calmed hyperactive children and adults. It also seems that music stimulates the regions of the brain responsible for memory, motor control, timing, and language. The impact of music on early learners seems to be even more profound. Preschool and primary children exhibit growth in math and language when singing and music are regular parts of the curriculum. So if you do nothing else, get a radio, tape or CD player, and float some tunes over your kids' heads while they're working. When you shift from one activity to another, change to a lively composition, and let them march, slide, tip-toe, or gyrate to the music as they transition. Even the dawdlers will be more animated, and focusing on creative movement reduces the chances that kids will attempt to use each other as sports equipment.

Rhythm—No Blues

Making music draws on kinesthetic intelligence, but it also has a mental health benefit. The sheer physicality of performing music can act as a stimulant and relieve stress. When your kids get mired in academics and need a lift, bring out the rhythm band and take a music break. Actually, you don't even need instruments to use music as a mood elevator. Your classroom is a veritable orchestra pit—dozens of surfaces that will give up interesting sounds when kids pat, tap, or rub them. They can drum with pencils, shake boxes of paper clips, crank the pencil sharpener, zip and unzip jackets, open and close a three-ring binder, and the beat goes on. You'll create an energetic, spontaneous classroom environment if you make invented music part of your learning plan. Just stop everything when kids least expect it. Tell them to grab an invented instrument. Then clap a rhythm, sing a simple song, or put on a CD and have them play along for two minutes. Just two minutes can release pent-up energy and refuel the brain for classwork. Soon you'll discover that these breaks don't take time, they make time—for learning.

The Body Orchestra

There's more music to be made with the addition of hand, foot, and mouth sounds. Stamping, tapping, clumping, shuffling, brushing, marching, and jumping in a variety of shoes can produce a veritable fiesta of sounds. And don't forget tongue clicking, clucking, whistling, oohing, aahing, and doo-wopping, just to name a few. This can become a real adventure as kids work arduously with their tongue, lips, teeth, cheeks, and vocal chords to produce designer sounds that can be used for music breaks or as sound effects in read-aloud stories or student skits.

The Science of Sound

Sound is one of those ubiquitous elements that's tough to analyze because there's nothing to see. But you can make music a bit more visible by helping your kids to set up a Soda Bottle Symphony. Gather eight large glass wine bottles. Measure a small amount of water into the first container—maybe four ounces, then double that amount for the next bottle. Strike the two bottles and let your kids discuss what they hear. Let them finish filling the bottles, increasing each by four ounces, so that the final container has thirty-two ounces. The result is a scale that can be played by striking the bottles lightly. Encourage experimentation and invention. Some bright student will wonder out loud, "What if we dumped the water and used tomato juice?" Then vegetable oil, syrup, and dish detergent. Press your kids to be very precise about their observations and pose theories for the difference in the sounds they produce. Set aside time for water glass compositions to be performed for the whole class. Students may want to invent a notation system to preserve their compositions.

Recycled Orchestra

Once upon a time, every school had closets full of rhythm instruments and a full orchestra for eager young musicians. If you've searched high and low and can't find so much as a pitch pipe, let your kids make their own instruments with recycled materials. Then they can play along with selections of multicultural music or move on to composing their own pieces. Once your kids get the knack of music making, the variations are endless. Try the following suggestions.

- Oatmeal box drum with wooden spoon drumsticks

- Milk carton or bleach bottle struck with chopsticks
- Tin cans filled with varying amounts of rice, sunflower seeds, nuts, rocks, pasta, or beans
- Toilet paper tubes with objects inside then tape placed over the ends
- Two plastic cups taped together at the lips with rice, beans, or dried peas inside
- Two tea strainers taped together with marbles inside
- Rubber bands around a box or stretched between two doorknobs
- A scrub brush dragged over a piece of screen or the rough sole of a shoe
- Keys on a shoestring
- Bells sewn on old gloves
- Kazoo, New Year's Eve paper whistle, or noise makers

Songs from Historic Periods

Songs are a powerful way to teach about people and events in the past. Analyzing lyrics can help children sense the hope and hardship of slaves, or the optimism of novice revolutionaries.

American Memory (http://memory.loc.gov/ammem/award97/ncdhtml /hasmhome.html), sponsored by the Library of Congress, is a huge and utterly amazing website, loaded with resources for this adventure. Start with The Historic American Sheet Music collection, which presents multiple perspectives on American history and culture through a variety of music types including minstrel songs, protest songs, patriotic and political songs, plantation songs, spirituals, dance music, songs from vaudeville and musicals, and songs from World War I. The collection is particularly strong in Civil War songs and music.

Helping Students Learn Through Art

When I was about two and a half years old, I'd sit in my highchair long after mealtime, content to scrawl tiny lines on bits of paper. My grandmother thought my stillness was a sign of anemia and urged my mother to bundle me off to the doctor. Mom sensibly resisted and by three years old, I'd moved on to my sister's wooden easel. So I really can't recall a time when I didn't draw or paint. I still do, rarely, and instantly remember how much I love the scrape of pen on paper, and the deep, almost magical pleasure of watching an image slowly emerging from nowhere.

You may enjoy art as much as I do, but still cringe at the thought of an afternoon of painting with twenty to thirty kids. Who can blame you for avoiding lessons that require a fair amount of prep time and even more cleanup, with nothing to show for it but wasted materials and bad art? But there are other kinds of art that take a minimum of preparation and produce maximum brain development. The process and the product are all about learning. With a few simple strategies, the visual arts can become the unofficial second language in your classroom.

The Two Best Things About Putting the Visual Arts in Your Curriculum

1. Art brings the images and objects of other eras and cultures into your classroom, adding details and dimension to history, anthropology, social science, and multicultural studies.
2. Art is a medium for ideas and emotions, allowing students to create images of things that do not exist.

No-Mess Outdoor Art

Painting is one of the purest delights of early childhood. Accidental color mixing is nothing short of magical. But painting can be messy, so it's a perfect outdoor activity. You don't need those heavy wooden easels or even a tabletop. It's easy to make a hanging easel with a piece of stiff cardboard and a flat wooden hanger with a metal handle that rotates. Glue the hanger on the cardboard so the hook sticks up over the top edge of the board. Hook the handle on a fence, railing, or gate. Two clothespins will hold the paper in place. Set the cartons of paint on the ground in a bucket or shoebox so they won't tip over. Then kids can paint away with only the pavement running for cover. Even that can be protected with newspaper, plastic garbage bags, or an old tarp.

Disappearing Paintings. All you need for this painting activity are water and brushes. Gather up toothbrushes, pastry brushes, house painting brushes, old makeup brushes, bottle brushes, and a few buckets of water. Your kids can paint water images on the sidewalk, brick wall, or playground and watch their masterpieces evaporate. When they're all done, empty the buckets into the garden. No mess. Lots of fun. But don't stop with pictures. Do your phonics or spelling lessons outside. Give all your kids a brush and a cup of water. As you call out buh, buh, buh, they paint giant Bs, capital and lowercase. Using large muscles for literacy tasks helps kinesthetic and visual learners retain more information longer because they build up muscle memory. Use this to practice for spelling tests, or have a competition to see who can write the longest sentence. Kids really reach for every adjective and adverb when they're trying to write a ten-foot sentence.

Chalk. Drawing on the sidewalk or playground with chalk is a full-body experience. As the chalk stumbles and grinds over the rough surface, it sends shock waves all the way up the arm. The dull, pedestrian surface suddenly comes alive and there's virtually no space limit. Kids can chalk from the classroom to the cafeteria with complete abandon. Any kind of chalk will do, but look for the chunky sidewalk chalk because it's easy for little kids to grip and it doesn't break. Time, rain, a hose or a broom will erase their gallery or prose. Yes, chalk is an irresistible tool for literacy.

No-Mess Indoor Art

Lots of kids want to make art but they're afraid to paint or draw. Actually, they're just afraid to fail saying, "My paintings look stupid. I can't draw people." Kids also go through a phase around eight or nine years old when they aren't happy with their pictures unless they're very realistic, and few of them possess that skill. But they can make wonderful no-paint images if you introduce them to the art of collage, quilts, and masks.

Collage. Collage is a process that combines found images to create a work of art. It's a cut-and-paste approach to art that costs exactly nothing because the materials are all recycled: a pile of old magazines, newspapers, letters, photos, cloth, colored paper, wrapping paper, bark, pressed flowers and leaves, comic books, junk mail, ribbons, box tops, labels, lace, gum wrappers, and of course, scissors and glue. Kids love collage because they can create realistic looking images of almost anything they can imagine. It is especially appealing to kids with a quirky sense of humor. Using this technique, they can easily create surreal, fantasy, or humorous art. Bodies with two heads, faces with three eyes, medieval creatures such as griffins and gargoyles.

Making collage portraits is a wonderful way for kids to show who they are, inside out. Explain that a face can't tell all the really important things about a person—memories, dreams, talents, ideas, interests. But a collage portrait can. Have your kids outline a head on stiff paper, then fill it in with all the images that tell about who they are. They may want to mix features—eyes, nose, and mouth, among the objects. They can include words, phrases, advertisements, products, and patches of pure color. The portrait can be used as the cover for a journal or portfolio. It's also a great starting point for an autobiographical writing project.

Quilts

Throughout history, people have designed and used quilts for different purposes: to keep warm, to decorate their homes, to express political views, to remember a loved one, or to tell an important story through pictures. Appliqué and other old quilting techniques were brought to the United States by slaves from Senegal, Ghana, Nigeria, and Angola, and influenced quilting in the American South. Harriet Powers (1837–1911) was a famous African American quilter. Contemporary artist Faith Ringgold, author of *Tar Beach,* continues in the tradition with her painted and sewn quilts, which hang in many museums.

Traditional quilts are made with cloth—hundreds or thousands of pieces joined in elaborate patterns. If you want to do cloth quilts without investing months in the process, let your kids draw or paint on cotton or felt and hand-sew or glue the pieces together. Or bring a portable sewing machine in and have a parent or aide teach your kids to sew simple seams to join their blocks. Alternatively, you can make paper quilts with colored construction paper, wrapping paper, magazine illustrations, paint, marking pens, and tape to achieve a similar effect. Either way, students experience the process of making a single aesthetic object out of many small pieces. Quilts are excellent assessment tools, since they give visual learners a way to represent the most important images culled from what they've studied. Since quilts are often collaborative efforts, you may want to propose a class quilt, where each student creates a block as the culmination for a major unit of study.

The Edsitement website (http://edsitement.neh.gov/view_lesson_plan .asp?id=241) has several sections that can augment quilt studies in your classroom. Look at the links for History in Quilts and Family and Friendship in Quilts. The lessons in these units can help your kids recognize how people of different cultures and time periods used cloth-based art forms to preserve their traditions and history.

Masks

Masks intrigue people because they hide and transform at the same time. Kids who are shy or working on a second-language acquisition often find the courage to speak when they're disguised as animals, villains, heroes, or monsters. Masks are a powerful way to develop narrative ideas and speaking skills in all students. First they have to visualize a character and create a face to match. They can lift the inspiration for their masked characters from familiar stories, historic events, or literature. Then they need to make the masks talk, so they write dialogue. When it's time to perform, they can hide behind the mask and use a big voice, mimic animal sounds, and express a range of emotions, protected and liberated by a false face.

Before you start making masks with your kids, take some time to explore what students already know about masks by asking:

- What is a mask?

- What are masks used for?
- When have you worn a mask?
- Who else wears masks?
- Where have you seen masks used?
- Why do you think people like to wear masks?

Discuss how masks are used in the United States and in other cultures. Link the masking tradition to your history lessons by examining masks used by Native Americans. Ask your students if they know that the people who staged the Boston Tea Party before the Revolutionary War wore buckram masks or painted their faces to protect themselves from prosecution.

Paper is an excellent mask material because it's malleable and accepts attachments easily. It's also plentiful, cheap, or free. Think recycling and you're on your way. For starters, gather up shopping bags, paper plates, large envelopes, wrapping paper, newspaper, construction paper, advertising flyers, and magazines. Cereal boxes also make a great foundation for a mask. Just add scissors, glue, tape, staplers, marking pens, and imagination.

- *Five Minute Masks*   A pair of sunglasses or goggles become a simple mask when bits of paper, feathers, sequins, or yarn are added. Kids can make dog or cat masks starting with industrial paper masks used to filter out dust or paint fumes. Add pipe cleaner whiskers and a tongue. Other masks can be made from skin-diving, hockey, or ski masks embellished with hats or wigs.

- *Figure 8 Masks*   This mask looks like old-fashioned opera glasses or a lorgnette—a figure eight on a stick. Cut a rectangle of paper to cover eyes and nose from ear to ear. Draw a block numeral eight and cut out the eye openings. Hold the mask in place with a piece of elastic around the back of the head.

- *Paper Bag Masks*   Giant shopping bag masks are fun because kids can really hide inside. Make the bag sit all the way down on the head by trimming it to fit around the shoulders or fringing the bottom. Cut wide eyeholes so kids can move safely and a big mouth for easy breathing. Then let kids add earrings, hair, glasses, eyelashes and eyebrows, freckles, and rosy cheeks. Try adding pipe cleaners, yarn, paper strips, curling ribbon, cotton, steel wool, or string. Cut ears, lips, teeth, and eyebrows out of a magazine to make a collage face. Add a variety of hats—baseball, fireman, feathered—to define the character.

- *Tin Foil*   A very simple, contour mask can be made by pressing a sheet of tin foil gently over the face and smoothing the foil along the nose ridge, chin, and under the jaw. Then press in where the eyes need to be, remove the mask and cut generous holes. Make nostril holes and a mouth slit if the character needs to speak. These masks can be tinted with colored felt marking pens. Everyone can be in disguise in minutes.

Recognition

Recognition is often in short supply in elementary schools. You teach amazing lessons all day but you don't get showered with roses on your way out the door. Kids knock themselves out but may only get a passing nod—especially the artists. But since you know that the arts are ways of knowing and ways of showing, why not make a big deal about the talented kids in your class? Mount an exhibit. Art exhibits are exciting and your kids can do most of the work. Let them decide which pieces they want to include in the show and be sure everyone has something on display. Older kids can be in charge of mounting, framing, and hanging the show. They can design invitations and write press releases. Show them the art announcements and reviews in your local paper as samples. Invite parents, administrators, board members, and as many local artists as you can round up to the exhibit. Kids talking art with real artists is the most authentic assessment you can devise.

Getting published is a very, very big deal. That's how professional artists and writers get their ideas out into the world. Students achieve a level of self-esteem that you can't buy or rent when they see their work in print. Help them research the process, starting with *Skipping Stones*, an award-winning, international, nonprofit magazine that showcases child authors and artists. To find out more, write to:

> Skipping Stones Magazine
> P.O. Box 3939
> Eugene, Oregon 97403–0939

Enclose a legal-sized, self-addressed stamped envelope and ask for their guidelines and brochure. Try to get a copy of *The Market Guide for Young Artists and Photographers* by Kathy Henderson. It contains more than 100 markets and contests for people under eighteen years old. This could be the new bible for some of your students. And remember, while they're scouring the pages for contests with cash prizes, they're reading with high comprehension.

When All Is Said and Done

Busy teachers rarely plow through the National Standards on anything, and when the do, they're likely to discover that it's about as exciting as watching paint dry. The major benefit for most readers is a quick snooze. However, the National Standards for Arts Education are remarkable for their vivid imagery, passionate language, and dire predictions for societies who ignore the arts. Take a look for yourself.

The arts have been a part of us from the very beginning. Since nomadic peoples first sang and danced for their ancestry, since hunters first painted their quarry on the walls of caves, since parents first acted out the stories of heroes for their children, the arts have described, defined, and deepened human experience. All peoples, everywhere, have an abiding need for meaning—to connect time and space, experience and event, body and spirit, intellect and emotion. People create art to make these connections, to express the otherwise inexpressible. A society and people without the arts are unimaginable, as breathing would be without air. Such a society and people could not long survive.

> All art involves the physical organs—the eye and hand, the ear and voice: yet it is something more than the mere technical skill required by the organs of expression. It involves an idea, a thought, a spiritual rendering of things and yet it is other than any number of ideas by themselves. It is a living union of thought and the instrument of expression.
>
> —John Dewey

The arts provide a tool for appreciating all of our cultures and dealing with life. They're a basic way to understand ourselves and others. More important, the arts give students the tools to learn in every possible way—not just reading, writing, and calculating, but also feeling and moving, drawing and singing, dancing and creating, not as entertainment or relaxation, but as a unique way of developing all their intelligences.

Resources

Books

Gardner, Howard. 1984. *Art, Mind, and Brain: A Cognitive Approach to Creativity*. New York: Basic Books.
———. 1990. *Art Education and Human Development*. Los Angeles: J. Paul Getty Trust Publications.
Grady, Sharon. 2000. *Drama and Diversity*. Portsmouth, NH: Heinemann.
Jensen, Eric. 2000. *Arts with the Brain in Mind*. Alexandria, VA: ASCD.

Online Resources

Artsedge

Curricular materials, professional resources, and lesson plans on a huge range of arts-related topics and integrated lesson plans from the Kennedy Center for the Arts. http://artsedge.kennedy-center.org

Edsitement

National Endowment for the Humanities' teacher resources on art and culture, literature and languages, history and social science. http://edsitement.neh.gov/

Yale–New Haven Teachers Institute

Hundreds of detailed lessons on the arts and ideas that can help you integrate art appreciation with other content areas. www.yale.edu/ynhti/curriculum/indexes/a.x.html

SECRET #10

Great Teachers Are Insurrectionists

Learning Through Social Action

In This Chapter:

- Meet Barbara Henry, Ruby Bridges' Teacher
- What's the Big Idea About Social Justice?
- What Kids Learn from Social Justice
- Planting the Seed
- Taking Sides: How to Choose a Social Justice Project
- Prepping Students for Action: Politics 101
- A Social Activist's Toolbox
- Getting Smarter About Social Justice Through Primary Source Documents
- Literature and Social Justice
- Click for a Cause
- The Downside of Social Justice
- Improve Yourself, Improve Your Community

Meet Barbara Henry, Ruby Bridges' Teacher

When the superintendent of the New Orleans School District called Barbara Henry in November of 1960, he didn't say, "I have the perfect job for you."

But it was.

He also didn't say she would have to run a gauntlet of parents, demonstrators, reporters, and police to get to the front door of her new school. Nor that there would be a cordon of jeering, abusive, sign-toting housewives who would gain international fame as "the cheerleaders."

The city was holding its breath. No one could predict that opposition to school integration would be so intense that Barbara Henry would have federal marshals posted outside her classroom door for a year and a police escort each afternoon when she headed for home.

The superintendent simply asked this new bride, recently arrived from Boston, if she would like to teach first grade. Barbara was thrilled because she had experience in first grade and felt secure about the curriculum. Then came the question she would never forget. "Would it make any difference if it was in an integrated school?" Her first thought was, "What a strange thing to ask me."

Barbara Henry was an avid reader. She loved history and politics and followed current events in the daily newspapers. In the south of the 1960s, that meant freedom riders, sit-ins, boycotts, demonstrations, and violence. So Barbara knew that the September deadline for integrating the New Orleans schools had come and gone unheeded, but to any outside observer the end of segregation was near. What puzzled her about the superintendent's question was why any teacher would mind an integrated classroom. What did race have to do with teaching?

Barbara Henry had been preparing all her life for her role in this momentous event—preparing to be the teacher of six-year-old Ruby Bridges, the first African American child to attend all white William Frantz Elementary School.

Barbara was raised in Boston. When it was time for junior high school, she went to Boston Latin—an historic public school in the heart of the city.

> Kids came from all over the city. From seventh grade on, I was in classes with immigrants from Russia and Poland. There were black kids, Irish, Italians from the North End, Catholics, Jews, and Protestants. Kids came from everywhere. There was never any down-looking on anyone. It was a melting pot. Everybody was eager to learn. No matter what race, color or creed, I saw the other students as being just like me because they were all willing to learn. We did everything together. There was no distinction, so without being explicitly taught about racism or tolerance, we learned to appreciate what we had in common.

Barbara's multicultural education continued once she became a teacher. "I spent two years teaching the children of Air Force personnel in Europe. The service was integrated, so I taught children of every race. Whoever was in the service, I taught their children. And it was a wonderful experience. So I just could not believe the social injustice of the events in New Orleans. To me it was outrageous. How could any one deny a child an education?" She was truly puzzled.

When Barbara arrived at the William Frantz School on November 14, her puzzlement turned to shock and indignation. The scene outside the school was chaos. Police kept a surge of demonstrators behind wooden barricades.

Reporters, photographers, and cameramen jostled for positions on the sidewalk, forming the embryo of a media frenzy that would bring national attention and shame to New Orleans. Barbara and her husband pressed through the mob, cloaked by their whiteness and air of purpose. "I thought, 'How am I ever going to get to that front door?' But we were the same color as the mob, so they didn't know who was entering the building." At the barricades, Barbara gave her name to the police. "Of course, they were adamantly opposed to what was happening, so they weren't particularly enthusiastic about facilitating my role. Eventually, they let me go through and make my way alone up the front steps of the building." When she reached the door she was mistaken for a reporter and the media-shy staff wouldn't let her in. Finally she gained entry, and was ushered to a classroom that had been stripped bare by the exiting teacher who chose to leave the school rather than teach a black child.

Barbara spent the day transforming the stark room that would become the arena for one of the greatest friendships of her life. Unbeknownst to her, Ruby Bridges and her mother sat downstairs in the office all day, waiting and watching as white parents reacted in angry disbelief to the long delayed implementation of *Brown vs. The Topeka Board of Education*. At the end of the day, Ruby returned home through a hail of jeering protesters, and the principal informed Barbara in a tone that was both challenging and skeptical, "*If* you return tomorrow, you'll meet your student." Barbara observed, "I think they hoped I'd go home and never come back."

By late afternoon the crowd outside had grown. A meeker person might have called it quits. But the noise and insults and fundamental injustice of the situation strengthened Barbara's resolve. "I could not understand how anyone could yell at a child like that. I could understand that they felt a need to protest in some formal manner. But to direct it personally at a child? I was so appalled that I was determined to come back. I'd given my word." The next morning she returned and waited.

Outside the school, the streets throbbed with anger and fear. The demonstrators now displayed crosses and a coffin with a black doll in it. Ruby arrived, as she would each morning, accompanied by four armed federal marshals, and mounted the steps, walking with dignity, composure, restraint, and courage. Her demeanor captured the admiration of a watching world, and prompted Norman Rockwell to paint *The Problem We All Live With*, his only work to comment on contemporary social strife.

Inside the school were rows of abandoned classrooms, freshly emptied by white parents frantically rescuing their children from the unimaginable—sharing their school with a black child. Down an echoing hallway, Ruby Bridges was greeted by her mirror image, Barbara Henry. The date was November 15, 1960. "It was love at first sight. Once she took my hand, there was no turning back."

Barbara was still a relatively new teacher when she walked into the eye of the national storm over integration, yet from that first day in November until June of 1961, she conducted herself with dignity, composure, restraint, and courage. Despite the daily line-up in front of the school, the antagonism of the principal and pariahlike treatment of the staff, she taught her single student every day, every subject, with only a marshal at the door for company. "Ruby was my territory and no one else would come near us."

"I often think of Robert Frost's poem, 'Fire and Ice.' 'Some say the world will end in fire, some say ice.' I often think that outside Frantz school it was the fire and anger, inside the school it was the quiet cold, the apartness that was as frightening as the hatred outside." As the nation struggled to eradicate segregation, the great social scourge of twentieth-century America, Barbara created a sanctuary in which Ruby could learn. Her explanation for her performance is simple: "A teacher's charge is nothing less than changing the world."

That's what comes through when you meet Barbara—the strength of character and goodness that made her the perfect fit for Ruby Bridges during that tumultuous time. Barbara says, "One of the great things in my life is that I was able to be there for her when she needed someone. I was in the right place at the right time. So I'm very thankful for the gift of that year with her."

The other element that ensured Barbara's success was her passion for teaching. When I asked why she became a teacher, she said,

> For me it was a natural thing. I always thought that not being in an academic atmosphere was just not a life worth living. I admired the teachers with whom I studied. I love learning. I love children, so it seemed a perfect thing. I just think it's the best job in the world. It's also one of the hardest. I can't think of anything I would have preferred to do.
>
> And teaching Ruby was such a joy. She was a quick learner so we didn't have to do much repetitive work. I would get books out of the library because she loved to be read to about places that were different from where she lived. We learned a lot about other countries and I told her stories about my life when I was teaching in France and Germany. We did art and music and math together. Ruby and I sat side by side—learning.

Throughout the winter in this solitary classroom, a very close relationship blossomed. "I didn't have any children of my own. It was like Ruby was my child." And Ruby thought of Mrs. Henry as her best friend.

> I really think it was Ruby's interest in learning that kept the peripheral hurts and unpleasantness away from us during the day. We could never leave the building. We had no gym, no library, no lunchroom. We had nowhere to go but that room. What was it Plato or Aristotle said—two people on a log is all you need for learning. We were able to create our own world.

But outside the classroom, there was no visible thaw in the arctic climate of the school. As the year progressed, no teachers stopped by to see how Barbara was faring. "The principal would step to the threshold occasionally and look around very imperiously to make sure we were engaged. Then she would leave without a word. I was the foreigner, the stranger." Her visits to the staff lounge were greeted with stony silence by teachers idled by the boycott. Some sat and smoked or busied themselves sorting textbooks. One teacher filled her time by giving impromptu piano lessons. Barbara was simply "that northern woman." "I think they saw me as an instrument of integration, not as a person who was simply there to teach." But she's very philosophical about her treatment. "I understand. They were scared. They had lived in that community all their lives so they were under a lot of pressure. Befriending me would have been dangerous."

She was not so tolerant of the passive-aggressive administrator whose sympathies clearly lay with the four hundred or more white parents maintaining their boycott. One day, as Barbara walked through the nearly deserted school, she was enraged to discover another first-grade class tucked away in a little room off the basement. Four white children lounged about while their teacher listened to the radio.

> I went to the principal and demanded to know why Ruby wasn't in that class. Integration meant in the same room, not just the same building. The principal refused to include Ruby despite my threats to go to the superintendent. She said, 'That teacher won't teach them.' I said, 'Well, I will!' So Ruby stayed with me all morning but in the afternoon the other first graders joined us. We did things that were very communal—science projects and social studies. Ruby was in her glory because she finally had other children in her class. And it was amazing to see their reaction, how they came in so timidly because this was something new for them. They'd never been in school with a black child, but it took about one day—you know how children are. There really is no hate in their hearts.
>
> Ruby was such a wonderful child. So sweet. How could your heart not go out to someone so alone? I used to think, how sad for those other teachers. They missed this wonderful child. She came to school so cheerful every day after having walked through that ugly mob, yelling and protesting. The federal marshal would bring her to the door and I'd be there waiting for her. She always had that beautiful smile and those gorgeous eyes, and she was always so enthusiastic about anything we did. She never seemed sad, which is an amazing thing. Just think of the courage it took. Neither of us ever missed a day. We were always there for each other.

Novelist John Steinbeck was drawn to New Orleans in 1960 by the media stories about the "cheerleaders" and went one morning to see for himself. He made his way to William Frantz school and witnessed the spectacle unfold as Ruby arrived. In his book *Travels with Charley*, he chronicled the experience—his revulsion at hearing the obscene comments of the mothers, the sight of the coffin, the carnival atmosphere surrounding these very public displays of racism. In the end he asked, "Where were the good people?"

There were many good people in New Orleans. Ruby's neighbors watched her house for prowlers and walked behind the car that took her to school each day. A group of concerned women formed Save Our Schools (SOS) with the goal of keeping the schools open. They organized carpools to safely transport white students to the newly integrated schools. Ruby was surrounded by many strong supporters who believed in social justice and had the courage to act—especially her parents and Barbara Henry.

At the end of the year, Ruby and Barbara parted with a big hug. But there was one last battle for Barbara at William Franz School. When she turned in Ruby's grades, the principal insisted that Ruby didn't deserve such high marks "since she'd been the only student in the class."

The next fall, Barbara Henry returned to Boston to have her first child and resume her teaching career. But that was not the end of Barbara's career in social justice. True to form, she met with leaders of the black community and Jonathon Kozol to help implement the Metropolitan Council for Educational Opportunities (METCO), a project to reduce segregation in Boston's city schools and integrate suburban school districts, providing multicultural experiences that would benefit both minority and majority students.

Forty years later, Ruby is an activist for social justice. She created The Ruby Bridges Foundation to promote parent involvement in the very school where she broke the color barrier. Her foundation is bringing educational opportunities to the children at William Frantz School, now almost completely re-segregated. It is as black as it had once been white. She also travels the country talking about her childhood experiences and helping students and teachers tackle the still-difficult topic of "the problem we all live with"—racism.

When I asked Barbara what she thought she'd given Ruby during their year together, she said she was proud that Ruby did not become a prejudiced person.

> I helped her realize as a young child that not all white people were ugly and poisonous, like the crowd demonstrating outside the school. There was something good about some white people. She knew she was loved and cared about in school and that helped her feel good about learning. That joy of learning went through her life—she was always a good student. Most important, I think I nurtured the good qualities that she already had and didn't let them get subsumed in an angry hostile world. They were allowed to flower.

Then I asked what Ruby gave her. "Courage," she said, "Throughout my life, whenever I had to face something difficult I would just tell myself, 'If Ruby could go through all of that, I can do this.' And then I would be strong."

In the quiet hallway of Barbara's home in Boston hangs a copy of Norman Rockwell's painting of a little black girl in a white dress, flanked by four large men. Across the bottom is the inscription—*Dear Barbara, I couldn't have made it without you. Ruby.*

Ruby Bridges and Barbara Henry are fast friends.

What's the Big Idea About Social Justice?

Great teachers like Barbara Henry are social activists at heart. They believe that every child has a right to be educated, and they spend their days delivering on that promise through their dedication to excellence. But they are also keenly aware that despite *Plessy vs. Fergeson, Brown vs. the Topeka Board of Education,* and all our collective efforts to create a more just society, the world is still ripe with opportunities for social action, so they use their classrooms and their curriculum as a platform for social justice education.

These teachers realize that most of their students observe, experience, or think about issues of social justice every day. Great teachers do not ask kids to leave their life experiences at the door each morning. Nor would they expect students to trust them if they ignored the reality of racism, poverty, abuse of power and neglect, and its crippling impact on their community. The credibility gap created by this charade would be unbridgeable. They also know that their students long to address social injustice, but they need adult mentors to help them translate their ideas into action. They can't do it without us.

When you're teaching social justice, the curriculum is ourselves. Younger students may not be able to name the specific elements of social justice that the citizens of our country expect, but they surely can list the values that underlie our fundamental relationships—human-to-human. Friendship, responsibility, equality, fairness, mutual support and encouragement, collaboration, and caring. For students at the 99th Street School in Los Angeles, social justice meant being able to live without the fear of gun violence.

Early one warm afternoon, a band of second- and fifth-grade students crowded the curb, shouting and gesturing at the approach of an ice cream truck. It was a typical scene on 99th Street, where several brightly painted trucks regularly troll for hungry customers. But this afternoon was different. As the truck slowed to a crawl, preparing for a brisk round of open-air sales, the students raised a flutter of hand-lettered signs demanding, *No more guns. Don't sell guns. Throw away guns.* The hopeful vendors sped away with a freezer full of Popsicles and a complete selection of toy guns. These students had decided that their community didn't need another gun—real or lookalike, so they campaigned for their fellow students to boycott the gun-toting sweets distributors.

These students and scores of other courageous children all over the planet have decided that business as usual is not good enough. School must be about more than worksheets and recess. It needs to be about their world and their lives. They're demanding social justice and getting it, one small victory at a time.

Waking Students Up

When you introduce your students to social justice education, you encourage them to look at the real world inquisitively, boldly, and from various points of view to observe how other people, particularly children, exist.

Sometimes, it's not a pretty sight. That's what Valerie Roach's third-grade students discovered when a classmate brought in an article about the child slaves working in cocoa bean fields in the Ivory Coast, where 43 percent of cocoa beans are grown. Adult workers in the cocoa fields are paid wages that leave them at the edge of poverty and starvation, so in desperation they sell their children into slavery. Then eight-, nine-, and ten-year-olds work twelve-hour days, are undernourished and mistreated, simply to satisfy the cravings of chocolate lovers around the world and the greed of cocoa farmers.

As her students began their investigations, they got their first glimpse of a phenomenon known as Fair Trade Chocolate, in which candy manufacturers agree to pay cocoa farmers prices that allow them to do business without relying on slaves. Armed with this information, Ms. Roach's students went right to the top of the food chain. They wrote the President of M&M/Mars, and laid out their consumer concerns in no uncertain terms. "I will not eat any of the candy that has been picked by child slaves. I like your company's candy but I will not be eating any until you stop. I am also going to suggest to my friends that they stop eating the chocolate that has been made by the cocoa beans picked by child slaves." They pressed his company to use only certified fair trade chocolate or cocoa beans. The students also gathered up all their M&M/Mars Halloween candy and sent it back to the company.

With little prompting, students arrive at the notion of socioeconomic status, exploitation, and the uneven distribution of wealth. They won't use those words, but they'll nail the concept. They'll notice that some people seem to be treated unfairly more often than others but without good cause. They may notice that more men or minorities seem to be homeless. Be prepared. They'll discover suffering and injustice without ever leaving their town. And now that Internet access is commonplace in classrooms or school libraries, it won't take long for them to discover sweatshops, toxic dumps, discrimination, and the devastation of the natural environment.

All of that would be emotionally daunting for kids, if it were just an exercise in cataloguing misery. But social justice education encourages students to do something about the injustice they discover. Actually, it goes well beyond encouraging; it asserts responsibility. When you embrace social justice as a pillar of learning in your class, you send a message that we're all responsible for improving the world in which we live.

With your help, kids go from passively spectating their way through a text, to focusing their energy and skill on a solution that could save a childhood, a species, or a life. They identify the strategies they need to sharpen, the people they need to meet, the resources they need to gather, and they do it without hesitation because something real and terribly important is hanging in the balance.

What Kids Learn from Social Justice

As educators, we often talk about the importance of letting students solve real-world problems through hands-on activities. Then we turn around and design projects that begin with the phrases, "Pretend you're _____ . . . Imagine you heard that _____. . . ." We do a lot of simulating, while keeping a fair amount of yardage between our kids and the real world. But great teachers put social justice on their classroom agenda and keep it there, because they believe it's one of the most effective ways to teach skills, nurture active citizenship, and promote planetary stewardship. Not bad for a morning's work!

Students in pursuit of a cause grow prodigiously. Once they get their teeth into a real problem, they routinely meet and exceed their academic goals, without goading, threats, or artificial inducements. The following are some of the skills kids develop while working on social justice projects.

School Skills

- Application of knowledge to a real-life problem
- Problem solving and decision making using multiple intelligences
- Critical thinking
- Learning from experience
- Use of persuasive speaking and writing

Life Skills

- Openness to new experiences and roles
- Willingness to take risks and accept challenges
- Realistic ideas about the world
- Awareness of community needs

- Awareness of personal convictions
- Awareness of personal abilities
- Belief in the power of the individual to make a difference

Skill development could be reason enough to steer your kids toward social action. But there's a second reason to pursue this brand of education, and quite frankly, this is the one that sent me to the barricades: citizen apathy. I was teaching my kids about the ancient world, raving on about the Greeks, the invention of democracy and the wonder of citizens-as-decision-makers, when I got a reality check that was more like a body blow. Our local election failed to attract one in three of my neighbors. A scant 31 percent of the eligible voters managed to carve fifteen minutes from their day to mutilate chads. It appeared that for the fine citizens in my community, democracy was a spectator sport. At that moment I decided that my kids wouldn't just know their way around a democracy. By the time I got through with them, they'd be able to redraw the map if they decided it was the right thing to do.

As a classroom teacher, you hold the next generation of voters, politicians, and corporate leaders in your hands. Teaching children about interdependence and responsibility through social action is a lesson that can stick. With your guidance, kids discover their power to help people, animals, or the environment through the political process. Active, inquisitive citizenship can begin when kids are very young. They should act out early and often, until championing worthy causes becomes a habit they can't break.

Planting the Seed

The best social action projects are like an earthquake. One minute you're comfortably ensconced in your classroom, earnestly working through your curriculum, and the next minute, the ground shifts. Even before the room stops rocking, you sense that you're in new territory—face-to-face with a genuine adventure. You may not love it right away, but you know you've got your arms around something important and real. The best projects come organically from the work and conversations you have with your students every day. Sometimes a kid will burst through the door on red-alert and demand that his peers sit up and take notice.

But suppose your kids don't seem to have a clue about activism. Their idea of social justice is being first in the cafeteria line at any cost. It's not hopeless—they're probably just not paying attention. But you don't have to wait around for them to "discover" social justice on their own. One way to get their attention is to lure them with examples of what ordinary kids just like them are doing. It won't take long for them to catch the activist bug.

A wonderful tool for this is a book by Phillip Hoose called *It's Our World, Too: Stories of Young People Who Are Making a Difference* (Little Brown, 1993). It has biographies of fourteen kids who saw problems in their world and worked for change. They're heroes, and your kids will be dazzled from the very first page. There's Justin Lebo, who rebuilt bikes from used bicycle parts and gave them away to kids without wheels—children who were homeless, or had AIDS or were orphans. He made nearly 200 recycled bikes using donations and all his spare time. They'll read about James Ale who saw his friend get hit by a car while they were playing ball in a busy street, and wondered, "Why do we have to play ball in the street, while the kids in the rich part of town have parks?" The more he thought, the madder he got, until finally he persuaded city officials to build a park in his poor neighborhood. Read this book aloud to your students to inspire them, fire them up, and prove that kids can be powerful change agents. It is their world, too.

After reading parts or all of this book, ask your students, "Why do you think these kids were successful? What did they know or learn how to do?" Have your students begin to list the traits and skills that helped these students reach their goals. Keep that list posted as you move toward your own goals.

I've used Hoose's book dozens of times, with adults and children, and the reaction is always the same—awe and discontent. Students recognize that these kids are doing something real and very important. That's the awe factor. But they're filled with questions. Could I do that? Would I? Are there problems like that in my community? How would I find them? Do I have the courage to act? The status quo has been replaced with a new standard of behavior, and kids wonder if they can measure up. That's what causes the discontent, and that's a perfect platform for learning.

Social Action Autobiography

Now you want to draw parallels between all those amazing kids in Hoose's book and your students by helping them recognize all they ways that they have already been social activists. One way to find out what your kids already know about social justice and what they've done about it is to have them do a Social Action Autobiography. Ask them to remember a time when they acted to help someone or something else—to change a situation for the better. In effect you're activating their prior knowledge and doing a quick assessment of their skill level in one activity.

For younger kids, the prompt might be something like: Think of a time when you helped someone else. The answer could range from taking care of a neighbor's cat to playing with a child that had no friends. They can respond by writing or drawing a picture, or by making an annotated drawing with images and words. Even kindergarteners can do this reflective activity, by drawing a picture or a series of pictures, and then narrating details to a scribe, perhaps an older student, parent, instructional aide, or the teacher. If you can't arrange for scribes, just have them share their pictures in small groups.

For older kids, ask them to think about a problem that involved other people, the community, the environment, or animals, and what they did to help solve it. You can pose a series of questions to help them remember details and analyze their actions. Ask:

- How did you find out about the problem?
- What did you think was a good solution?
- What did you need to do to make it happen?
- Did other people help you?
- How did you feel about the solution?
- How did you feel about yourself?

As students work their way through these questions, they begin to identify the ways that they are powerful, so they have a platform from which to work the next time they decide to take action. Their previous experiences become a template for more action, and with your help their skills grow, so they can take on more challenging problems.

Taking Sides: How to Choose a Social Justice Project

Since you are the person who bears the ultimate responsibility for educating your kids, you must evaluate every project to see if it has the potential to promote social justice *and* guarantee learning, by allowing students to apply their school skills to a real-world problem. And not just a few enthusiastic students. All kinds of learners must be able to get involved. Does the project need writers, designers, speakers, thinkers, coaches, artists, advocates, or devil's advocates? The following are a few more questions you need to answer before you settle on a social justice project.

- Is it an issue that is within your students' experiences, or can be directly related to their lives?
- Is firsthand, direct investigation possible?
- Are there sufficient resources for students to do research and take action to achieve their goals?
- Is it related to your curriculum goals?
- Is it sensitive to the local culture and the cultures of your students?

- Does it represent a cause or issue that adults feel is worth the time that students will invest?
- Is it a project where parents can participate, support, or learn from their children without feeling defensive (as in antismoking campaigns)?

Another consideration relates to learning. We know learning is most effective when kids start with what they know and build on that. Social justice learning is no exception. Since children are the experts on how children live in their own community in the twenty-first century, your social justice efforts will be more compelling if your students' focus on projects that directly affect children. They can compare and contrast their lives with other children, and take action if they feel some kids are being treated unfairly.

For example, Canadian students decided to help children in Africa and Afghanistan by raising money to remove landmines from schoolyards. Another way that kids help kids is through Amnesty International Kids (www.amnestyusa.org /aikids), a subset of a global organization to ensure human rights. Each month they post an Urgent Action on their website, usually a call to help save a child. For example, a recent request for action focused on Hmong children in the Laos jungle who are starving and wounded. Each Urgent Action is issued with instructions about how your kids can help, including tips for writing letters and who to contact.

If you are looking at any issues that raise questions about the rights of children, tell your kids about the UN Convention on the Rights of the Child, written in 1989. It is very explicit about the protections that all children, everywhere should enjoy. It is an amazing document, widely embraced by nations around the world. Students can research this document at www.unicef.org/crc/convention or simply type in keywords UN Convention on the Rights of the Child.

The following are two resources you should investigate while you're prospecting for a project. The Rethinking Schools website (www.rethinkingschools. org) is loaded with ideas about effective teaching for a better world.

Rethinking Globalization: Teaching for Justice in an Unjust World (2002) by Bill Bigelow is a 400-page teaching resource. Sections cover colonialism, global sweatshops, child labor, along with culture, consumption, and the environment. The book is available from Rethinking Schools.

The Green Teacher (www.greenteacher.com) is a magazine by and for educators to enhance environmental and global education across the curriculum at all grade levels. Each issue contains ideas for rethinking education in light of environmental and global problems; reports of what successful teachers, parents, and other youth educators are doing; cross-curricular activities for various grade levels; book reviews; and announcements of events.

Once your kids begin to close in on a problem with action in mind, ask some questions that will help them focus their research and come up with a plan.

- What do we need to know if we want to help?
- What's already being done? Who's doing it?
- What's still needed for a solution?
- What skills or resources do we already have to lend to the effort?
- What skills/resources/information will we need to learn/acquire?
- What problems might we confront?
- How will we handle them?
- Who else may want to help us?

Teachers who are bold enough to embrace an activist approach to teaching find themselves scrambling to *add* to the standard curriculum—impromptu lessons in trickle-down economics, writing a press release, how to make an effective speech in under three minutes, graphic design principles for poster artists, and the fundamentals of negotiation. Their students cover all the educational "standards" in the process of making a ruckus and contribute something of permanent value to their community.

What skills do kids practice while they're working on social action projects?

- Research
- Communication
- Organization
- Goal setting
- Media literacy
- Group process
- Division of labor
- Consensus building

What personal traits will they develop in the process?

- Courage
- Persistence
- Ingenuity
- Intelligence
- Diplomacy

This interconnectedness of curriculum echoes the global interconnectedness of people, communities, and the environment, which are some of the fundamental underpinnings of social justice education.

Prepping Students for Action: Politics 101

If your kids decide to abandon their classroom for a more public learning venue, they'll be playing with the big boys. And no matter how patronizing adults are to kids when the cameras are on, I've yet to meet an entrepreneur who will sit idly by while a band of well-coached ten-year-olds derails his plans for yet another strip mall. So you will need to teach your kids to think politically about both the causes of problems and roadblocks to solutions. Because they're young and rather innocent, they'll formulate solutions that are logical and doable, even affordable, but haven't been done. At first glance they may wonder why it's so easy for kids to find solutions, and so hard for adults. Before they start congratulating themselves for being brilliant, step in. It's time for Politics 101.

Thinking politically requires kids to focus on the *who* rather than the *what*. Problems don't just exist like natural laws. Most of them are the result of human behavior. So your kids need to uncover the *who* behind social problems. Understanding an individual or group's motivation can help kids get the leverage they need to create change. For a start, challenge your kids by asking them to consider the following questions about their project:

- If so many people know about this problem, why do you think it still exists? One way to decide if a problem is common knowledge and discover what's already been tried is to check the number of citations on an Internet search engine such as Google.
- Who might be benefiting from this situation as it currently exists? Who else?
- What values might be motivating them? What do they want or need?
- Have they already tried to block solutions? How? What happened?
- What kind of solutions would appeal to them?
- What kind of pressure or action might move them to change and cooperate with a solution?

Questions like these hone analytic thinking and encourage research. But be prepared for some disillusionment. As the veil is lifted, your kids may conclude that many adults are good, and some are even heroic, but a disappointingly large group behave as if they live in a community of one—themselves. That doesn't mean kids have to give up. Remind them of all the other kid-warriors who have succeeded. Then teach them how to fight fire with fire by using politicians' tools, and if necessary, using politicians as tools.

A Social Activist's Toolbox

Successful student activists use the following tools to get their message out and achieve their goals.

- Write petitions and collect signatures
- Organize letter-writing campaigns
- Create an education campaign with flyers, bulletin boards, and displays
- Follow-up with surveys to gauge public interest and awareness
- Give speeches to interested groups
- Organize fundraising
- Target spending effectively
- Call a press conference
- Contact the media
- Write a press release
- Contact sympathetic foundations and individuals
- Lobby for their cause
- Campaign with elected officials who support their cause
- Demonstrate, protest, and boycott
- Negotiate

Meet the Press

You know the riddle about if a tree falls in the forest and no one is there to hear it, right? Well, the same applies to social justice campaigns. Your kids can be smart, organized, and energetic, but if the word about their cause never gets out, little will happen. Smart activists know the power of the press and they use it. A critical element in your project work is to identify local news outlets—press, television, and radio. Get the names, fax and phone numbers of the reporters who cover local happenings, education, or human interest stories and get their attention. Your students have an advantage because the press likes to run occasional feel-good stories, and remarkable kids are always popular subjects. The difference this time is that your students have gone where many adults fear to tread. That's a hook that could capture a reporter's attention, giving you a chance to inform the public and garner support for your cause.

Breaking through to the front page or prime time is very difficult. Stories are prioritized from minute to minute up to press time. *If it bleeds, it leads,* means that every time there's a high-speed chase or a natural disaster, your story will be cut. Your kids need to be prepared for disappointment and just keep on trying. If you're having trouble attracting the press, try an oblique approach. Most board of education meetings and almost all city council meetings are televised, and members of the press routinely show up looking for a story. If your students speak during public comments about your project, they will get the word out and perhaps attract a reporter or two in the process.

The most important thing about press coverage is credibility. You may only have one shot at an article in the newspaper or a two-minute feature on television, so when the opportunity comes around, your kids need to be ready. Whether they're on camera or face-to-face with a reporter, they must be clear, accurate, articulate, and serious. Message discipline is essential. No freelancing. No mugging for the camera. So before you go public with your campaign, you need to rigorously train every student in research techniques, critical thinking, and public relations skills.

Do mock interviews and critiques with your whole class—not just a few hand-picked speakers. You never know who will capture the limelight. All students need to be ready to think on their feet and speak for the cause.

If you do snag some press time, don't miss the opportunity to compare the coverage to the real event. Have your students analyze articles or television spots in which they appear to see if their message was distorted, diluted, or came through loud and clear. Ask, What was their goal? What was the reporter's goal? Did the reporter's view match what they said and did? If there is a gap between their presentation and the reporter's version of things, guide your students to think about the implications for other things they read in the press or see on television. Once students begin to take a critical look at media based on personal experience, they will be much more discerning media consumers.

Getting Smarter About Social Justice Through Primary Source Documents

One of the most direct and powerful ways to help your students think about social justice issues is to take them to the scene of the crime through photographs. Staring into the eyes of a six-year-old, twelve-hour-a-day carpet weaver or recoiling at the sight of young civil rights protesters being mowed down by high-powered water hoses can do more to define social ills for your students than a dozen manifestos. Students feel empathy for people who are being treated unjustly, and they're motivated to investigate and act. Most of the social justice movements of the last two centuries have been documented in photographs that are available on the Internet. You can literally click on the major events that have shaped the social landscape and have your students investigate with their eyes.

Using Photographs to Learn About Child Labor

One of the most photographically compelling issues of modern times is the problem of child labor, an issue that seems to worsen as the gap between the first and third worlds widens. The appetite for affordable clothing, sports equipment, and shoes has sent manufacturers to countries where families are struggling and children are part of the equation of survival. You and your students can take an historic look at the issue of child labor through the photographs of Jacob Riis and Lewis Hine. Go to *The Campaign to End Child Labor: Child Labor Photographs* by Lewis Hine (www.boondocksnet.com/gallery/nclc /index.html). Use the following sequence of questions to help students investigate this issue.

- How have things changed in America since Jacob Riis took those photographs?
- Why did they change?
- What are the laws about child labor like today?
- Do any children in America work? Under what conditions?
- How is child labor different in other countries? Why is it different?
- What kind of work do children do in other countries?
- What happens to children who run away from their jobs?
- How can we decide what work children should and shouldn't do?
- How can people from many countries protect all children from unfair work?
- Are there any rights of children that are still being ignored or unfulfilled in the United States? (hunger, education, poverty)
- What needs to be done?
- What might we as students do to help?

Then compare and contrast the situation as Hine portrayed it with the current conditions of child laborers. Your students can use the Internet to find out if children are still part of the labor force, performing dangerous jobs, underpaid, or exploited.

Other Sources of Photographs and Primary Sources for Social Justice Discussions

The History Place—Child Labor in America, 1908–1912 (www.historyplace.com/unitedstates/childlabor/) includes sixty photographs by Lewis Hine, including the original captions.

How The Other Half Lives by Jacob Riis (www.cis.yale.edu/amstud /inforev/riis/title.html) includes photos of child laborers in New York in the 1890s.

Stolen Dreams, photographs by David Parker, M.D. (www.hsph.harvard.edu/gallery/). Images of child laborers in the United States, Mexico, Thailand, Nepal, Bangladesh, Turkey, Morocco, and Indonesia.

Afghan Child Labor Photographs by Chien Min Chung (www.digitaljournalist.org/issue0208/cc_intro.htm).

Sweatshops: The Triangle Factory Fire in New York City (www.ilr.cornell.edu/trianglefire/narrative1.html).

Photographs of the Civil Rights Movement (http://afroamhistory .about.com/library/blphotos_civilrights_index.htm).

The Civil Rights Photography of Charles Moore—Powerful Days (www.kodak.com/US/en/corp/features/moore/mooreIndex.shtml). Charles Moore was one of the unsung heroes of the Civil Rights movement. Without the publishing of his dramatic photographs in *Life* magazine and the work of other photojournalists, the public perhaps would not have been galvanized into action against the atrocities of segregation.

Newsfile: The Civil Rights Movement (www.time.com/time/newsfiles /civilrights/).

Soup kitchen photos (http://hazel.forest.net/skjold/photo_pages /soup_kitchen.htm).

Poverty in the United States (www.plu.edu/~poverty/hist/1930.html).

Homeless awareness and advocacy group (www.unm.edu/~willow /homeless/links.html).

Sleeping New York Homeless (www.artcarmuseum.com /tepperhomeless.html).

Literature and Social Justice

Another way for students to discover what it takes to be an effective activist is to research people who have displayed leadership in fighting to protect the rights of people and preserve the environment. If you ask your students to name people who were leaders in their own time, you'll probably hear about Harriet Tubman, Rosa Parks, Cesar Chavez, and Martin Luther King Jr. In addition, there is a long list of lesser-known social activists who have distinguished themselves in battles to help agricultural workers, displaced Native Americans, exploited factory workers, and victims of racial discrimination. Researching these courageous people can give students the vicarious experience of being a crusader, and teach them about the skills activists use to create conditions for change.

- **Ida Wells-Barnett** (1862–1931) was a full-time journalist in 1891 who defied mob violence and terror to expose the national disgrace of lynching.
- **Nellie Bly**, a journalist, exposed inhumane conditions in mental institutions, sweatshops, and jails.
- **Dr. Ralph Bunche** mediated the first Arab-Israeli war in 1950, and he played a major role in the formation of the United Nations.
- **Fannie Lou Hamer** was a lifelong activist who worked to secure federally guaranteed voting rights for African Americans.
- **LaDonna Harris** founded Americans for Indian Opportunity and crusaded for the rights of children and women, and for the elimination of poverty and discrimination.
- **Dolores Huerta**, co-founder of the United Farm Workers of America (UFW), directed the UFW's national grape boycott taking the plight of the farm workers to the consumers.
- **Aung San Suu Kyi** is a Nobel Peace Laureate currently under detention for her commitment to human rights and democracy in Burma.
- **John Mercer Langston**, the first black American elected to public office in the United States, worked for the fair and equal treatment of black soldiers in the Union Army and struggled for black voting rights.
- **Russell Means**, an Oglala Lakota, brought worldwide attention to the injustices and privation faced by American Indians past and present.
- **Lucretia Mott** was dedicated to achieving equality for all of America's disadvantaged and disenfranchised, including Indians, women, slaves, and free blacks.
- **Frances Perkins** (1882–1965) witnessed the infamous Triangle Shirtwaist Factory fire, which claimed the lives of 164 female workers. She spent her life as an activist for industrial reform, tackling worker safety, child labor laws, and wage and hours regulations.
- **Mary Ann Shadd**, the first black woman editor of a newspaper in North America, worked for racial integration in the United States and equal education for people of color.
- **Dr. Daniel Williams** earned his medical degree in 1883 and fought so that black doctors would be allowed to operate at Chicago hospitals.

- **Emma Yazzie**, a Navajo shepherd, challenged the Four Corners Power Plant in New Mexico, which was strip-mining Navajo land around her hogan, and destroying the desert environment. You can read about her in *Red Ribbons for Emma* (1981), written by Deb Preusch and published by New Seed Press.

If you are looking for images of social activists, try the website for Picture History (www.picturehistory.com). This site has photographs of sixty social activists and reformers with short biographies of each.

Click for a Cause

One of the more amazing aspects of the Internet is its ability to connect people and social justice causes, simply by clicking a button. Here's how it works. Social justice organizers enlist sponsors for their cause. Every time you click a button on their websites, the sponsor gives a specified donation to the cause—sometimes just a penny or two, but it adds up. You can log on once a day, every day, and if you round up friends, colleagues, and parents, together you can make a difference. Here are five websites that welcome you to click once a day for a cause. Bookmark these sites and let your students take turns being the designated donor each day.

> www.clearlandmines.com   Each year 26,000 people are killed or mutilated by landmines. Eight thousand of these are children. You can help support the foundation that is trying to eradicate landmines, by clicking on their site once per day.
>
> www.thehungersite.com   Each year approximately 31 million Americans are food insecure, meaning they were either hungry or unsure of where their next meal would come from. Twelve million of these Americans were children. Once a day, you can click on the Give Free Food button and fund the purchase and distribution of a cup of staple food for a person in need.
>
> www.therainforestsite.com   According to The Nature Conservancy, 8 million square miles of tropical rain forest used to encircle the planet. More than half of it has been burned, bulldozed, and obliterated. Funds generated by your daily click are used primarily to purchase land for preservation.
>
> www.theanimalrescuesite.com   The Animal Rescue Site is an online activism site that gives Internet users the daily opportunity to help an abandoned or neglected animal awaiting adoption. Visitors to The Animal Rescue Site can click on the "Feed an Animal in Need" button and provide at least one bowl of food.

www.thechildhealthsite.com   According to the United Nations, over 10 million children die annually from preventable causes, and many millions more are severely injured. The goal of The Child Health Site is to save and keep healthy the lives of at least 1,000 children per day.

The Downside of Social Justice

Clearly there are some pretty compelling reasons to include social justice in your curriculum. You may already be regretting some missed opportunities and turning over a new leaf. But it's only fair to warn you about the downside. Social justice projects don't just push the envelope—they're several leagues outside of the box. You may feel intense discomfort when your kids first seize upon a cause. You might think, What will people think if they see my kids parading up and down the sidewalk chanting and carrying signs? There is intense professional pressure in some schools or districts to color inside the lines when it comes to curriculum.

There's another challenge. You're convinced that your kids have learned more through one social justice project than they would in a year of text-driven lessons. But to prove that you'll need to do some task analysis that shows how authentic learning addresses the course of studies for your grade or subject. For example, take a look at the standards for language arts. Then think of all the talking, researching, speechwriting, demonstrating, lobbying, leafleting, and cajoling your students have done on behalf of their cause. You will be amazed at how many standards have been mastered—not covered, but mastered. And here's a thought. What if your kids save a life—human, animal, or arboreal—but don't finish the science book? It's worth pondering because that's a potentially rich dilemma created by social justice education.

Another daunting reality of social justice projects is that the work can be very emotional—intensely invigorating and profoundly sad. There is so much that needs to be done, even in our own cities, and many projects turn out to be a tiny first link in a long, arduous chain of effort to achieve one change. Think of all the discrete actions required over decades to achieve civil rights for minorities in this country. So your kids may never have the thrill of seeing a bill signed into law, or a shelter renovated, or even a municipal code modified to allow public feeding of the homeless. They may fix one part of a problem only to discover that they've uncovered a greater injustice or need. Social activists eat disappointment for breakfast, then go on to a full day of trying. Learning to manage emotions and persevere is one of the challenges of embracing social justice projects.

Parents may be confused by social justice projects. What does collecting canned goods have to do with first grade? A few may even say it's inappropriate, but most will be impressed. They see kids tackling difficult problems head-on and making a difference, where adults have only cynicism to offer. Some adults are moved by their kids' passion and sincerity: "I used to feel like that." You can also run into trouble if kids go home and start challenging family purchases or talking boycotts. Some parents simply don't appreciate projects that obligate them to action, so expect a few phone calls.

The biggest challenge of social justice education is that there are very few right answers. For every earnest protester there's a countervailing voice explaining why the situation can't or shouldn't change. Those voices are often well-educated and well-funded. So you have the difficult yet intoxicating task of grappling with the question: Are there some behaviors or conditions that are simply unjust, no matter the culture or the situation? When students begin to advocate for change beyond their own borders, they run straight into the daunting task of sorting out what is a cultural practice and what is a human rights issue. This is complex and subtle work that confounds adults, but you must bring it to the front of the conversation to keep students from falling into the trap of thinking that their culture and practices are the moral standard for the world, and judging all other situations from that lofty peak.

Finally, in an era of shrink-wrapped, germ-free curriculum, social action is amorphous, messy, and potentially dangerous. Herbert Kohl, a veteran educator, tells the story that one of his students warned him, "You know, Mr. Kohl, you could get arrested for stirring up justice." You have only to look at the history of the Civil Rights Movement in this country to know how right he was. Utah teacher and author Barbara Lewis received threatening letters when her kids went after the toxic waste polluters in their neighborhood. You may launch a project that has deep underground opposition in your own community. If you don't know the behind-the-scenes players, you could irk someone who's very connected to the power structures of your district or community. A heavy-weight donor. A close friend of the school board president. It's politics—largely invisible but very real. A wonderful project can blow up in your face with almost no warning.

If that happens, you may find that you're suddenly the recipient of some industrial-strength criticism. The most puzzling thing may be how indirect it all is. Rather than saying you should refrain from social justice activities, you may just get a flurry of questions about why your curriculum is "so different" from the other teachers at your grade level. Or there may be comments about your test scores, with the suggestion if you spent more time teaching and less time trying to save the world, your kids would be better served. At the time when you need support the most, you may find that there aren't many people who know how to handle the landmines. But thanks to the Internet, you can connect with colleagues who are experienced in social justice issues, and they'll gladly share their strategies and success stories.

You can inoculate yourself against some of the potential criticism by keeping your administrators informed from the minute your kids start sniffing around a cause. Principals are often dying to find new life in their schools, and will feel proud as a new parent about your efforts and successes. But they don't appreciate being blindsided by an irate phone call or oblique inquiry from a board member. Prepare a press packet for your administrators with a concise description of the problem your kids have chosen, an outline of your plans, and the skills your kids are learning through this project. Ask for your administrators' support early and invite them to every discussion or event. That way they're in the loop if the going gets rough, and in the limelight when your kids are triumphant.

The other form of insurance you can give yourself is to be sure your teaching is exemplary, even on your worst day. Plan, research, and teach your butt off. That way your kids will be exceptional, too. It's the price you must pay for courageous teaching. Actually, it's the price of greatness.

Improve Yourself, Improve Your Community

I adore Ben Franklin, one of the earliest global citizens, and a social reformer if ever there was one. He organized the first lending library, the first volunteer fire department, and plied the Atlantic Ocean countless times, working for peace. One of his guiding principles was *Improve Yourself, Improve Your Community.* Through the virtual revolution, we've all been rendered global citizens. Every day you and your students can flip on the television or fire up your computer, and there's the world in living color. You can read about famines, landmines, and infanticide, with a simple click. The question is, Will your students be planetary eavesdroppers, aware but unmoved, or embrace their vastly expanded citizenship through action? It's your call, but believe me, you won't regret a minute you spend guiding your students to discover their roles as stewards of the environment and champions of human rights.

> *We must be the change we want to see.*
> —Mahatma Gandhi

Resources

Books

Bridges, Ruby. 1999. *Through My Eyes.* New York: Scholastic Press. The autobiographical account of Ruby Bridges' experience as the first black child to attend William Frantz School in New Orleans with a detailed history of the Civil Rights Movement.

Hoose, Phillip. 1993. *It's Our World, Too*. Boston: Little, Brown.

Krull, Kathleen. 2000. *Lives of Extraordinary Women: Rulers, Rebels (and What the Neighbors Thought)*. New York: Holt.

Kuklin, Susan. 1998. *Iqbal Masih and The Crusaders Against Child Slavery*. New York: Holt.

Lewis, Barbara. 1991. *The Kids' Guide to Social Action: How to Solve the Social Problems You Choose—and Turn Creative Thinking into Positive Action*. Minneapolis: Free Spirit.

Parker, David L. 1998. *Stolen Dreams: Portraits of Working Children*. Minneapolis: Lerner Publications.

Organizations

S.T.O.P. Slavery That Oppresses People
This organization was founded in 1998 by a fifth-grade class in Denver. Its goal is to take action on behalf of children held as chattel slaves in the Sudan. www.anti-slavery.org

Free the Children
This international organization's focus is to combat child labor. www.freethechildren.com

The Student Environmental Action Coalition
(www.seac.org)

Tree Musketeers
Contact this organization, which is dedicated to empowering young people to lead environmental improvement movements, such as tree planting programs. www.treemusketeers.org

Heifer International
In its efforts to end world hunger through "living loans" of animals to impoverished families in 128 countries, this organization helps families learn to survive. The project transforms families, communities, and the environment. www.heifer.org

SECRET #11

Great Teachers Speak in Tongues

Mastering Communication in the Information Age

In This Chapter:
+ What's the Big Idea About Communicating with Parents?
+ Ten Essentials of Effective Communication
+ Cross-Cultural Communication
+ A Parent Conference Kit
+ Public Relations or Self-Defense?
+ What's in It for You?

In this age of instant messaging, why is it that conveying a simple message about Back-to-School Night seems to require the skill and manpower of a presidential campaign, complete with bumper stickers and buttons? You've probably spent more that a few restless hours in the middle of the night wondering how to capture all your parents' attention in under six tries. Will five reminders about parent conferences do the trick? Ten? In your more desperate moments you may have considered carrier pigeons or singing telegrams. How about food? I never met a parent that didn't respond well to a tasty morsel. Perhaps wrapping your weekly newsletter around a candy bar or a slab of pound cake would work? On second thought, you could just end up with a rash of "my dog ate the newsletter" responses and fervent requests for more.

Establishing and maintaining a connection with parents can be as challenging as trying to crack the secret of the Enigma Machine. One week your message gets through, and Family Math night is a smashing success, with standing room only. The next parent evening is a dud—just you, a mountain of refreshments, and three shy parents staring awkwardly at you across an empty room, and wondering what the other parents knew. It's puzzling at best.

And sadly, parents sometimes feel the same level of frustration when they try to communicate with you. Your voicemail box is full. Email bounces back. Or there's just no response, so they give up. When this happens, everyone loses, because parents and teachers are natural allies in a young child's life. Both are working on the same precious, precarious task of helping a young person grow up successfully. Yet parents and teachers may have only a vague sense of each other's efforts. Their collaboration is dominated by long periods of silence interspersed with one-way messages—mostly unacknowledged, sometimes undelivered. A parent scratches a hasty note explaining her child's unfinished homework. It flutters onto the playground and is scooped up in the weekly litter-abatement drive. The teacher's weekly newsletter, earnestly composed at midnight, sails across the soccer field or soaks up juice in the bottom of a backpack. Mom never sees it.

The result is that teachers and parents often feel like ships passing in the night. Their paths intersect momentarily in a parking lot or hallway. They semaphore across a sea of blacktop. Occasionally there's an awkward encounter in the checkout line of the grocery store. Mostly there's just the daily exchange of cargo—a child. Then they disappear in opposite directions.

What's the Big Idea About Communicating with Parents?

Great teachers have perfected a dozen different ways to communicate with their students' parents because they believe that each world—home and school—is hugely important to a full and successful childhood. Knowing about one world can help the adults who are working with a child in the other. So for great teachers, parent–teacher communication is about enlightenment. Their goal is to seek and convey enlightenment about their kids. Enlightenment is possible in even the briefest encounter if you keep these two objectives in mind.

1. You want to *learn* as much relevant information as you can about each student in the context of their home and family. Parents can share vital information that will help you be more effective with their child. They give you the big picture of their child as a learner in the world.

2. You want to *share* information with parents about their child as a learner in a specific educational system that has its own criteria for success—high school exit exams, standardized tests, grade-level expectations, behavioral norms—which may be very different from home.

Every time great teachers encounter parents, they ask themselves:

- What can I learn from this parent that will help me teach his child more effectively?

- What can I convey to the parent that will help them appreciate what their child knows and can do?
- How can I express my appreciation for what they have already taught their child and encourage them to do more?
- What do they need to know about my classroom to help their child?
- What forms of communication are most effective for them?
- What communication strategies don't work, confuse, or overwhelm them?
- Are there cultural factors that will influence the effectiveness of our communication?

When enlightenment is the goal of parent–teacher communication, parents are seen as unique resources of personal, particular knowledge about kids. Every conversation holds the potential for revelations that can explain unusual talents or puzzling behavior. Grandma is a painter. Dad rebuilds engines. Three languages are spoken in the home. Great teachers scoop up that kind of information as clues for understanding who their kids are and how they learn best.

Enlightenment communication involves parents in their child's learning. Parents quickly discover that by talking to the teacher they get a more accurate picture of their child at school and what they can do to encourage learning. When parents convince their kids that learning is important, interesting, even fun, kids bring those attitudes to school, and the teacher is the beneficiary. If the parent takes a very specific interest in your classroom activities, you become allies and now there are two adults with a vested interest in a child's efforts and progress in school.

Ten Essentials of Effective Communication

If you're determined to reach every parent, remember that one size doesn't fit all. You will need to communicate around the clock, in writing and in person, with and without visual aids. Orchestrating an effective parent communication plan is a lot of work, but it's a very powerful way to multiply learning opportunities for kids. Here are ten points for honing your communications with parents. Your messages need to be:

1. Proactive
2. Positive
3. Frequent
4. Clear

5. Basic
6. Attention grabbing
7. Appealing
8. Inclusive
9. Timely
10. Error-free

1. *Proactive*

Make contact as early in the year as possible, before there's an incident that makes either of you reluctant. Send a personal note to all entering students and their families, welcoming them to your class. This makes a huge impression on parents. Do a little research on your kids. Find one strength listed in their student record and mention it in your note. That student enters your class on the first day with a sense that you know him or her personally and you like what you know.

2. *Positive*

All communication, whether written or verbal, should start on an upbeat note. Prospect for anything good you can say first, then build a bridge to the rest of your message. The trick to finding and keeping a positive voice in your written communications is visualization. Whenever you're writing to all of your parents, visualize one that you really like—a parent who "gets" what you're doing and is totally supportive of your work with kids. Picture that person's face. See him smiling and nodding as he reads your letter. Now relax and let your ideas flow out to that cheerful recipient. Try to include in every article and newsletter a reference to all the ways that your kids are smart, and a lively anecdote to illustrate your remarks. If you do that consistently, you'll gain readership, and that's the goal here.

3. *Frequent*

Establish a regular schedule for your parent notices, classroom newsletter, homework packets, and requests. Parents learn to watch for them and your rate of completed passes soars. But I know there are some weeks when you feel like you just can't crank out one more newsletter or Friday update. So put your kids to work. Let them take over the writing duties once in a while. Periodically have an entire issue that's just written and illustrated by kids. That one will get read over and over, and you'll get a rest.

4. *Clear*

Keep your writing simple. Use bulleted points instead of full sentences whenever possible. Think of the Ws—who, what, where, when—to make sure you hit all the high points. Then work in the details of why this event or announcement is important to your students or their parents. That way parents won't stare at the bottom line and wonder, "So what?" If you like to use clever headlines for your articles, like Make a Face, be sure to add a very concrete subtitle—Jack O' Lantern Contest Tuesday. That way readers get the message by line 2. Otherwise, they may skip to the next heading without ever reading your message. Put all dates and student names in boldface, to catch a few more eyes. If you need a reply, be sure to tell parents how and by when you'd like to hear from them. A simple tear-off sheet increases the chances of a timely response.

5. *Basic*

It's impossible to tell parents everything you're doing with their kids. But there is some basic information that all parents should know, for example: schedules, dates for report cards, procedures for field trips, what to do when a child is absent, what to do if a natural disaster strikes during school hours, where kids wait when parents are late picking them up, what tests are given and when, what to do if your child is having trouble learning, what about health care at school, what if a child is being harassed, what if a child is gifted. Be sure to cover these topics in the first month of school, so you don't hear, "Why didn't anyone tell me?" from the parents.

6. *Attention Grabbing*

A great way to start your newsletters is with a fresh anecdote from your classroom that illustrates your theme or your point. If you're not sure how to do this, just pick up your local newspaper. Half of the articles start with something like *Bob didn't think of himself as special, but on Friday night, his neighbors were convinced he was a hero.* People are hooked by the human element in a story, and what could be more human than a room full of kids.

7. *Appealing*

It goes without saying that written materials need to be readable, but they should also be attractive. Avoid small or Baroque fonts. Parents frequently read your newsletters after midnight or in heavy traffic, so make it easy on their eyes. Try to include student artwork and writing in every newsletter. Instead of using those generic borders and moronic computer graphics, put your students to work. Intersperse your text with their designs to give the reader's eyes a rest and a treat. Be sure to include students' names or initials in their designs so they can show off when they get home. That's another way to get parents' attention and hold it.

8. *Inclusive*

Make sure all parents are in the know by developing a multichannel system of communication. Email can be great, or it can be an invitation to be buried electronically. The last thing a busy teacher needs at the end of the day is fifty email messages ranging from vitally important—"We changed Jared's seizure medication over the weekend"—to the inane, "Did Sarah eat all of her lunch today?" You may want to establish some ground rules. If you decide to set up an e-mail grapevine to provide reminders, good news, or rapid information in a crisis, distribute a parent contact form at the beginning of the year with a line for email addresses. But remember, some families don't have email, so you need to distribute printed versions of all your messages at the same time, to avoid creating an electronic in-crowd.

A word of caution: Email is public property with an embarrassment potential exceeded only by the supermarket tabloids. Your hasty reply to one parent can be edited, quoted out of context, or forwarded to dozens of other people, including your principal or superintendent. Before you ever hit the Send button, scrutinize your writing as if it were headed for the front page of the *New York Times*. If you have any sense that your message can be misunderstood or misused, delete it and pick up the phone instead.

Now examine your communication plan to make sure you are reaching all families. What about noncustodial parents? The Education Code ensures them the right to all information about their child's education, even if they only see each other for two weeks during the summer. You may ask these parents to give you a stack of self-addressed envelopes. Each week when your newsletter is published, drop one in the mail to keep them in the loop. The same technique can work with co-custodial parents who alternate custody by the week, weekend, or even month. Keeping them informed can help fill the void in the absent parent's life. Instead of routinely interrogating their kids about what's going on at school and hearing the usual "Nothing," or seething in frustration because they missed the class play, parents can have detailed conversations drawn from the topics in your newsletter. This also helps kids who are traveling between two families by creating a sense of continuity from one household to the next.

One big challenge to any communications plan is when parents and teachers don't share a common language. You need to work hard to find some way to translate your messages for them. You may have an aide who can translate written messages or at least make phone calls that distill the most important ideas, dates, and events into a clear, concise message. Seek out a cultural organization in the community and request a volunteer to help you reach your families in their language. Call the local college and find out if there are any language students who would like to volunteer several times a month to do a communication package for you.

How about parents who work the night shift or two jobs? What's the best way for them to stay in touch? You might want to put important information on the outgoing message of your voicemail, so they can call in any time, day or night and catch up on all the news.

9. *Timely*

Most parents are full-time jugglers. Jobs, kids, community, school, church, and social events all compete for space in their calendars. So if you want parents to participate, you need to give them lots of notice. Put a rolling calendar in your newsletter, with two months worth of events. Keep announcing the events every week until they occur, and adding new ones to the lineup. As the big days get closer, pump up the volume with a variety of other reminders. Have your students design invitations. If you have a phone in your room, supervise students while they make phone calls to leave reminder messages for their parents.

There's one flavor of information that should always be served fresh—that's news about a child's progress in school. Most parents want to know immediately if there are academic or behavioral problems. "Don't surprise me with bad news!" If you wait, hoping things will get better and they don't, parents will inevitably ask, "How long has this been going on and why didn't you tell me?" That's not a good conversation starter.

In my experience, the best teachers are often the most reluctant to make these calls. Many of them won't contact parents until they've exhausted all possible interventions—and exhaustion is probably an understatement. Their professional pride drives them to succeed with every child. Other teachers avoid difficult calls because they're anticipating a parent's pain, anger, or demands.

So before you pick up the phone or write a note, take a few minutes to collect your thoughts. What is your goal in contacting the parent? What do you need them to know or do? What is your plan for improvement? Having these points in front of you will make it easier to stick to your message and end on a positive note. When you decide to contact a parent with your concerns, don't just leave a voicemail message and hope for a call back. It may never come. Parents are into avoidance, too, especially if their own school history was checkered. Send a brief note in the mail and keep a copy for your records. At a later date, you may be asked to show documentation that you tried to reach the parent.

10. *Error-free*

It's hard for parents to be confident in your skills as a teacher if every newsletter you send home has a sprinkling of spelling or grammatical errors. With spell check on your computer, you're halfway to perfect communications. But read your draft over carefully and pass it by another adult, just for good measure. Then do a quick polish. Throw in some dynamic verbs, sharpen those adjectives, and always proofread one more time before you print and send it. Try to make every written communication a small masterpiece.

Cross-Cultural Communication

Even the most ambitious communication plans can draw a blank or actually harm your relationship with families if you're unaware of cultural practices. The goal of understanding cross-cultural communication is to reduce accidental violations of cultural rules. If you're a busy teacher in a multicultural community, the first puzzle you may have to solve is the issue of time and promptness. The dominant culture in America is time-obsessed. Time is divided into tight compartments and allotted in increments of five to ten minutes. This is especially true in schools where many activities are driven by the dual forces of a clock and a bell. So if you make an appointment with a parent for 3:00, you won't want them to be hanging around your door at 2:30, but you will definitely expect an appearance by 3:10. If you live in a traffic-clogged area, you may have an unspoken grace time of ten minutes, but beyond that you begin to feel stood-up. If this is the second time you've scheduled a meeting with a no-show parent, you may have even started a list of adjectives to explain their tardiness. None are complimentary.

Suppose, then, that the immaculately attired parent casually arrives at 3:45, just as you're reaching for your keys to go home. Now you're on the horns of a dilemma. You still want to have a conference—that was the whole point. This parent clearly has taken pains to look professional for the appointment. You may even feel a little grubby by comparison, after a day in close quarters, with clinging children, tuna sandwiches, and ripening tempera paint. But then there's the part of you that resents waiting almost an hour, with no explanation. You're not going to cancel, but you're not pleased, so your long-awaited conference could get started on a very sour note and go downhill from there.

So what do you need to know about time? Glancing at your watch only tells you local time. You also need a quick lesson on cultural time zones. In some cultures, saying "yes" to an invitation to really means "maybe." It will take several more attempts to make it a reality. In other cultures arriving thirty to forty-five minutes late isn't late at all because appointment times are approximate. Finally, in some cultures promptness is seen as "apple polishing." So your challenge is to understand the meaning of time in various cultures, and help parents understand that American schools are time-driven institutions. Here are some other practices that differ from one culture to another. Knowing about them can help you communicate successfully with all the families in your community.

Attentiveness During Conversations

Constant eye contact while listening to a person who's speaking can violate a conversational rule in some cultures including African American and Hispanic. In contrast, Americans expect eye contact, head nods, and verbal interjections like "Uh huh" and "I know"—behaviors that show interest and attention. In Asian cultures, nodding and saying "yes" does not mean that people agree with you. It simply means that they hear what you are saying. "Yes" can mean "no," "maybe," or "we'll think about it." Most Asian parents are too polite to disagree with you directly.

Distance Between People During Conversations

In some cultures, speakers stand close enough to touch each other often while talking. In other cultures, distance is maintained to denote respect. You'll need to be a good observer to discover what's comfortable for different adults. In general, try not to have a barrier such as your desk between you and parents, but avoid being casually chummy.

Objects, Characters, and Symbols That Reflect Different Beliefs

Red is the color of death or unfriendliness in the Korean culture, so notes to parents should not be written in red pen. Opening a folder of student work festooned with red marks—or even a red A plus —can be very unsettling. The confederate flag is offensive to many African Americans because it represents the culture of the South and by extension, the institution of slavery. When offered a gift, it is impolite to refuse in some cultures and impolite to open it in the presence of the giver in others. Also, avoid admiring an item to excess, as some parents may feel obligated to give it to you.

Different Rules for Taking Turns in Conversations

In some cultures "breaking in" to reinforce or disagree with the speaker is permissible, even desirable, while in other cultures it is considered interrupting and unacceptable.

Different Use of Gestures

In many cultures, the thumbs up or okay hand gesture is offensive. Touching or patting a child on the head, a standard gesture in many primary classes, is sacrilegious in some Asian cultures, because the head is the seat of the soul and is therefore sacred. Gesturing, touching objects, or eating with the left hand is considered unclean in Middle Eastern cultures, so don't use your left hand to offer a child's portfolio to a parent for review. Pointing or beckoning with one finger is rude, and crossing your legs during a conversation is unwise, since exposing the sole of your shoe is very offensive in some Middle Eastern cultures.

Different Standards for Silence, Responding, and Speed of Speech

Americans tend to be impatient. The phrase "In a New York minute" indicates that even sixty seconds can be compressed into more efficient performance units. Our conversations tend to be ping-pongish. We use short utterances and expect a rapid response from the listener. Many Native American cultures place a high value on contemplation, and therefore, don't feel compelled to make immediate responses during conversations. They're comfortable with silence and long pauses. In Middle Eastern cultures, pauses are the norm, and high-status individuals may choose not to speak at all.

Comprehension

When you're speaking to parents who have learned English as a second or third language, it is both wise and considerate to adjust your language. If you are speaking to parents who are still learning English, monitor your speed and pronunciation. Even if parents speak fluent English, they may have difficulty understanding your accent, no matter what you are saying. If you throw in idioms, jargon, or slang, the conversation can feel like a concentration test. Use direct, clear language, particularly if you are conferencing with the help of a translator. Stop periodically to ask parents if they understand what you have said up to that point, if they have questions or need clarifications.

Affective Filters

Even if you observe cultural rules closely when communicating with parents, there are also affective or emotional factors at play, especially in face-to-face conversations at school.

- Feelings of apprehension or lack of confidence are common when experiencing another culture. Parents don't want to make a mistake with their child's teacher, so they may be very quiet. That doesn't mean they're not interested. Culture shock can even look like apathy, when it is probably just overload.

- Differences between cultures are often experienced as threatening, particularly when parents see their children assimilating rapidly, picking up habits that are unacceptable at home. They may also be concerned if your style of teaching and disciplining students differs radically from their own school experience. Parents from some Asian cultures expect corporal punishment in schools. They find American students' behavior shocking and the schools lawless.

- Parents may not have attended school and feel shy or inadequate about discussing their child's academic progress. It is vital to acknowledge them as the experts about their child and point out all the ways that they have already helped their child learn, regardless of their level of formal education.

- What is logical and important in one culture may seem irrational and unimportant to an outsider. For example, a Korean family may be very upset if their child is assigned to Room 4, and insist that he be changed to another teacher. This could feel like a personal rejection unless you understand that the number 4 is seen as so unlucky—like our number 13—that in Korean hotels and hospitals, there is no fourth floor. The word *four* in Korean is a homonym for death.

- When parents come to school, you are in the role of "expert" and for various reasons that may increase their discomfort. In some parts of the world—regrettably not here—teachers are high-status individuals. If parents come from those cultures they may seem overly tentative and deferential, while you are hoping for a robust dialogue. Or you may meet gender resistance if parents hail from a culture where women are supposed to be subservient, and you are trying to conduct a conference as if all parties are equal.

It may seem like there's a universe of cultural practices out there just waiting to be discovered, but with very little time on your hands, you may worry that you'll never learn enough fast enough to avoid cultural gaffes. But remember, parents are eager to help you. They're very forgiving when they realize that you have an authentic interest in their cultures and are passionately committed to the education of their child.

A Parent Conference Kit

There are many kinds of conferences that you have all year—the most common, especially with younger students, being the mobile variety—at the gate, at the carnival, even at the farmers' market on Saturday morning. It's amazing how much you can accomplish with a bag of tomatoes in one hand and a cantaloupe in the other! But when most of us think of conferences, it's the formal meetings early in the year that come to mind, where you sit down with parents to have a detailed conversation that replaces or augments written progress reports.

These face-to-face conversations are extremely important, but unfortunately, the reality is sometimes a brief and unsatisfying encounter. The twenty-minute affair is divided into predetermined topics—math facts, reading scores, cursive writing, name the fifty states, and don't forget PE! The presentation is about as personal as a newspaper horoscope. Half the time, teachers seem to be speaking in code—IEP, AYP, Star-9, and critical pedagogy. It's no surprise that when you finally ask, "Do you have any questions?" parents are dazed and unresponsive.

Many parents are dismayed to discover that the Parents-As-Partners banner hanging over the front of the school means that every time they talk to the teacher, they'll leave with a To Do list that looks like a pre-Harvard prep course: Practice multiplication tables every night. Check math homework. Correct spelling errors. Read the classics aloud for fifteen minutes. Speak English, Latin, French, Esperanto. More than a few parents have complained, "One simple question and now I have a part-time job. What's that teacher doing all day, anyway?"

Some conferences are downright painful. Parents endure a litany of their child's behavioral and cognitive deficiencies, with a none-too-subtle hint that DNA may be at the root of the problems. They slink away, filled with school-hating memories. For these parents, conferences are an annual event where they are robbed in installments of any hope for their child.

If parents find their stress level soaring at conference time, just let them try being the teacher. After weeks of preparing portfolios, writing narratives, and sprucing up the room, you cheerfully plow through several dozen meetings that resemble anything from a therapy session to a quiz show—occasionally, target practice with live ammunition. Seasoned teachers bring tissues and wear body armor.

For every conference that goes well, there's the potential that the very next one will be a rout. Before you ever open your folder or your mouth, a vitriolic parent seizes the agenda and demands to know why "her extremely bright child is wasting six hours a day, bored to tears." This is followed by threats of going to the principal, board members, or a state senator, depending on the IQ of the child. Can't you feel your stomach twisting into a Gordian knot?

Sometimes teachers discover that instead of holding a conference, they have a front-row seat at a long-running custody battle. More than a few divorced parents drag their disputes into the classroom, vigorously arm wrestling over who supervises homework best. Then they turn in unison on the wary teacher, demanding that he crown the better parent, so they can move on to Round Two. Others parents seem so nervous or eager to please that they upstage the teacher completely, monologuing about themselves until time's up. Some don't show up at all.

Experiences like these make conferencing a season of dread. Anxiety is high. Advil consumption is higher. After thirty or more maximum-intensity dialogues packed into a single week, bruised and word-weary teachers can be found trolling through the classifieds or staring at the want ads on the supermarket bulletin board and musing softly, "Dog-walker . . . I could do that." Others quietly chuck their ambitious parent education plans for the year and head for the nearest happy hour. Why even try? Don't give up. Conferences may be the single most important event you stage all year long. So let's take a look at some ways that great teachers do it right, and even enjoy the process.

Preparing for Enlightenment Conferences

Great teachers see conferencing as one of the prime opportunities for enlightenment. A well-prepared, well-organized conference can be a two-way information exchange that will make parents partners in the learning process and give the teacher a trove of information to use all year. But nothing will happen if parents don't show up. So the first thing you need to do is publicize conference season over and over, in newsletters, reminders, and phone calls. You're going for 100 percent attendance, so pull out all the stops in as many languages as necessary.

Conference Information Sheet

Parents are more likely to attend their conference if they feel like they know the rules of the road. Craft a clear letter to send out when conference time approaches. It should contain:

- Greeting/looking forward to meeting with you
- Goal of conferences

- Your conference appointment (date/time/location/length of meeting)
- Confirmation response tear-off
- Q&A about conferences
- How do I reschedule if I can't keep my appointment?
- What if we don't finish the conference?
- What if I need a translator? Can I bring my own translator?
- Can my child come?
- How do I share conference results with my child afterward?

Parent's Preparation Packet

It will come as no surprise to you that great conferences take a lot of preparation on your part. But they will be much more fruitful if parents do some preparation, too. Here are some items that you can use or modify to help parents hone in on their child as a learner, and in the process generate valuable information before your conversation ever starts.

- Student Self-Survey (keep a copy for self)
- Parent's Student Profile

Student Self-Survey. Conferences are really a three-party affair—teacher, parent, and student. Some teachers have student-led conferences at least once a year to help kids realize that they are the experts on how they're doing, and

---

Student Self-Survey (Vary the content for different grade levels)

I am smart about

What I like about school

What I do best in school

What I have learned to do

How I'm doing in math

What I like to read

What I like to write

I'd like to learn more about

I'd like to be really good at

My best friends at school are

How I help my class

they are also the only real beneficiaries of their effort. But in many schools students are not invited to conferences, even when they reach the upper grades. Nonetheless, you can include the students' point of view by helping them think through their progress and goals using a self-survey. Sharing this with parents gives them the bigger picture about their child and may provide some positive insights that parents will truly appreciate. Remind parents that this is not a report card, but a self-assessment, which is one of the most powerful tools for growth.

Parents' Student Profile

Now it's the parents' turn to have a good long think about their child as a learner—inside and outside of school. They may want to discuss the profile with their kids as they fill it out, and the resulting conversation could be enormously interesting. However they decide to complete the profile, the time spent will be great preparation for the serious business of parent–teacher conferencing. This is much better than having parents who breeze in expecting a glitzy but not overly taxing performance from you, after which they can delete you from the To Do list in their palm pilot.

If you have parents who do not write well, set up a time when they can meet with community liaisons or classroom aides to dictate their answers.

Parents' Student Profile

The most important thing to my child (passions, interests) is

My child is most sensitive about

My child has strengths or talents in

My child's hobbies are

My child's personal qualities include

My health/safety concerns are

Issues that could affect attendance or learning are

The most important thing you should know about my child is

What I wonder about my child as a student is

Before Conferences Begin

Organize examples of student work to go with each point you want to make about a student. Parents should not have to take your comments on faith, especially if the student needs help from home and school. You need to be concrete in your statements and use examples to show the student's whole range of achievement, not just the worst papers to drive home your point, or the best to avoid a confrontation.

Be prepared to answer questions—lots and lots of questions. Whenever possible, cite specific examples to illustrate your answer. If you don't have an answer, say so immediately. Don't hem and haw. It wastes time and spoils your image. Don't say, "I'll try to find out." Lean in. Say enthusiastically, "That's a great question. I'll find out and let you know. Shall I call you or do you prefer e-mail?" Keep a clipboard handy during conferences and jot down follow-up chores. Parents might ask:

> How does my child get along with other students?
>
> Does my child participate in class discussions and activities?
>
> How can I know on a daily basis what homework has been assigned?
>
> How do you accommodate for learning differences?
>
> Do you know that my child has an IEP or 504?
>
> How are special education services integrated into the regular day?
>
> How will I know if my child is falling behind the rest of the class?
>
> Does my child get into trouble?
>
> How do you prevent kids from teasing my child about his disability?
>
> What kinds of tests will my child have to take this year?
>
> Can I sign a waiver to exempt my child from the tests? Do you recommend that?
>
> Can my child's educational therapist work with him here during the school day?
>
> Can my child get all his special education services after school so he doesn't have to miss class time with you?
>
> How does my child handle taking tests? How can I help her prepare?
>
> How can I help my child improve in math, reading, and so on at home?
>
> What is the best thing I can do to help my child succeed in school?

Take a few minutes to find out who's who in your students' lives. Scrutinize the school directory, review information on emergency cards, or look at enrollment forms for information on parents and guardians. Some children have different last names from at least one parent. It's awkward to start a conference by calling a parent or stepparent the wrong name, or not knowing that the child's mother is actually an aunt who is acting as guardian. Knowing the players makes a positive impression and gives you helpful information about the family.

On Conference Day

Signage.   For some parents, this could be their first time in your room or even at the school, so help them find their way. Many working parents arrive separately. You don't want to sit waiting with mom for fifteen minutes while dad wanders around the campus. Put a big sign on your door, or set an easel at the end of the hallway. If you room is really difficult to find, put signs by the school entrance or include directions in your conference preparation materials. If for some reason you're not meeting in your classroom, be sure everyone in the office knows where to find you.

At Ease.   Don't barricade yourself behind your desk. Choose a table where all the participants can be comfortable and try to find chairs that will accommodate a normal-sized adult, even if you have to borrow some from the library or nurse's office every afternoon and return them by morning. It's hard for a six-footer to perch on a kindergarten chair and then concentrate. Have a table large enough so you can look at student work together.

Be Prepared.   Have a basket of bite-sized candy on the table and a box of tissues. Everyone appreciates a sugar boost during intense moments, and occasionally there are tears. Most teachers have heard stories about divorce, death, or family illness during conferences. Be empathic and then refocus on the student as quickly as possible.

Look Professional.   Think about how you'd feel if you went for your annual health exam and the doctor arrived looking as if she'd just rolled out of bed. Not a confidence-boosting image. Parents come to conferences with similar expectations. They want to feel that the person who spends the better part of 180 days per year with their child is a professional. The way your room looks and the way you dress speak volumes. So tidy up. Make sure your room is clean even if you have to sweep it yourself, and put up current, substantive displays of student work. Then dress up. It may be tempting to show up in casual gear—after all, you'll be sitting for hours and sweating if the going gets rough. Don't do it. Professional dress promotes better behavior, and contributes to an atmosphere of mutual respect.

Set the Agenda.   Having a simple, generic agenda will keep the conversation focused on the child and his work. Give a copy of the agenda to the parents at the beginning of the conference, and refer to it during the meeting as a way to stay on your message. If the comments become too tangential or a parent is a bit long-winded, you can point to your agenda and say, "I really hope we can talk about all of these points because I need your input. Maybe we can loop back to this topic at the end of the conference." The agenda could be as simple as:

Parent Conference Agenda, October 2004

1. Tell me more about . . .
2. Your child as a learner
3. Strengths and interests
4. Where we need to focus
5. Next steps together

Lead with Good News. Always start with the student's strengths—social, emotional, or academic. You may want to have an index card for each student on which you jot anecdotes or comments to share with parents at conferences. If you can't think of anything positive about a student, you need to adjust your glasses. It may be a sense of humor, unbridled curiosity, love of classroom pets, leadership skills with younger students on the playground, artistic ability, or simply that she loves to drive the broom and dustpan around the room. If you gave parents a student profile to fill out, this would be a good time to segue to their observations, adding more positive fuel to the conversation. Or just ask and take notes as they tell you about their child's hobbies, talents, or special experiences that help you understand more about your student.

Pick Your Battles. The forty or so minutes you've set aside for a face-to-face parent conference are prime time for learning. Don't waste ten minutes obsessing about how a student still can't make a cursive capital G. Or that he's messy. Or "young." This is childhood we're dealing with here. It's the messy, experimental, sometimes painful process of getting from young to old, in whatever time it takes. Criticizing nonessentials is self-sabotage. You may as well stick great wads of wax in the parents' ears once you start down that negative road. They're deaf from then on. And hurt. So choose a few areas for improvement and give the parents concrete examples of what it will look like when their child makes progress in that area. Give them at least two ways they can help. Now you have an ally, so there are two people working to achieve your goals. You'll get little support if parents leave the conference feeling wounded and bad-mouth you at every opportunity.

End on an Ascending Note. At the end of each conference agree on a plan of action for school and at home to help the student improve. Decide on a way to stay in touch to monitor progress. Set up a next meeting if it seems necessary. Thank the parents for taking time to come and talk with you, and cite specifically one item that you learned from them that will help you teach their child more effectively. Parents who have enjoyed their conference with you may end with a shower of compliments. Don't say, "Oh, it's nothing." Deflecting a compliment diminishes both you and the person offering it. Just say, "Thank you, I truly enjoy my students," and smile. Accepting positive remarks, and really hearing them, is a way to nurture yourself. And you deserve all the nurturing you can get.

After Conferences Are Finished

When the last parent heads into the sunset, you may be tempted to heave a huge sigh of relief and not think about conferences for another year. But great teachers have one more strategy that helps them get maximum mileage out of all those hours of chin wagging. They send out thank-you notes—individual or an open letter to all parents. Thank them for taking the time to come and teach you about their kids. Mention how much you appreciate their efforts to follow-up on your suggestions—"I saw improvement the very next day." Finally, invite them to contact you if they have any additional questions or concerns and review the directions for the best way to reach you.

Public Relations or Self-Defense?

In a recent survey, 90 percent of the parents responding said that their child's teacher was just fine. Ninety percent! Given that number, you'd expect teachers to be up to their intercoms in thoughtful gifts, fresh flowers, or at the very least, thank-you notes. The reality is that happy parents are quietly grateful, while the unhappy few noisily devour your time and peace of mind. There are years when you seem to have a handful of parents—or maybe just one—who arrive in an antagonistic mood. Many new teachers have been grilled to within an inch of their lives because parents just don't trust novices. Or there's a curriculum change—new math or literacy initiatives—and parents see their kids as guinea pigs in a doomed experiment. Some parents were educated in another country, and find American education puzzling or inferior. You become the sounding board for their fears and questions. If they're carrying personal scars of racial or ethnic discrimination from their own school experiences, they may be worried that their child is in for the same treatment. Trust will be a huge factor with those parents. All of these concerns take time and thoughtful communication, but they can be successfully addressed.

Occasionally you get parents who are bent on enlightening you about education in a tone of voice that could cut through sheet metal. In extreme cases, they may "put you on notice," announce that they "won't tolerate it," or allude to their lawyer. It's never fun. In fact, it often has the heat and sting of a slap in the face. You can't gasp audibly, say "Ex-cuuuusssse me?", or blurt out, "How very rude! Now I know why your child has no friends." So, what's a teacher to do?

Setting Boundaries

As a teacher, you deal with the good, the bad, and the ugly. The good is you're the prime mover in dozens of kids' education. That's hugely important. The bad—there's one of you, and lots of them. Thirty kids times two or more parents, depending on the number of divorces and remarriages, makes easily 100 people who crave your attention. The ugly is that teachers, as public servants, are increasingly subjected to abuse and threats from parents, students, and members of the community. You need to learn to set boundaries with parents to keep yourself sane and safe.

Overly Dependent Parents

There are people who want to be good parents, may even be good parents, but they missed out on the confidence gene, so they second-guess themselves to death. When that doesn't work, they attach themselves to you like a survivor clinging to a lifeboat. They send five ponderous emails a day, some only minutes apart, then corner you after school and bend your ear until it juts out from your head at a right angle. They want to talk to you every day, but have a hard time getting to the point, so when they open with, "Do you have just a second?" you know it will be fifteen agonizing minutes replaying old issues that never seem to die like:

- Can you make sure my daughter eats all her lunch before she goes to play?
- Can you send me an email every day to let me know what he's supposed to do for homework? He's always confused about your assignments.
- Can you put him at a table with some kids who aren't too smart, otherwise he feels bad?
- Can you help him get into the dodge ball game? Nobody picks him.
- Can you please tell my husband that the way he talks to my daughter about her homework isn't helping her?
- Can you let her stay in the room with you during PE because she's too shy to do team sports?

They ask parenting advice, like how much television their child should watch and what you think of various offerings on cable stations. They want reassurance that video games don't cause irreversible brain damage, but could you please tell their son to stop playing them so much because he never listens to them. A few parents of young children are struggling with their own separation anxiety, so feeling connected to you helps them feel less distant from their child. Becoming your "best friend" blunts the full force of reality—that their child goes away for five or six hours a day and they don't know exactly what's going on.

As sweet and benign as these people may seem at first, you really need to set boundaries. They may need a good therapist, but you're not it. Be quite clear about the number and kind of contacts you think are appropriate and then stick to it. If you agree to one email a day and you get seventeen, just answer one and delete the rest. Don't do a stand-up conference at your door every afternoon—make appointments. If they try to slip in just one question, say you have a colleague waiting for a planning session or you're due at the district office for a meeting. When you meet for an appointment, help shape the conversation. If they start to ramble, giving too many details, ask: What's your goal? How can I help you achieve that? Finally, be sure to set a time limit and make another appointment directly afterward so you have to stop. This may seem a bit harsh, but you are the teacher to an entire class and your time needs to be spent on thinking and preparing to be the best teacher for all of your students. That's your first obligation.

Overanxious Parents

Some parents are highly competitive and eager to have their kids succeed, often in ways that bear no resemblance to the goals you've set for your students. They do Internet research every week on what's new in reading techniques and want to share it with you. They can't tolerate it when their child makes mistakes. Some are perfectionists and their neuroses are driving you and their kid crazy. They may resort to doing most of the homework for their kids just to ensure high marks. Or they want you to give extra homework that they think is more challenging and fills up their child's time. Be careful. Overanxious parents seem overly critical of you and really get under your emotional radar. They may bring back papers that you corrected and show you where you went wrong, or recalculate test scores until you want to scream, "Get a life!" But then you realize—this kid is their life.

Some overanxious parents want to be classroom volunteers but spend most of their time helping their kids do their assignments or observing other students to see how their offspring are faring in the classroom competition category. Some just want to keep an eye on you. These parents may also spend a fair amount of time camped outside your room, taking impromptu surveys, or sharing their latest observations about your curriculum with any parents they failed to reach during a two- or three-hour telephone marathon the night before. It's like having your own personal Wal-Mart greeter, but not nearly as much fun.

Overanxious parents ask questions like: How do you make sure that the smart students don't get bored while you're spending all your time with the slow ones? Last year my son learned everything that you covered this month. When are you going to teach something new? I heard that the other fourth grade is already doing long division. How will our kids ever pass the state tests if you don't catch up?

These parents need strict boundaries. And while we're on the subject, yes, you do have the right to limit their access to your room and you. Diplomacy is a good way to start, but if that doesn't work, you may need to ask your principal for support.

Abusive Parents

Your job description probably contains the phrase *and other duties as assigned*, which may encompass cleaning up vomit or trapping an escaped gerbil, but it never includes accepting verbal abuse or physical assault. Yet teachers routinely encounter parents so explosive that they can clear a room. Not to mention the garden-variety drunks, bullies, and people with Diminished Capacity stamped on their foreheads. Even if you maintain the face of a Buddha and the composure of Ghandi, these clashes are mega-stressers. Since it's impossible to eliminate these heart-stopping encounters, here are some techniques to use when bad behavior goes ballistic.

- Never respond to provocation. When the fight-or-flight instinct kicks in, the answer is *never* fight. Even if you have to shove your fist into your mouth up to your third knuckle, don't say what you're thinking. My mentor John Shambra's advice was "Keep you hands in your pockets and say the fifth thing that comes to your mind."

- If tempers and volume escalate, or language takes a threatening turn, even if the atmosphere just gets too tense or rude for your comfort level, end the meeting. In a calm voice, explain that you will be happy to reschedule, "But please understand. I don't feel we can have a productive meeting at this point."

- Stand up and walk toward the door or exit. Say, "I'm sorry that our meeting has to end this way. I truly hope that we'll be able to continue the conversation at another time." If the person refuses to leave the room, walk out anyway. That puts a stop to the encounter.

- Alert someone on the staff of the problem, and ask them to stay with you until the angry party departs.

- If the person tries to provoke you—"So you're calling my kid a liar"— or peppers you with questions to restart the conversation, use the broken record technique. Just repeat again in a calm voice, "I can't talk to you anymore, but I hope we can continue on another day." It feels weirdly robotic, but you're winning by maintaining control.

- If the person refuses to leave or becomes more agitated, tell him or her that you will need to call campus security or the police. Then, follow through. Better safe than sorry. If the police arrive and write a report, get a copy.

- Document the entire incident in a short memo as soon as your hands stop shaking. Give it to your supervisor and ask him or her to send it to the person at central office who handles legal matters.

- If the behavior is repeated or escalates, the district can obtain a tempo-rary restraining order (TRO) against the person, barring him from coming on campus without your administrator's expressed permission. This is a last resort and a real low point for school-family relations. If you are pushed to this point, make sure that the student is insulated from the skirmishes and that your feelings toward the parent don't taint your relationship with the child.

After an encounter like this, get help. Debrief with your school psychologist, a counselor, or your therapist. Don't keep the trauma bottled up where it can create a reluctance to meet with any parent. It's also good to go out and do something unusually nice for yourself. You always deserve it, but especially after shoddy or frightening treatment by a member of your school community.

What's in It for You?

Communicating with parents can feel like a second job, but great teachers seem to relish it. They've mastered a dozen ways to get the word out, over and over again. It's not just that they have a hyperactive PR gene. There is much to be gained when teachers and families connect.

First of all, parents want to believe that teachers are effective and caring. They also read the newspaper and watch television. I don't have to tell you that the media is not your best friend. While you're quietly knocking yourself out to help your kids, parents are hit with film-at-eleven about the latest school failure. Good personal communication combats bad generic press.

But more compelling reasons to get parents in the loop and keep them there are that it's good for your kids and it achieves your goals. In a recent review of the literature about parent involvement conducted by the Center for Law and Education, Anne Henderson and Nancy Berla (1994) found that

- When parents are systematically involved, economically disadvantaged students' achievement not only improves, but can reach levels that are standard for middle-class children.
- Students whose parents are involved are more likely to stay in school.
- Schools that work well with parents have improved teacher morale and higher ratings of teachers by parents.

Here's the most impressive finding that should have you running to your computer to pound out a newsletter or plan a parent meeting: A teacher's efforts to keep parents informed and involved have a greater impact on inner-city parent involvement than other factors such as marital status, family size, parent's level of education, or the student's grade level. Bottom line: Parent involvement—and that means all kinds of parents—improves student achievement.

> *Education is the ability to listen to almost anything without losing your temper or your self-confidence.*
> —Robert Frost

Resources

Dresser, Norine. 1996. *Multicultural Manners: New Rules of Etiquette for a Changing Society.* New York: Wiley.

Henderson, Anne, and Nancy Berla. 1994. *Beyond the Bake Sale: An Educator's Guide to Working with Parents.* Washington, DC: Center for Law and Education.

White-Clark, Renee, and Larry Decker. 1996. *The "Hard-to-Reach" Parent: Old Challenges, New Insights.* Charlottesville, VA: Mid-Atlantic Center for Community Education at University of Virginia.

SECRET #12

Great Teachers Are Lifelong Learners

Reaching, Recharging, and Moving On

In This Chapter:
- What's the Big Idea About Teaching as a Famine Culture?
- Connecting with Colleagues
- Collaborating and Coaching
- Meet Anne Brown, Mentor Extraordinaire
- Connecting with Professionals Beyond Your Campus
- Rethinking—The Moving-On Questionnaire
- Job Searches and Sources
- Moving On

Most of the teachers I've worked with are intelligent, dedicated, and relentlessly optimistic, despite the fact that their primary employment perk is unlimited access to wide-lined manila paper and airline-type meals—without the annoyance of e-tickets or security screenings. Their schools are often located in neighborhoods that are desperately antiscenic or downright unsafe. While a few schools have ample parking arrangements, many feature lots the size of a postage stamp. Late arrivals begin their workday cruising the neighborhood, praying to the parking-space gods, then sprinting in a beat-the-clock fashion to campus. Once inside, they navigate darkened corridors that bring to mind a hospital in the third world—we're conserving electricity—before scooping up a gaggle of students clustered outside their classroom doors.

Classrooms vary from school to school. Some are sunny, some efficient and hygienic, at least until the kids arrive. Many, no bigger than a living room, evoke memories of those 1950s bomb shelters with the added luxury of aging texts, antiquated audio-visual equipment, and a chalkboard. Sometimes not even that! I heard of a teacher whose board was so slick from years of use and weekly washings, that it was chalk-proof. Simple notations during lessons produced a stutter of codelike dots and a sound that resembled squealing tires. Her first graders cringed every time she went for the chalk, but pleas for a new board fell on deaf ears. In desperation, she scrawled *Fuck You* across the useless surface with a permanent marker and promptly reported the vandalism. A new board appeared within days.

A veteran teacher confessed that she staked out her room for two days during the summer while it was being cleaned for fear that her furniture, stacked in the hallway, would be stolen. It wasn't even great furniture. Some of it resembled fire starter, but it was all she had. And she's lucky compared to first-year teachers who may rove from bungalow to portable classroom every three weeks, looking more like an itinerant encyclopedia sales force than professionals with advanced degrees. Lots of teachers work for decades in decaying rooms that are alternately sweltering or frigid, depending on the season. Nonetheless, these ingenious people have discovered a thousand ways to turn a World War II Quonset hut into a stylish and convivial space. Most of them involve butcher paper.

So many rooms. But no room service. In fact, schools are notoriously bad food zones. There's usually a cafeteria of sorts that distributes bag lunches or serves up a carbohydrate buffet—entrees and desserts guaranteed to make you waddle, with a little something green that most kids will discard without so much as an exploratory nudge from their plastic "sporkette." Most teachers spend half their lunch hour looking for lost milk money, returning phone calls, or begging for cuts in line at the copy machine. Is it any wonder that many of them survive on a steady supply of diet Coke stashed in a desk drawer?

Things are no better in the supply room. Teachers prepare and teach a demanding curriculum in an environment of unrelenting scarcity, so hoarding is a survival tool. Holiday-colored anything (red and green for Christmas, orange and black for Halloween), brand-new glue bottles, and scissors so dull they could pass inspection by an airline security screener—it all disappears within hours of delivery and is stored like nuts for winter. Scrounging and recycling are right up there with behavior management skills in the guide to successful teaching.

Self-sufficient teachers routinely stock and furnish their classrooms at their own expense, while cash-strapped administrators pore over requests for conference registration fees—a mere $79—like bank examiners, and scrutinize textbook requisitions as if they were financing a condo. Scarcity has been such a constant in education for so long, it has achieved the status of a natural law. As a result, teachers have learned to appreciate the low-level ecstasy of a supply closet brimming with colored markers and yarn.

What's the Big Idea About Teaching as a Famine Culture?

Beyond the lack of material resources and creature comforts, there are more serious conditions in education that create an atmosphere of famine, turning teachers' thoughts from success to self-preservation or simply survival. Teachers endure low salaries and lower status, even in eras of economic boom. When the economy goes south, you can bank on larger class sizes, smaller paychecks, fewer professional development days, and rationing of essentials. Teachers have limited autonomy over their schedules and even less over instructional programs. Despite their degrees and credentials, they're deprived of authentic input on critical decisions that directly affect the nature of their work. Research and policy making are routinely carried out with no direct participation from the very teachers who are being researched and regulated.

In short, educators live with a persistent scarcity of materials, information, and power, not knowing if or when more will be available. It's a professional famine with no relief in sight. As a result, many exhibit symptoms associated with people who live in a time of unrelenting famine. In his book, *Man and Society in Calamity* (1942), the researcher Pitirim Sorokin observed that victims of a natural disaster like famine don't feel that they possess the means to change the situation. They're at the mercy of the elements and unresponsive political systems. Teachers often feel the same way, resulting in a what's-the-use attitude, a mixture of powerlessness and loss of hope. They stop fighting for best practices or simply stop thinking.

Famine victims and teachers often feel that they have to make choices that involve personal sacrifice. For teachers, this usually means giving too much of their time, money, and effort for too little in return. So they shut down, refusing to engage in professional growth of any kind, under any conditions—even with the inducements of stipends, extra pay, or release time with a substitute teacher—in order to conserve their limited personal resources. This withdrawal from professional life may be broken by periodic attacks on the district, the system, the principal—anyone responsible for not providing nourishment or the means to improve the situation. Eventually, some teachers simply cannot go on without regular, sufficient sustenance, so they quit the profession or endure the slow death of burning out on the job.

But not all teachers. Not the great ones. Despite the fact that they teach in a famine culture, great teachers never go hungry.

The trick to thriving in a famine culture is reaching out and making connections with people and activities that can nourish you—your peers, your principal, and professional organizations beyond your campus. In effect, you need to feed yourself and grow by constructing your own professional development programs.

The first hurdle you'll need to overcome is isolation. This is no small feat since school schedules and even the architecture reinforce the privatization of practice. It's tough to collaborate with talented peers if you're all teaching in self-contained cubicles, at the same time. The teacher in Room 2 often has no idea what's going on in Room 3. If she inquires, she may get a quizzical look or the cold shoulder. Despite years of reform efforts emphasizing teamwork, "Don't ask—don't tell" is still a more common guideline than collaboration.

Happily, on every campus and beyond, there are people eager to help you. The trick is finding them. Whether you're a novice teacher struggling through your first challenging year in the classroom, or a veteran hungry for collegial support, you need to get smarter about finding colleagues who can help you construct a vigorous, satisfying professional development plan.

Connecting with Colleagues

Great teachers are perpetually curious about the process of teaching and learning, so they're always prospecting for fresh faces, fresh ideas, and challenging conversations. Rather than circling the wagons in the lunchroom, they explicitly seek out new teachers, even student teachers, as a pipeline to the latest in research or best practices. The great ones believe that their professional power and value come from innovation, sharing, and inventing solutions. This behavior is in stark contrast to teachers operating from a famine mentality who see power and knowledge as finite commodities. They maintain their status by hoarding, trading, or cautiously doling out their craft knowledge. Famine teachers believe that ideas, especially the good ones, must be closely guarded, like the last bag of rice on the shelf. I once worked in a school where a dispute over "ownership" of a poetry lesson led to a six-month rift in the third grade team. Don't let that happen to you. There's a banquet out there, and here are some ways to find your place at the table.

Informal Alliances

Walk and Talk. Find a partner who wants to walk for thirty minutes or so before or after school. Bring your tennis shoes, head for the sidewalks, and while you're exercising you can swap stories about what you're doing with your students. Or don't talk about work. Just get some endorphins pumping through your system. As the character Elle Woods said in the film, Legally Blonde, "Exercise creates endorphins. Endorphins make you happy. Happy people don't kill." That should be a comfort to your students and their parents.

Book Clubs. It's wonderful to live in a time when books are chic and your local bookstore is the "in" place. So if you mention starting a book club at your school, you'll probably get lots of takers. There are hundreds of educational titles that could be on your list, but don't limit yourselves to books about teaching. Choose a wonderful new novel or a classic. Reading great books can help you escape from your environment long before vacation rolls around. That's a good thing in itself. But more important, talking about good literature reinforces the skills that you must teach your students if you want them to become lifelong readers.

Meet and Eat. Organize Brown Bag Seminars for anyone who's interested. Pick a room. Announce the topic. You all bring your own lunch and one person presents on an area of expertise that can be taught in one or two short sessions. For example, I had a colleague who trained us in the high points of "Handwriting Without Tears" during forty-five minutes over sandwiches. Everyone got smarter, and later that week our kids were the beneficiaries.

Theme Dinners. This sounds like something you'd find on a cruise ship, but in this case the theme is a topic that really deserves some undivided attention. One year my school had an influx of autistic kids who were fully included in regular classrooms. Suddenly there was a desperate need for current information on autism and practical strategies for behavior management. We invited a district specialist to dinner, cooked up some pasta, and our knowledge base took a big leap.

Mutual Support

Sharing Bin. Some teachers have accumulated so much precious stuff that they can't see the floor in their garage, and their basement is the Smithsonian of teaching devices. When that's full, they resort to renting a storage space. Raised eyebrows usually get the response, "But what if I have to teach first grade again? I'll need this." You can help counteract this particular brand of hoarding in yourself and others by establishing a sharing bin—like a tag sale or a swap meet, but everything's free. Just designate a table or shelf at school where people can drop off unwanted materials for the taking. Novice teachers will be forever grateful.

Pass-It-On. If you find a wonderful website loaded with fresh art ideas and science freebies, bookmark it, then forward it to three other people on the staff who will welcome the resource. Encourage them to pass it on.

Connecting with Your Principal. Great teachers have concocted a dozen ploys to lure busy principals into their classrooms, and as a result they get recognition, support, and guidance. In short, they get fed. I'm not talking about kissing up. I mean get that principal into the room so you can do some work together. If this statement elicits howls of laughter or derision from you and your colleagues, I understand. Many teachers view their administrators with suspicion, or even contempt. And really, who can blame them?

There's the principal who glides through the school, waving and smiling like royalty but avoiding any contact. Or the instructional leader who abandons his staff to teach unevaluated for years, but won't let them into the supply closet without an escort. If you're long on kids and short on texts, he posts an armed guard at the bookroom. These portraits in leadership don't inspire confidence, but they're the exception. Most principals are passionate about education and they'd pounce on the chance to have a professional conversation with you. It beats the hell out of shuffling papers in a dreary office.

I know. I was a principal.

I taught for twenty-three years, mostly for great principals whom I loved, but for the life of me I couldn't figure out what they did all day. Then I became a principal, and some days I was still puzzled. But I can tell you this much: Principals don't spend nearly as much time as they'd like in classrooms, unless an enthusiastic teacher says, "You *have* to see what my kids are doing." This is a moment of supreme joy for an administrator. It may even feel faintly indulgent—like a little holiday. Suddenly they feel energized. They remember what's great about their school—it's you.

So get to know your principal. Invite him to look at student work or listen to individual kids read. Ask her to observe a child before you have an IEP or 504 meeting. Then she can help make the tough decisions or support you if you have difficult information to share with a parent. What else do you get out of courting your principal? He knows firsthand about the quality of your work, so when a parent calls to complain that you never teach science, and he's seen your kids knee-deep in the scientific method, he can counter with eyewitness accounts. And when the principal starts popping in regularly, you have someone to witness your brilliance. Then you get the praise and appreciation you deserve, so you never need to go hungry at school.

Collaborating and Coaching

Tag Team

There are probably a dozen great teachers at your school who could model skills that you want to learn, but it won't happen if you can't break free. So develop a tag team. Pair up with a kindred spirit, introduce your kids to each other, and build a schedule of collaboration. Think of ways your two classes can learn together. Start with short mixers that emphasize getting to know each other and cooperative skills. When the kids get good at it, one of you slips away to observe a peer while the other conducts an activity with both classes. You can team at the same grade level or do a cross-age pairing. Keep reading for suggested activities that work well for cross-age groups.

Cross-Age Projects

This is similar to the tag-team concept, but with the twist of deliberately finding a colleague who teaches a different grade. The idea here is to learn by teaching together. Cross-age collaborations allow you to pierce the grade-level boundaries that are sometimes a part of a school's culture. Your kids escape the social limitations of their age group and build relationships with younger or older students. Older kids feel competent. Younger kids find role models. You can attempt a broader range of activities when you have older students to model and assist. Here are some activities that work well in cross-age settings:

- Pair-share reading in the library
- Board games such as checkers, chess, Monopoly, or Chinese checkers
- Campus beautification and gardening
- Music appreciation and movement
- Building models
- Collaborative drawing
- Letter-writing campaigns and community service

Student Teachers

Having student teachers can be nerve-wracking. They watch you like a hawk and pepper you with questions laced with phrases like *critical pedagogy, accountable talk,* and *fluctuational instructional expedients.* They quote Vygotsky with confidence and ask if you agree. They make you think.

Then they take their ideas for a test drive. You watch them like a hawk, then pepper them with questions about why Matthew seemed so confused, and Haley unraveled the sleeve of her sweater, and "What do you think Mario meant when he said that pumpkins have juice inside, even after you'd cut open that pumpkin? How could you explore that with him?" You make them think.

Both of you go home with throbbing heads, determined to do it even better on the morrow. On the best days it's intense, so if you're thinking you'll finally get a coffee break once the student teacher moves in, think again. Your work will actually double because you have to provide the richest teaching experience for your student teacher—including the occasional failure—without compromising learning for your own students. Even if you have to give up coffee completely, training student teachers is one of the most significant contributions you can make to the profession.

The Fine Art of Mentoring

Even after a great student teaching experience—and some are arrestingly dire—new teachers still need support. First of all, novice teachers frequently inherit a group of students affectionately known as the "dump class." And they're facing an academic agenda that seems to be powered-by-locomotive. Even seasoned teachers struggle to meet their goals, since year after year they are subjected to rapidly changing reform plans that reduce them to the status of crash-test dummies. It's little wonder that novices turn in their keys at an alarming rate. So think about becoming a mentor. It's another great way to grow professionally and raise a crop of excellent colleagues. The success rate of new teachers jumps about 50 percent if they're assigned to a mentor. If that mentor is Anne Brown, the novice is on the way to greatness.

Meet Anne Brown, Mentor Extraordinaire

If you ask Anne Brown how she became a great teacher, she'll tell you, "It all started in the backseat of a car. When I was a new teacher, I carpooled with four other teachers. Nina Cole was a second-grade teacher and a mom with four kids. She was my mentor." Everyday Nina and Anne would talk on the way to school and debrief on the way home. "She'd ask—how did that go? Maybe you could try it this way? I've got some books you could borrow." This motorized mentoring program may seem a bit unorthodox in an era of bureaucratized everything, but for four years it provided Anne with daily support, curriculum ideas, trade secrets, a cheering section, and survival skills. "That's how I learned to teach."

That's why Anne was the perfect candidate to be a mentor when my state adopted class size reduction and our school hired eleven new teachers over a single summer. As a longtime teacher, I knew the value of a high-quality mentoring program. As principal of the school, I wanted the best person for the job. So I left a small note on Anne's desk: "Please apply. You'll only regret it some days." God bless her, she did, and eleven novices got the opportunity of a lifetime!

For a start, Anne makes killer pumpkin bread. It's so hearty, it feels like a meal, and so delicious that people beg shamelessly for the recipe. That's why it was perfect for her lucky novices. Like everything Anne offered, it left them well-nourished and hungry for more.

Anne was a matchmaker, linking people and ideas. Her greatest joy came from putting the perfect resource in the outstretched hands of new teachers. I wish I had a nickel for every time I heard her say, "Oh, I have just the book for you! Do you know Lucy Calkins?" Instantly, the book or article would appear

Anne Brown's Pumpkin Bread

Preheat oven to 350 degrees and lightly butter two large loaf pans.

In a large bowl beat until smooth:
2½ cups white sugar
1 cup light brown sugar
1 cup corn oil

Add and beat until smooth:
3 eggs lightly beaten
1 16 oz. can of cooked pumpkin

Mix the dry ingredients together and add, alternating with 1 cup buttermilk until the batter is smooth.
3½ cups all-purpose flour
2 teaspoons baking soda
½ teaspoon salt
1 teaspoon ground cloves, cinnamon, nutmeg, and allspice

Pour the batter into the loaf pans and bake for 55 to 60 minutes, or until inserted knife comes out clean. Let the loaves rest for 10 minutes in the pan, then turn them out onto a wire rack to cool.

from her capacious closets. Now that I think of it, Anne was a bookmonger, with a title for every occasion. If she didn't possess the title you needed, she would deliver the condensed version orally—like animated Cliff Notes—with commentary on the content and literary merits.

So what did Anne do with her squadron of novices? First she squired them around the school like a tour guide at an educational theme park. By the end of their junket, they knew where *all* the textbooks, art paper, and science kits were hiding. Also how to liberate books and art prints from the library after hours, and where to get industrial strength aspirin and Diet Coke on demand. Then the true work began. Mentor meetings started at 7:30 every Tuesday morning, always in a different classroom, so the new teachers could see each others' classes and glean ideas while they met. For the first semester, Anne chose topics based on urgency, and she invited veteran teachers to present with her. The agendas included parent conferences, report cards, the writing process, journaling, literacy resources, record keeping, and classroom management. Then there were those crucial unagendized topics: the ins and outs of faculty politics, when to speak up at staff meetings and when to just listen, how to handle aggressive parents and connect with the phantoms. "Those were the life lessons," recalls Anne. "I had to give them some defenses, help them master the tightrope, and sometimes just let them vent. But most important, we needed to talk about what counts. There was so much coming at them, and it's impossible to do it all. So I tried to keep their eyes on the prize—what would help them reach their goals with their particular kids—the bureaucratic stuff might have to wait."

During the second semester, the novices took the reins of the mentor program. They demonstrated lessons or lead discussions based on their own areas of expertise. But something was still missing. Anne and I knew that those eager acolytes could learn a lot more if we could free them up to observe the great teachers right on our campus. With no money for substitutes, I seized the opportunity to do what I love best—teach kids. We created Visiting Day. I would cover the new teachers' classes while they visited the classrooms of their colleagues. My assistant principal didn't want to miss out on the fun, so he started teaching, too. Soon veteran teachers heard about the project and decided they wanted to get in on the action, so visiting became a permanent feature of the school, and I was never happier.

Anne's Advice to New Mentors

Anne's cardinal rule for mentors is to think of your novices as learners, and then follow all your best teaching instincts with them. "You have to assess where they are and what they need. It will be different for each one, so you have to try to figure it out. Watch them and listen." Here are eight more suggestions from Anne for nurturing novices.

1. Maintain regular contact. New teachers who have regular meetings with their mentor feel like they have a safety net. Things may get bad, but they know they'll have a chance to sort it out with someone who cares and can help. Days may be grueling and parents ungrateful, but come Tuesday morning their mentor will talk them back in from the ledge. The pain or discouragement can't get too deeply ingrained and turn to trauma, if you have regular sessions—even if they're brief.

2. Don't overwhelm them. "I used to think you couldn't have too many books in a classroom, but now I know that new readers can get overwhelmed by thousands of volumes just waiting to be read. The same is true with new teachers." That's a huge insight from book-loving Anne. She recalls that when she moved to a new school, Marion Joy, the teacher next door simply said, "I have lots of materials but I don't want to overwhelm you. If you need anything, just knock on the wall." Anne knocked when she was ready and a friendship grew. Your goal as mentor is to grow successful teachers, but sometimes they just need to know what's going to work for them tomorrow and next week.

3. Offer information in bite-sized chunks. In the same vein, Anne suggests that mentors curb the impulse to explain it all. "Sometimes a new teacher will ask, 'How did you do that?' They're looking for the 101 version, not a graduate course. So you say, 'Here's the first piece' and then you watch and listen to see when they're ready for more. That way it can be assimilated."

4. Encourage independence. "You want them to be able to function on their own and grow confident," Anne insists. So she did nothing for her freshmen that they could do for themselves. But when they really needed her, she was there to coach them through their latest challenge.

5. Discourage perfectionism. Great teachers are risk takers. In fact, they fight for their share of the mistakes because they know that's the surest way to grow. So encourage your novices to share their hunches, the things they wonder about and their half-baked ideas. Have a true confessions segment, where they can tell their Titanic stories, or just puzzle out loud and get help.

6. Share your own failures. Anne recalls that in her carpool days, she learned that even veteran teachers had their dark days, so she was always generous with her tales of disaster. And then she'd laugh. The important question novices need to answer is: What will I do when things go wrong? They need to know that failure is normal—it shows they're trying something new. If a lesson flops, urge them to try it again—but tweak it, tear it down to the ground, and start over, or just dump it. Encourage novices to relax when they run into problems and focus on recovery strategies. Developing resiliency is one of the surest ways to avoid burnout and have fun.

7. Encourage them to balance their lives. This is ironic advice from a woman who can often be reached only by cell phone on Sundays, because she's in her classroom. But she also takes predawn runs, goes to movies, leads a book club, creates amazing pottery, and is devoted to her grandson. So Anne stresses the need for recreation, physical fitness, and just hanging out to balance the demands of a job that can be "like a black hole—no matter how much you do in your classroom, there's always more waiting."

8. Praise and encourage. Anne believes this is the most important part of the job. "If you give even a little bit of encouragement, they'll do amazing things." Mentors seem so powerful to their flock—experienced, calm, professional. A frown or offhand remark can send a bruising message. Outright criticism is deadly. "Leave evaluation up to the administrators and embrace the supporter role with all your heart. They may or may not remember what you say. They will remember how you make them feel."

Anne's Advice to New Teachers

What if you're a new teacher in a school without a mentor program? Are you simply doomed to wander in the wilderness until you stumble on the path to greatness or abandon teaching in a fit of frustration and become a telemarketer? Actually, no. There are dozens of ways to get smarter about teaching, even if you're on your own. Anne has a few suggestions:

Snoop around. Find out who the exceptional teachers are on your campus and then con your way into their rooms. Stop by to admire their students' paintings or a mural in progress. Mention that you heard they're great in social studies. Once you get your foot in the door, look around, ask good questions, and camp out. Most teachers, and certainly the great ones, are dying for a professional conversation. They're flattered that you admire them and more than willing to share. In time, you'll have a valuable colleague and maybe a lifelong friend.

Go online. A virtual university is out there just waiting for you online. Almost anything you want to learn can be delivered electronically to your desk—it's just a matter of Googling until you find a topic of interest. You don't even have to sign up for a formal class. Just read articles posted on the infinity of educational sites, or click on the *New York Times, Washington Post,* or other metropolitan newspapers and go to the education section. It's current events with a classroom slant.

Hit the chat rooms. Did you ever wonder if teachers in Florida are puzzled by the fourth-grade science standards, too? Or if anyone out there has a bright idea for fully including autistic kids? A chat room can be a goldmine of regional, national, and international information. You can hook up with colleagues who are grappling with similar issues and mentor each other across state lines.

Read professional journals. Teachers tend to avoid professional journals, discouraged by esoteric jargon, politically motivated mandates, or mindless craft activities meant to fill time that you don't have. But some professional publications routinely offer high-quality ideas for instruction and food for thought. Don't subscribe until you've sampled their wares. A good university library will have all of them, or check at your district office. Many journals are online so you can read and subscribe from the comfort of your laptop.

Cruise the educational catalogues. Lots of people are closet catalogue addicts. There's something fascinating about all those possibilities—fur-lined sneakers and see-thru bowling shirts—all delivered to your front door. Well, consider shifting your obsession over to professional catalogues to discover what's new and stylish in education. At least twice a year, educational publishers come out with glossy catalogues packed with their latest offerings. And you don't even have to give up a month's salary to get smarter. Just reading them can give you dozens of ideas without ever spending a dime. It's easy to get on their mailing lists, and don't forget to pass those catalogues along to curious colleagues when you're finished browsing.

Earn salary credit in diverse places. Novices in many states must keep taking classes to retain their credentials, and most new teachers take classes to earn salary points, hoping to boost their take-home pay above the risible level. Did you know that many museums, concert halls, and other cultural venues sponsor classes specifically for teachers, and they offer credit? For example, the county art museum in our city hosts Evenings for Educators. Once a month, after the museum closes to the public, it reopens just for teachers, who come to enjoy a tour of the latest exhibition in uncrowded galleries, lectures, and hands-on workshops. Food, music, and a fat packet of handouts, including slides of the featured art, are provided. All that and salary credit, too. As Anne says, "It's not just about your classroom. It uplifts you as a human being."

Spend your staff development time wisely. It's a rare day when a teacher gets to play learner by attending a conference. Rarer still if your district will pay your way. But whether you're footing the bill during the summer or lucky enough to snag a professional development day, you don't want to spend your precious freedom as a captive at a vendor festival, or stuck in a lecture hall with only a discreet nap to break the boredom. So choose well. Look for nationally recognized workshops and conferences. Many publishers put together annual tours of their best authors, who present their current ideas and sign books.

Read, read, read. Anne Brown is more than a bibliophile. She's a hog for anything between covers. The well-organized shelves and crates in her room are crammed with the cream of the literary crop for adults and child learners alike. Here are a few of Anne's favorites for your professional growth.

> *In The Company of Children* by Joanne Findlay
>
> *The Energy to Teach* and *Writing: Teachers and Children at Work* by Donald Graves
>
> *Lessons from a Child* and *The Art of Teaching Writing* by Lucy Calkins
>
> Anything about math by Marcy Cook
>
> Ditto on reading by Pat Cunningham

So You Want to Be a Mentor?

I asked Anne what she thought was the best thing about being a mentor.

> I learned from them. I'd say, "Wow, where did you get that idea? Can I borrow that book? Tell me more about that author." I think that's what cemented

our relationship. They respected me—maybe just for the grey hair—but when I let them know they had things to offer me, we became colleagues. If you're sincerely interested in their ideas, they're more likely to be receptive to yours.

By the end of the year, there was a well-worn, two-way thoroughfare between Anne's room and the eleven novices who simply adored her for her generosity, wisdom, and seemingly endless energy.

But mostly Anne inspired them with her unabashed love of children and teaching. "I knew in third grade that I wanted to be a teacher. I don't think I could have done anything else. School was a place where I felt safe and success-ful. In high school, I tutored in elementary classrooms, and in college I volun-teered in the inner city. One day we went on a field trip. The bus driver got lost in the Berkeley Hills and all the kids started to throw up. When we got off the bus I thought, 'I still want to be a teacher.'"

She still is—with every fiber of her being—and there are many superb teachers who have Anne Brown to thank for putting their feet on the road to greatness.

Last-Ditch Antifamine Strategy

Finally, if you do nothing else to nurture yourself at school, avoid colleagues who specialize in asserting their snivel liberties. Stay clear of the designated whiners who complain at every staff meeting that they can't possibly take on another responsibility because "their plates are full." In fact, they are end-stage famine victims, starving for professional sustenance but unwilling to reach out and take it.

Connecting with Professionals Beyond Your Campus

Reform is only a concept. Teachers are the ones who make education work. Yet teachers are often the last to know about policy changes that affect the very core of their work with kids. They're so removed from the educational decision makers that they may as well be manning a classroom in another galaxy. You can extend your professional horizons and let your voice be heard by joining in local, state, or federal efforts to improve your profession.

District Committees

Most districts want to develop leadership at all levels by including teachers in a broad array of activities. It's called capacity building. They also have more work than staff, so they can always use an extra brain. In my district last year, teachers served on committees to revise subject area curriculum, and develop a standards-based report card. They served on hiring panels for a new superintendent and did much of the heavy lifting for the high school redesign. To discover opportunities like these in your own district, pester your union president or the director of curriculum at your central office.

Local, State, and National Organizations

If you pay attention to the fine print on your pay stub, you'll probably notice a deduction that goes to your local teachers' union, and a piece of that goes to your state teachers' organization. There are also hundreds of national organizations that focus on issues from testing to bilingual education. Some create standards or promote professional development. Most have a small paid staff and rely on an army of volunteers and pro bono officers to work on conferences or campaigns. You can add a very interesting dimension to your career by getting involved.

Internet Tutors

You can actually get much smarter about teaching and learning with as little effort as it takes to stagger out of bed on Saturday morning, grab a cup of coffee, and flop down in front of your computer. No registration, no parking, no final exams. Just getting smarter on your own. The information highway is gridlocked with education resources. If I could only go to one website, I'd pick ERIC, the Educational Resources Information Center (www.askeric.org), a national information system funded by the U.S. Department of Education that provides accurate, fresh, detailed research on a broad range of education-related issues.

ERIC is a fabulous resource when you want to answer a difficult question from a parent or cite research in your weekly newsletter. ERIC can help you with term papers if you are finishing up your credential or getting an advanced degree. It has at least six different ways to access information.

1. *AskERIC* is an Internet-based service providing education information to teachers.

2. *Question & Answer (Q&A) Service* will send a personal email response to your education question within two business days.

3. *Resource Collection* has more than 3,000 resources on a variety of educational issues.

4. *Question Archive* has more than 100 responses to questions received through the AskERIC Q&A Service.

5. *Lesson Plans* contains more than 2,000 unique lesson plans, written and submitted to AskERIC by teachers from all over the United States.

6. *ERIC Database* is the world's largest source of education information.

Teacher Institutes

Teacher institutes are one of the best perks of your job. They give you a chance to be a learner in optimum conditions—expert instructors, great facilities, in-depth thinking, long lunches, no bells. For example, the Colonial Williamsburg experience invites participants to live in Williamsburg and take junkets to nearby Jamestown and Yorktown to gorge on American history. I was a fortunate Williamsburg fellow, and I never taught history so well as after that immersion experience. So I urge you to jump on the Internet and find yourself a summer dream. Start your research early, watch the time lines, and have fun. Here are the names of a few possibilities.

- Facing History and Ourselves Summer Institute
- Examining the Underground Railroad (An innovative summer institute for teachers)
- Environmental Education Institute
- Poetry Alive! Summer Residency Institute
- The Bronx Zoo Summer Institute for Teachers K–12
- The Crow Canyon Archaeological Center
- The U.S. Space Camp
- Primary Source, Inc.

Some institutes are invitational. You apply and if you're selected, you get instruction, a stipend, and often money for the learning materials of your choice. Sometimes you pay a fee to participate, but the learning is always superb. Most universities host teacher institutes during the summer, sometimes in foreign countries, so you get education, travel, and even graduate credit, all in one getaway.

Responding to the Call for Presenters

Another way great teachers grow is to share their expertise by making presentations at conferences. If you go on the Internet and use the key words *call for presenters teachers*, you'll get a Google of opportunities. Once you figure out what you're presenting and how, write up your presentation as if you worked for an advertising agency. You can fill the room with a great description. If you've never done this before, get a few conference brochures and study them for good models. Speaking professionally is exciting, and public applause can become an addiction after years of toiling in obscurity.

Publishing in Professional Journals

Most of the professional journals you read, like *Instructor* or *Teacher,* solicit articles from teachers just like you. Check their website for writer's guidelines and a calendar of themes and see if you have an idea that is a match. Editors are always in the market for exciting articles on any topic, so the next time you create a really impressive science unit or have a unique insight into literature circles, empty your head on paper, spruce up your prose, and send it off. Editors really appreciate down-to-earth, jargon-free writing that helps teachers get better at their craft. It's fun to find your name in print, and it won't hurt your resume, either.

National Board Certification

The National Board for Professional Teaching Standards (www.nbpts.org) is an organization that wants to enhance the quality of teaching and learning by describing high standards for what teachers should know and be able to do, and organizing a system to certify teachers who meet those standards. If you decide to apply for National Board Certification, you will compile a portfolio of videotapes, student work samples, and a written analysis that gives examiners a clear picture of your teaching practices. Finally, you'll complete a series of essays at an assessment center. Many teachers go through the certification process with a cohort, for moral support and to have a study group. If you can't find a cohort at the local university, invest in *The National Board Certification Workbook* by Adrienne Mack-Kirschner (Heinemann, 2003).

Rethinking—The Moving-On Questionnaire

All teachers have days where they shake their heads and muse, "There's got to be more to life than this." Indeed, there are times when teaching can feel like marathon burden bearing. But most teachers also experience deep satisfaction in the job—usually from their daily triumphs with individual students. The profession truly needs great teachers. It needs you, for as long as you can provide that intelligent, inspirational approach to learning that is an essential ingredient of healthy learning communities. Some teachers last for decades, and become legends in their own time. Others use their classroom as a springboard to the principal's office—great teachers frequently make great administrators. Some turn their prodigious skills into second or third careers. If you're rethinking your teaching career, it's smart to admit out loud that it's a huge step—

potentially so overwhelming that you might give up before you ever get to the resume-interview-I-love-my-new-job stage. So here are some steps to help you take stock of your situation, assess your needs, and pursue your options with the enthusiasm that a good adventure deserves.

What Do You Really Want?

First and foremost, you need to be clear about what you want. Poke around inside your head to identify the good, the bad, and the tolerable about your current job. Some people make lists of pros and cons to get clarity. I like questions. Try these.

The Moving-on Questionnaire

Do I still feel passionate about this job?

How often do I feel satisfied at the end of the day?

What special skills do I have that are untapped in this setting?

Is there a different audience that I want to address?

What do I love about my current job?

What do I hate about this job?

Am I making a difference?

Can I do this work and still be myself?

Is my family paying too high a price for my career?

Is my physical health suffering?

Is my intellectual life on hold?

If I could change one thing about my current job, what would it be?

If I accomplished that change, would I want to stay?

Do I have another dream?

What is my fantasy of a perfect job?

Be as truthful and specific as possible because your answers hold valuable clues for making your current job more satisfying, or preparing to move on. The solution to your dilemma may be as simple as changing grade levels, or as radical as heading for a primary school in Pretoria. Armed with your personal assessment, you're ready to start crafting a plan.

Job Searches and Sources

If you decide on Monday that you need to change jobs, you may wake up on Tuesday and freak out at the thought of doing a resume, especially if you insist on thinking of yourself as "just a kindergarten teacher." You might wonder, What do I put on my resume? Supervised snack time? Mixed paint in milk cartons? The reality is that you're an experienced professional in the field of education, and once you tackle your resume, you'll be surprised to discover how much you've accomplished.

So get started on your resume right now. Then you'll be ready to act when the perfect job comes along, instead of missing a deadline because you're still puzzling over which font to use. The easiest way to generate a resume is to hire someone. But you still have to collect all the dates, comb through your professional history, and then explain what all that jargon means to your resume writer. You could end up doing most of the work, and picking up the tab. If you're a do-it-yourselfer, go to the library or go online. First stop: www.headhunter.net. This website has lots of suggestions for making a career change, including the ten top resume mistakes. Here are some more steps to ease the process.

1. Make a list of every committee, commission, or taskforce on which you have served. Describe each in active, product-oriented language, such as: designed K–12 math assessment, created interactive science curriculum, analyzed achievement of minority students, and implemented interventions. Check your word processing software for a resume feature. With one click, you can choose from a variety of auto-formats, and then concentrate on content.

2. If you're applying for a job outside of education, increase your success rate by redefining your educational responsibilities and experience in nonschool terms. Analyze the tasks you've performed in the jobs you've held, and describe the *skills* they required, rather than simply relying on ambiguous educational titles like Program Specialist.

3. Identify key words in the job description and use them in your resume and cover letter to underscore the fit between you and the job you want.

4. Plan on tweaking your resume every time you apply for a job. Adding, highlighting, or deleting information can bring your job experience into sharp focus and catch the eye of your potential employer.

Letters of Recommendation and Other Job-Hunting Tips

Most job applications require at least three reference letters, including one from your most recent supervisor. Fresh letters. Recommendations have about a one-year shelf-life. Don't be afraid to ask your references to freshen up their letters with a new date and signature every year.

If you're asking people to write a reference letter about you for the first time, help them out. List all the things you've done that relate to the job you're seeking. Indicate the skills or characteristics you'd like them to emphasize. Give them a description of the job you're pursuing to put their comments in the right context. Some applicants even write a first draft of a reference letter as a prompt. It's a huge help to the writer—so much better than staring at a blank screen and wondering, Now what the heck did she do well?

Here are a few more ways to help your application.

- Draw on a broad group for your letters of reference. Three letters from the same school suggest that you don't get out much professionally, so the job may go to someone with a wider range of experience.
- Don't include letters of reference from subordinates or parents. Potential employers want to hear from your direct supervisors or colleagues.
- Fill out all parts of the application. Blanks raise questions.
- Watch for consistency in the dates on your resume. Unexplained gaps will stand out.
- If you list people as references, be sure their phone numbers are correct. Many Human Resource offices can't complete the hiring process until references are checked so a disconnected number can delay the process.

Now that you have a razor-sharp resume and a stack of sparkling letters, you're ready for the big adventure—your next job.

Moving On

If you're an educator seriously considering a job or career change, you may be hampered by a narrow view of what's out there. Take heart! There's a vast array of opportunities. You'll need to do some basic research and put your curiosity in overdrive, but searching for just the right job is an adventure in itself. Be prepared. It takes time and energy—of which you have little at the end of your teaching day. So think of this as a research project, with lots of little parts that you can do in your spare time. Start slowly. Make a file, go online, and keep notes. Then repeat after me: *All progress is progress.*

Location, Location, Location

Maybe you still like many aspects of teaching, but just need a change of venue. Rethinking your location is a great way to improve your outlook, and stay in a profession that truly needs talented, experienced teachers. Start with this math lesson. Take a minute to calculate the number of hours you spend commuting each week. If it's more than ten, imagine how you could use that time to improve your lifestyle. If it's approaching twenty, you're working half-time as a commuter. Look for a job closer to home.

Thinking that the grass is always greener can also lead to a successful school change. You could find educational nirvana and add years to your career, simply by moving to a school that's a different size, more compatible with your philosophy, or a magnet school with a focus on science, humanities, or the arts. Start by cruising the Internet. Most districts have websites listing all their openings and may even encourage you to apply online.

Independent Schools

If you've spent most of your career in public education, struggling with crumbling facilities, underfunding, and overregulation, you may not realize that there's a parallel universe, where educational philosophy, best practices, academic rigor, and meeting students' needs are the rule of the day. Maybe it's time to investigate independent schools. They're private, nonprofit schools governed by boards of trustees, and supported by tuition, private gifts, grants, and endowments. They range in size from several dozen to thousands of students, and their approaches to teaching cover the spectrum from team-taught, project-centered, experiential classes to industrial-strength academics. Independent schools are not perfect, but they may be a perfect fit for you. If this sounds intriguing to you, go online to begin your investigation at the website for the National Association of Independent Schools (www.nais.org).

Globe Trotting

Picture a classroom overlooking a colorful street market in Singapore, or nestled in a seventeenth-century villa in Florence. Imagine trying to finish your weekly newsletter, distracted by a sudden snowfall in Paris. It could happen to you, because there's a far-flung network of international schools that serve English-speaking students around the world. Every year they host bustling job fairs to lure teachers with a chance to see the world. The Internet is a perfect tool for exploring these daydreams or making them a reality. Start with International Schools Service (www.iss.edu) for a detailed description of their recruitment service, frequently asked questions, setting up a professional file, and time lines for selecting candidates.

Moving On Up

For those of you who long to see the view from the top of the organization chart, even for a few battle-scarred years, investigate life as an assistant principal or principal. You'll need a credential, a mentor, and good thick skin, but it can be a real adventure. Many districts, tired of searching for new administrators, have established their own farm teams. Promising teachers are recruited, tutored, and groomed until they are ready to step into an administrative position. If your own district doesn't have this, check others in your area for leadership academies. Or you can go the university route, often with financial support from your district.

The Business of Education

Teachers longing for a complete career change may lose heart, mistakenly seeing themselves as one-trick ponies. "All I've every done is teach. Maybe the classroom is my only option?" But many jobs in the for-profit world rely on people with the exact skill set that you've been perfecting for years. A logical place to start is in the publishing world.

Educational Publishers. Educational publishing is a billion-dollar industry that depends on a steady supply of writers, editors, trainers, and consultants. These companies hire armies of freelance employees who are paid very well compared to the in-house staff. The more you know about curriculum and best practices, the greater the possibilities for employment. Start your inquiries with any of the publishers who specialize in textbooks. A tour of the bookroom at your school will give you a short list, and as always, the Internet is a trove of information on textbook publishers. There's also a broad range of educational publishing aside from the business of textbooks. Check the AcqWeb Directory online for names and locations of companies in educational publishing.

Training, Workshops, and Speakers Bureaus. Education supports a vast constellation of companies in the business of helping teachers get better at what they do. To locate these companies, just monitor the junk mail that arrives in your school's front office each week. All those colorful flyers for conferences, seminars, and workshops were sent by potential employers. Pick up the phone and ask to talk to the Professional Development Director. If that doesn't work, ask for the recruiter or simply say that you're interested in being a trainer or presenter for their organization. There's an application process that may require some combination of the following: an outline for the seminar you want to teach, your resume, a list of seminars you have conducted for adults, the names of five or six individuals who have seen you present, a video of you presenting to adults. This may look daunting at first, but if you take it piece by piece, it can lead to a successful application, travel opportunities, and a chance to share your professional expertise.

Foundations with an Educational Focus

Foundations are often the philanthropic offspring of an individual with a passion for excellence in education and some disposable cash. In this era of uberphilanthropists, the list of foundations is growing, and all of them need experienced staff. Many of their positions require curriculum expertise; educational experience; writing, speaking, and organizational skills; so here's another opportunity for a career change. Start your Web investigation with the key words: *education foundations.*

Moving Day

Whether you leave your school in a cloud of balloons, bound for the sweet green hills of retirement, or you quietly announce that you've chosen another way to spend your passion for education, departing can be a truly bipolar experience—so liberating that you can scarcely contain your delight, and at the same time, tinged with loss, and even bereavement. Be prepared. After all, it's not like you're walking out of IBM or a high-rise office full of cubicles.

> *Life was meant to be lived and curiosity be kept alive. One must never for whatever reason, turn his back on life*
> —Eleanor Roosevelt

You've been at the center of a learning community, and you're an unofficial member of many families, whether you realize it or not. The roots of many a childhood are sunk deep in your soul.

As you turn the key in your classroom door for the last time, you may hesitate momentarily to wonder if a life among children was a life well spent. Should that thought cross your mind, run, don't walk, to your nearest video store and rent *Etre et Avoir,* a magnificent documentary film that chronicles life in a one-room schoolhouse in rural France. After watching this brilliant teacher, Georges Lopez, lovingly guide his students through his last year before retirement, you'll feel as proud to be an educator as the day you first stood before a room of expectant faces and announced, "I'm your teacher."

Resources

Schmidt, Laurel. 2002. *Gardening in the Minefield: A Survival Guide for School Administrators.* Portsmouth, NH: Heinemann.

Sorokin, Pitirim. 1942. *Man and Society in Calamity: The Effects of War, Revolution, Famine.* Westport, CT: Greenwood.